THE LIBRARY OF DISTINCTIVE SERMONS

VOLUME THREE

GARY W. KLINGSPORN
General Editor

QUESTAR PUBLISHERS • SISTERS, OREGON

Executive Editor
Stephen E. Gibson, B.A.

General Editor
Gary W. Klingsporn, Ph.D.

Associate Editor
Mary Ruth Howes, M.A.

THE LIBRARY OF DISTINCTIVE SERMONS, VOLUME 3
published by Questar Publishing Direct
a part of the Questar publishing family
© 1996 by Questar Publishers

International Standard Book Number: 1-57673-069-7
Design by David Uttley

Printed in the United States of America

All sermons in this book are used with permission of the individual writers.
No part of this book may be used or reproduced in any manner whatsoever
without written permission from Questar Publishing Direct,
except in the case of brief quotations embodied in critical articles and reviews.

Scripture quotations are from:
The Holy Bible, New International Version (NIV) © 1973, 1984 by International Bible
Society, used by permission of Zondervan Publishing House.

The New King James Version (NKJV) © 1984 by Thomas Nelson, Inc.; used by permission.

The New Revised Standard Version Bible (NRSV) © 1989 by the Division of Christian
Education of the National Council of the Churches of Christ in the U.S.A.;
used by permission.

The Revised Standard Version of the Bible © 1946, 1952, 1971, 1973, Division of Christian
Education of the National Council of the Churches of Christ in the U.S.A.;
used by permission.

The Revised English Bible (REB), © 1989 by Oxford University Press and Cambridge
University Press; used by permission.

The New English Bible (NEB), © 1961, 1970 by The Delegates of the Oxford University
Press and The Syndics of the Cambridge University Press; used by permission.

New American Standard Bible (NAS), © 1960, 1962, 1963, 1968, 1971, 1972, 1973, 1975,
1977, by The Lockman Foundation; used by permission.

ALL RIGHTS RESERVED
No part of this publication may be reproduced, stored in a retrieval system,
or transmitted, in any form or by any means — electronic, mechanical,
photocopying, recording, or otherwise — without prior written permission.
For information:
QUESTAR PUBLISHERS, INC.
POST OFFICE BOX 1720
SISTERS, OREGON 97759

96 97 98 99 00 01 02 03 — 10 9 8 7 6 5 4 3 2 1

TABLE OF CONTENTS

PREFACE 6
INTRODUCTION 8
CONTRIBUTING EDITORS 12

WHEN WE ARE LACKING DIRECTION
  Rev. D. Stuart Briscoe 15

UNNATURAL COMPASSION
  Rev. Dr. Martin B. Copenhaver 35

IN A NEW LIGHT
  Rev. Dr. J. Barry Vaughn 49

LORD, TEACH US TO PRAY
  Rev. Earl Palmer 59

I BELIEVE IN JESUS CHRIST
  Dr. Roberta Hestenes 71

MARTHA'S FEAST AND MARY'S PORTION
  Rev. Dr. Gilbert R. Friend-Jones 83

CROWD CONTROL ON PALM SUNDAY
  Dr. Bruce L. Shelley 101

CAN I SING WHEN THE GOING GETS TOUGH?
  Rev. Dr. William Powell Tuck 115

HOW "USER-FRIENDLY CHURCHES" GET USED
  Dr. William H. Willimon 129

PEACE FOR THE JOURNEY
  Rev. Dr. David C. Fisher 139

PILGRIM PEOPLE, PILGRIM FAITH
  Rev. Dr. Stephen Brachlow 151

JESUS THE WORD
  Rev. Dr. Mark D. Roberts 165

FINDING PEACE
  Rev. Dr. Gary A. Furr 183

THE POWER OF YOUR STORY
   Rev. Dr. Scott Walker 197
WHERE ARE YOU HEADED?
   Rev. Dr. Norman Neaves 207
THE NEARNESS OF GOD
   Dr. John Killinger 221
BLESSED ARE THE DESPERATE
   Dr. Gary W. Klingsporn 233
THE SCANDAL IN SANDALS
   Rev. Richard A. Davis 251
NO LOOKING BACK
   Rev. Rick Brand 265
KEEPING STRESS FROM BECOMING DISTRESS
   Rev. Rick McDaniel 279
TOPICAL INDEX 293
SCRIPTURE INDEX 296

For all who preach

How beautiful upon the mountains
are the feet of the messenger
who announces peace,
who brings good news,
who announces salvation,
who says to Zion, "Your God reigns."

ISAIAH 52:7

PREFACE

The idea of *The Library of Distinctive Sermons* originated in painful practical circumstances rather than in an academic context. A pastor friend of mine went through a prolonged ordeal of tension and conflict with a congregation before he was terminated primarily "because his sermons were dry and hard to follow." As a new, young pastor, he was doing the best he could without the benefit of much experience in ministry. By and large, however, he was not connecting with the congregation in his preaching. The congregation became impatient and was less than compassionate in handling the situation. This led to a bitter parting of the ways.

As a lay person sitting in the pew and aware of the tension, I felt the pain on both sides of the issue. I began to ask myself what more might be done to assist ministers in learning and sharing the insights which contribute to effective preaching. *The Library of Distinctive Sermons* originated from that experience. It is a resource designed to promote vital and effective preaching through the sharing of sermons and insights on preaching by working pastors.

The Library of Distinctive Sermons brings together a collection of powerful contemporary sermons of diverse style and content, along with careful reflection as to what makes each sermon effective, and how each sermon relates to biblical, theological, and practical ministry issues facing pastors today.

It is important to note that we have chosen not to engage in an academic critique of each sermon. No sermon is flawless. We have chosen good sermons and have asked some simple questions: What makes each of these sermons good? What can we learn from the creative elements of style and content in each sermon to assist us in the art of preaching?

Discussion of these questions in the Comment section following each sermon makes *The Library of Distinctive Sermons* unique among sermon publications. We have enlisted only working pastors for the task of commenting on each sermon. While there are many excellent books on homiletics, we discovered that few are written by pastors for pastors. The Comment sections are a means of sharing practical ideas and insights from pastor to pastor in a way that is helpful to pastors of all backgrounds and levels of experience. Our desire is that *The Library of Distinctive Sermons* will enhance your own process of developing new sermons and contribute to the continual renewal of your preaching ministry.

Many people gave of their talents to this series. First, we are deeply grateful to all of the preachers whose sermons appear in this volume. Their commitment to the proclamation of the gospel and their willingness to share their sermons "out of context" with a wider audience beyond their local congregations, have made this series possible. Special thanks go also to those pastors who shared their wisdom, perspectives, and insights in the Comment sections. Appreciation goes as well to the General Editor, Dr. Gary W. Klingsporn, whose special gifts and talents in communication and publishing are reflected throughout the series. Special thanks to Mary Ruth Howes, who, as Associate Editor, kept us all in line with her wonderful editorial expertise in the written word.

In a rapidly changing consumer culture which is increasingly visually oriented, the sermon "competes" as never before with a multiplicity of media and voices vying for our attention. In a culture where the entertainment world sets the pace and celebrities are often the measure of "success," preaching today is subjected to intense scrutiny and is regarded by many as outmoded, especially if it does not "entertain." And yet, since the beginning of Christianity, followers of Jesus Christ in every age have found preaching the most powerful and effective form of communicating the gospel. Indeed, there is something about the gospel that seems to demand this particular expression, this form of communication, and none other. Through preaching, lives continue to be saved and transformed, liberated, healed and reconciled. We pray that *The Library of Distinctive Sermons* will encourage you and help you create new and effective ways of proclaiming the gospel of Jesus Christ in today's world.

Stephen E. Gibson
Executive Editor

INTRODUCTION

Welcome to Volume 3 of *The Library of Distinctive Sermons*. As we did in the first two volumes of this series, we are pleased to offer here another twenty outstanding sermons with comment.

Much has been written on the subject of preaching. Seldom, however, do we find good sermons brought together with commentary on why those sermons constitute effective proclamation of the gospel. Among the literature available today, we can read sermons. Or, we can read about preaching. But seldom do we have the opportunity to do both at the same time: to read good sermons, and to reflect on the art of preaching as it is embodied in those sermons.

The Library of Distinctive Sermons is designed to promote the enrichment of preaching through the sharing of good sermons and careful analysis of their style and content. The purpose is to read a sermon and ask, "What makes this sermon effective as the proclamation of God's Word?" The philosophy underlying this series is that, whether we are novices or seasoned preachers, we can always learn from others who preach. One of the best ways to do that is to "listen" to others, to observe how they preach, and pick up on some of the best of what they do in a way that is natural and appropriate in our own preaching.

Each of the sermons in this volume is accompanied by a Comment section. Here working pastors reflect on what makes each sermon distinctive and effective. To some extent, of course, this is a very subjective undertaking. What makes a sermon "good" or "effective" to one person is not always the same in the opinion of others. Given the subjectivity involved, it would be easy to avoid ever undertaking the task of serious reflection about our preaching. However, in the Comment sections in this volume, the writers have taken the risk of opening the dialogue about what constitutes effective preaching. There is much to be gained in this process: new ideas and techniques, new perspectives on texts, creative forms and structures, new stories and illustrations for preaching.

It is one thing to hear or read a good sermon and to have some sense of why we like it. But how often do we give serious analytical reflection, asking what we can learn from a sermon? *The Library of Distinctive Sermons* provides an opportunity for the enrichment of preaching through thoughtful consideration of why each sermon has been done in the way it is done.

In the Comment sections in this series the writers reflect on the style and content of each sermon. They look at such things as the genre and structure of the sermon, its use of biblical texts, illustrations, literary or rhetorical techniques, tone, and language. They also comment on how the content of each sermon proclaims biblical faith; remains true to the biblical text; reflects sound theology; deals with faith questions; addresses ethical and social issues; and shows the relevance of the gospel in today's world.

The Comments are presented in a fairly nontechnical way. The focus of this series is not on an academic analysis or critique of sermons, nor is the focus on theoretical aspects of communication and homiletics. The purpose of this series is to offer practical reflection aimed at stimulating our thoughts and improving our preaching in very practical ways.

The format of this volume is simple. Each sermon is presented as closely as possible to the original form in which it was preached. Obviously, in moving from the original oral medium of preaching to the written form represented here, some editing has been necessary to facilitate literary style, clarity, and comprehension.

The Comment following each sermon assumes that every effective sermon includes at least three basic elements. First, every sermon addresses questions relating to the problems and needs of the human condition. Second, every good sermon has a thesis and makes an assertion. It proclaims truth from the Scriptures using one or more biblical texts. Third, every good sermon invites people to respond or motivates them to think, act, or believe. These preaching elements can be described in many different ways using varieties of language. In their Comments the writers commonly use the terms Text, Problem, Proclamation, and Response (or Invitation) to refer to these elements of sermonic structure and content.

In the Comments, then, you will notice frequent discussion of the following items which are intended as helpful tools of reflection and analysis:

1) Text. How does the preacher interpret and apply the biblical text(s) in the sermon? What techniques are used? What insights into the text(s) are found in the sermon?

2) Problem. What human problem, need, question, or life situation does each sermon address? How is the problem of the human condition understood and presented in the sermon?

3) Proclamation. How does the sermon proclaim the good news of the Christian gospel? What is the truth or "kerygma" drawn from the Scriptures and applied to the human situation?

4) Response. How does the sermon invite us to respond? What does the preacher invite, urge, or encourage us to believe or to do? What motivation is there to act or to change, and how does this flow out of the interpretation of the biblical text(s), the human problem, and the proclamation of the gospel?

5) Suggestions. Each Comment section concludes with some practical suggestions for thought or discussion, for further reading, or for incorporating some of the insights from the sermon into one's own preaching.

The Library of Distinctive Sermons features a wide variety of sermon styles and subjects. This is important in a series designed for the enrichment of preaching. You will undoubtedly like some of the sermons more than others. You will react differently to different sermons. You may agree or disagree with some of the Comments. But all of these reactions can be learning experiences. So as you read, ask yourself: "What do I think about this sermon? Why do I feel as I do?" Interact with the material! Reflect on your own preaching and ministry as you enjoy this volume. Then the sermons and Comments will become a valuable resource for your own ministry.

It is important to remember that each of the sermons in this volume was preached in an original context, most of them in congregations on Sunday mornings. Each was spoken with the presence and guidance of the Holy Spirit to a particular people in a particular time and place. Each sermon had a life of its own as the Word of God in that specific moment.

While the sermons that appear here are removed from those original contexts, there is much we can learn from them. Whenever possible, the attempt has been made to acknowledge significant aspects of the original context. But now these sermons appear in a new context. God can use them in this context to speak home to our hearts and to create new understanding and possibilities for ministry.

The apostle Paul wrote, "So then faith comes from what is heard, and what is heard comes through the word of Christ" (Rom. 10:17). It is in and through the preached word of Christ that God directs us to faith in Christ and imparts to us the gift of faith. In preaching, the wonderful work and mystery of God take place: the living Christ becomes present through the preached word. Bonhoeffer said, "The word of Scripture is certain, clear, and plain. The preacher should be assured that Christ enters the congregation through those words which he [or she] proclaims from the Scripture...."[1] Preaching is a holy calling filled with the mystery and promise of God. We do well to give all the careful time and attention we can to this holy task, while always giving ourselves to God. As Augustine said of preaching, "Lord, give me the gifts to make this gift to you."

Gary W. Klingsporn
General Editor

Note
1. Dietrich Bonhoeffer, *Worldly Preaching*, ed. Clyde E. Fant (Nashville and New York: Thomas Nelson, Inc., 1975), p. 130.

CONTRIBUTING EDITORS

Dixie Brachlow is a recent graduate of Louisville Presbyterian Theological Seminary (M.Div.) and a candidate for pastoral ministry in the Presbyterian Church (USA). Her professional experience includes college administration, grant writing, public speaking, program development and high school teaching. She is a graduate of the University of Minnesota (B.S.) and Augustana College (M.A.).

Richard A. Davis is Teaching Pastor of Hope Presbyterian Church in Richfield, Minnesota. A graduate of the University of Minnesota (B.A.), Luther Theological Seminary (M.A.), and San Francisco Theological Seminary (M.Div.), Davis has served Presbyterian churches in Minnesota and Belfast, Northern Ireland. He has contributed a number of articles to various publications and is author of *The Prism Project: A Survey of the Bible for Adults*.

Gary W. Downing is currently Evangelism Pastor of Faith Covenant Church in Burnsville, Minnesota. He has previously served as a seminary instructor, executive minister of Colonial Church, Edina, Minnesota, executive director of Youth Leadership, and area Young Life director. A graduate of Bethel college (B.A.), Bethel Theological Seminary (M.Div.) and Luther Theological Seminary (M.Div.), Downing is author of *One Man's Heart,* a book on male spirituality.

David C. Fisher is Senior Pastor, Colonial Church, Edina, Minnesota. He served previously as senior pastor of Park Street Church, Boston, and Crystal Evangelical Free Church, Minneapolis. A graduate of Bryan College (B.A.), Trinity Evangelical Divinity School (M.Div.), and The Southern Baptist Theological Seminary, Louisville (Th.M.), he holds a Ph.D. in New Testament Interpretation from Southern Seminary. He is the author of *The 21st-Century Pastor: A Vision Based on the Ministry of Paul* (Zondervan, 1996) and serves on the Board of Ministry, Harvard University.

Gary A. Furr is Pastor of Vestavia Hills Baptist Church in Birmingham,

Alabama, and adjunct instructor in New Testament at Samford University. The author of numerous articles and book reviews, Furr is coeditor of *Ties That Bind: Life Together in the Baptist Vision*. He has served churches in Texas, Georgia and Alabama, and is a graduate of Carson-Newman College (B.A.), Southeastern Baptist Theological Seminary (M.Div.) and Baylor University (Ph.D.).

Debra K. Klingsporn is an author and former public relations and marketing executive who has served as executive director of marketing for Word Publishing, and as a vice president of Carol DeChant & Associates, a public relations firm based in Chicago. A graduate of Texas A&M University with a bachelor's degree in journalism, she is the coauthor of *Shattering Our Assumptions: Breaking Free of Expectations — Others and Our Own; Soul Searching: Meditations for Your Spiritual Journey;* and *I Can't, God Can, I Think I'll Let Him;* and coeditor of *The Quickening Heart* and *The Remembering Season*.

Gary W. Klingsporn is Teaching Minister of Colonial Church in Edina, Minnesota, and serves as General Editor of *The Library of Distinctive Sermons*. He has served churches in Texas and Minnesota and has taught religious studies at Baylor University and Metropolitan State University in Minneapolis. Formerly a writer and editor with Word Publishing, he is a graduate of St. Paul's Lutheran College (A.A.), Oral Roberts University (B.A.), and Baylor University (Ph.D.).

Peter J. Smith is Pastor of First Congregational Church of Thomaston, Connecticut. A graduate of Trinity College (B.A.) and Gordon-Conwell Theological Seminary (M.Div.), he has served United Church of Christ churches in Indiana and Minnesota and has been active in Habitat for Humanity, the United Church Board for World Ministries, and other ministry endeavors.

David Williamson is Pastor of Care and Counseling, First Presbyterian Church of Hollywood, California. Licensed Marriage and Family Therapist, he previously served as Counseling Minister of Colonial Church, Edina, Minnesota. A graduate of the University of Minnesota (B.S.B.), Fuller Theological Seminary (M.Div.), and Luther Seminary

(M.Th., D.Min.), he is the author of *Group Power; Opening Doors to the Job Market;* and *Unemployed, Unfulfilled.*

When We Are Lacking Direction

2 CORINTHIANS 5:14–21

REV. D. STUART BRISCOE
ELMBROOK CHURCH
BROOKFIELD, WISCONSIN

Rev. D. Stuart Briscoe

When We Are Lacking Direction

2 CORINTHIANS 5:14–21, NIV

I was talking to a futurist friend of mine not so long ago. He is a man who lectures to corporations all across America, predicting trends and that sort of thing. Two things that bother people the most today, he observes, are a lack of time and a lack of direction. It seems that a lot of people's lives are not really going anywhere. A question I often ask people, slightly tongue-in-cheek but also seriously, is "What do you want to be when you grow up?" Some people who have done quite a bit of growing still are not sure what it is they want to be. In other words, they lack a sense of direction.

I want to talk about finding a sense of direction this morning as we look at Paul's second letter to the Corinthians. In chapter 5, the apostle Paul makes a very significant statement: "For Christ's love compels us, because we are convinced that one died for all, and therefore all died. And he died for all, that those who live should no longer live for themselves but for him who died for them and was raised again" (2 Cor. 5:14–15). Notice particularly the word *compel*. "Christ's love compels us." The original Greek word translated "compel" is found in other instances in Scripture which give us a little insight into what Paul means.

For example, when Stephen was preaching to a crowd in Jerusalem, he wasn't getting a very good hearing from the people. He knew that was true because the people put their hands over their ears. They "covered" (NIV) or "stopped" (KJV) their ears (Acts 7:57). That is the same word as "compel."

The apostle Paul wrote about being "hard pressed" (NRSV) or "torn between" (NIV) two options — to stay and minister to the Christian churches, or to depart and be with Christ (Phil. 1:23–24). Pressure from two choices, two hands pressed against one's head — being hemmed in. "Christ's love hems us in," Paul is saying in our text. What does this have to do with losing a sense of direction? Let me give you an illustration.

One of the great rivers of the world is the Yangtze in China. It has two distinct phases. In its earlier route it is a deep river flowing through high narrow gorges with tremendous drive and phenomenal force. But as it moves down to the plains, it becomes wide, shallow and sluggish, meandering on its way to the coast. What makes the difference? It's obviously the same volume of water. The difference is that in its earlier stages it is hemmed in. But in its lower reaches, it is no longer hemmed in. The river is free to spread out and become broad, shallow, sluggish, lacking direction.

I suspect that there are people in this world who meander through life, whose lives are sluggish and shallow. They haven't been hemmed in to a specific focus. They need, if you like, to get into the early reaches of the Yangtze experience. They need to be hemmed in.

The apostle Paul explains the drive, the depth and the direction of his life quite simply: "It is the love of Christ that hems me in." He is like the Yangtze in the gorges. Any person today who rightly appreciates the love of Christ and applies it appropriately will also find themselves hemmed in and, accordingly, their lives will not meander, or be sluggish and muddy. Their lives will be deep, they will have definite direction and they will have tremendous drive.

In order for us to understand how this happens, let me refresh your memory concerning what Paul tells us about the love of Christ. "Christ's love compels us," he says, "because we are convinced that one died for all" (v. 14). He is relating the love of Christ to Christ's death. Paul goes on to say, "God was reconciling the world to himself in Christ, not counting men's sins against them…God made him [Christ] who had no sin to be sin for us" (vv. 19, 21). The love of Christ is manifested in the cross, in the fact that Christ died for all. Christ's death for all is directly related to the human sin problem. If we are going to understand the love of Christ so that it will hem us in and give us drive, depth and direction, we must understand what it was that motivated God to do something about the human sin problem.

I know it's not politically correct in many quarters to talk about sin. But let's not be concerned about being politically correct. Let's be concerned about being biblically accurate. And if we are biblically accurate, we will discover that the Bible talks unapologetically about the underlying social problem of sin as being in the hearts of individuals.

The reality of sin is that there is something within us that much prefers disobedience and independence to dependence on God. We have an attitude problem. It's not uncommon to find people who will say quite honestly, "I know what God says. I know that what God says is right. I know that I should do what God says. But I'm not going to do it." Why? "Because it's too hard." It's relatively easy to do what we want to. But we find it very difficult to do what God says. Why is that? It is because there is a built-in attitude, an attitude of resistance. It is often an attitude of resentment that will manifest itself in all kinds of rebellious activity.

Not only is sin an attitude, it is an aptitude. There is in each one of us a sort of bias, a tendency, that will almost inevitably draw us to do what we should not, and keep us from doing what we should. We are guilty of sins of both commission and omission.

I don't have to belabor the point. We all know it's true. God tells us, "If you want to live wisely and well, this is what you have got to do: Love God with all your heart, mind and strength and your neighbor as yourself." But if we check ourselves on any day and ask ourselves, "Did I love God with all my heart, mind and strength today, and did I love my neighbor as myself today?" we will probably get the answer "No." We have not done what we ought to have done. And our omissions will spill over into various activities where we do what we ought not to do. God has made it very clear that, for our own good, there are certain things that we should not do. But incredibly, we will go ahead and continue doing things that we know, before God, are not in our best interest.

So we have a sin problem. Some people want to write sin off as institutionalized sin. They look at all the things that are wrong in our world — with government, with big business, with education, with institutions. If we could just change government, they say, change big business, change education, we would get rid of sin. But who makes up the government? How is big business constituted? Governments and institutions are all made up of individuals. Yes, there is institutionalized sin. But there is institutionalized sin because there is individual sin. We have got to face up to our own sin. We have got to accept the fact of our failures and call sin, *sin*.

Hundreds of schemes and billions of dollars have been expended trying to solve societal problems. Some have served to alleviate the problems. But any attempts to solve society's problems that do not address the sin issue, that do not see the problems as fundamentally spiritual in nature, are damned and doomed to fail.

The good news is that God has taken the initiative and has instituted a remedy for the human sin problem. "Christ's love compels us, because we are convinced that one died for all" (v. 14). In other words, the great, good news of the Christian gospel is that God has made a sovereign choice, taken divine initiative and moved into the sin situation. He has effected a remedy for the human dilemma. Now the thing that is important to us in consideration of this text is simply this: God's action was predicated on love.

If you think about it, God had a number of options open to him (that's how we think from our human standpoint). God could have looked at the situation down here and said, "It's hopeless. Press the button and blow them into extermination." Or he could have said, "I gave them a chance, they blew it, let them stew in their own juices. They asked for it, they can have it. I'm done with them." Or God could have gone off and created another world somewhere. In actual fact, he did not choose any of these options, if indeed, they were options. God chose to love us. Love is more than a fuzzy feeling. Love is to be deeply concerned about another's well-being and to be willing to do something about it. What he did was to send his Son, Jesus Christ, into the world.

Notice what it says about Christ in verse 21: He was the one "who had no sin." The Scripture tells us that Jesus was tested or tempted at every point, just as we are, but made it through the tests without sin (Hebrews 4:15). There is no temptation that may come our way that Jesus was not also subjected to. He was different from us because he did not succumb to temptation.

What does it mean for us that Jesus Christ was sinless? As human beings, we have a tendency to look around us and find people who are worse than ourselves. So we arrive at the inevitable conclusion that we are better than they are. Then we take an illogical leap and say to ourselves, "Since I am better than they are, I'm all right." On one occasion, a young man told me, "If those people think they are going to go to heaven, I don't want to go there. Because if God wants those kinds of people there, I find myself far superior and I don't want to mix with them."

That young man's fundamental mistake was to measure himself against the wrong thing. We are to measure ourselves by the sinlessness of Christ. Christ is a model to us of the character and nature of God. He shows us what God is looking for in normative human behavior. When we measure ourselves against Christ what do we discover? We discover our utter sinfulness.

The little town where I grew up, Millum in Cumberland, in the north of England, was known for only one thing — its rich vein of iron ore that was smelted in the furnaces belching out smoke that covered our little town. All around town we had big, ugly, black slag banks, all the waste from the smelting of the iron ore. One day a lady living in a little miner's cottage did her laundry and hung it outside on the laundry line against the backdrop of the slag banks. She prided herself on her beautiful job of clean laundry. That night she forgot to take her wash in and overnight it snowed. The next morning, she looked at her yellow, off-white, not very clean laundry. It hadn't changed at all. She was seeing it now against the pristine, virgin snow. It looked pretty good against a black slag bank. But it looked pretty awful against the driven snow.

Measure yourself against someone else who is worse than you, and you come out smelling like roses. Measure yourself against Christ, and it is a very different matter indeed.

Jesus, who had no sin, was sent by a loving God into our world to deal with the sin problem. How did he do that? We are told in verse 21 that "God made him who had no sin to be sin for us." What that means, as I understand it, is this: the sinless Christ, through the action of God, has taken responsibility for the sins of the whole world. There is no sin for which Jesus is accountable or responsible in himself, because he has none. But now, Jesus accepts responsibility for the sin of the whole world. The consequence of sin, the Scriptures tell us, is death. "The wages of sin is death" (Romans 6:23). When God reckons to Christ the sin of the whole world, Christ accepts the judgment of God for our sin; he assumes our sin and dies our death. This is not a merciless father crucifying an innocent victim. This is God himself, in Christ, assuming our sins, accepting the judgment against our sins, in order that we might be forgiven our sins.

But not only that. Paul goes on to say, "God made him who had no sin to be sin for us, so that in him we might become the righteousness of God" (v. 21). In other words, in the same way that God reckoned to Christ my sin and dealt with it, God then reckoned to me Christ's righteousness, and he sees me forgiven in Christ. What was behind God's action? Nothing that I deserved. Nothing that I earned. Nothing that I merited. Simply love. The unbounded love of God in Christ makes available to me what I don't deserve.

Has God's love touched you? Has it gotten through to you?

Because Christ died for us, the apostle Paul tells us, the person whose sins have been forgiven and to whom the righteousness of Christ has been imputed, is like "a new creation; the old has gone, the new has come" (v. 17). The forgiven sinner never forgets that he or she is a sinner, but doesn't spend time brooding over the past, because the past has been forgiven. It has been cast into the depths of the sea. God says, "Your sins and iniquities I will remember no more" (Hebrews 10:17, KJV). So you don't spend your time being guilt-ridden by the past. It is forgiven. You look now to the future, because you have become a new person, indwelt by the Spirit of the risen Christ, embraced by the love of God, showered with the grace of God. "Old things are passed away;...all things are become new" (2 Cor. 5:17, KJV).

This new life is what God has made available to people, and the appeal now is to be reconciled to God. The table is laid, the provision is made. God presides and he invites you to join him, to become reconciled to him. The response is entirely up to you.

You remember the famous story told by Jesus in Luke 15. A man had two sons. The younger one said to him — this is the modernized version — "Dad, you're getting on in years. One of these days you'll pop off, and when you do, I'll get my share of the inheritance with my older brother. But, if you don't mind, Dad, it looks like you're hanging on a little too long. Would you give me my inheritance now?"

The father, a very benign character, says, "Okay, son," which doesn't seem like a very smart thing to do. He gives the money to his kid, and off the kid goes. He blows it! Messes up! Gets himself into a real bind. Talk about a screw-up, he was a screw-up to end all screw-ups. He ended up in a pig pen.

As he is sitting in the pig pen — and the pigs won't even cooperate with him because they don't like him very much — the great news is that "he came to himself." That is the wonderful thing that happens to this human being. He sees himself as he really is. And he says to himself, "I'm being stupid. I'll go back to my father, and I'll say, 'Father, I have sinned.'"

So he sets off on his long, laborious journey home. His father sees him coming and does the most undignified thing for an elder in a Middle Eastern country. He rushes down the main street, grabs his son, publicly embraces him, forgives him, reinstates him and sets him up in a new life. Father and son have been reconciled.

God, our Father is waiting for each of us to come home. Our Father is waiting for us to come to ourselves. He has never stopped loving us, but he gives us incredible freedom to mess up, on the understanding that when we come to ourselves, because Christ has died for us, we can be reconciled to him. What great, good news this is!

All that leads us to the heart of what I wanted to say this morning. The apostle Paul tells us that this great love of Christ "compels us" — hems us in. Proper appreciation of the love of Christ appropriately applied will hem us in. It will do so in three ways.

First, the love of Christ hems us into a *solid conviction*. Verse 14, "Christ's love compels us because we are *convinced* that one died for all, and therefore all died" (emphasis mine). Notice that I emphasized the word *convinced*. We are talking about conviction. Do not confuse sentiment with conviction. Do you remember the three whales that got stuck under the ice off Alaska, whose story the news media picked up on? Do you remember how the resources of the United States, the Soviet Union and Canada were pooled together? Planes and helicopters went out there, ice breakers plowed through the ice, and all kinds of effort went into releasing those three whales. The world stopped everything and watched with bated breath to see if the whales would get out. "Save the whales!" they said. Ironically, at the same time that was going on, tens of thousands of people were dying of starvation in the Horn of Africa and nobody was doing a thing about it. Why? Because one can be sentimental about whales and it doesn't hurt too much. But to get around to doing something about tens of thousands of starving people in the Horn of Africa, costs. It hurts. And therein lies the difference between sentiment and conviction.

There is no shortage of sentimentality in the American church today. People get very sentimental about Jesus. They can get very sentimental about all kinds of things. But there is a marked lack of conviction, because we are not hemmed in by the love of Christ. We do not have a solid conviction that will change a person's life. What is a solid conviction? "We are convinced that one died for all, and therefore all died. And he died for all, that those who live should no longer live for themselves but for him who died for them and was raised again" (vv. 14–15). Let those words sink in.

Let me just touch on a couple of implications of this truth. If I believe that Christ died for my sins, I will have no difficulty understanding that there were some things in my life for which it was necessary that Christ die. If I carefully think through that position, I will come to this solid conviction: I am no longer free to live with or in the sins for which Christ died. Let me run that by you one more time. If I am convinced that there were things in my life that made it necessary for Christ to die, I will arrive at this conviction: I am no longer free to live with them. Do you believe that?

Perhaps you have adopted a different attitude: "Yes, there are a whole lot of negative things in my life, a lot of garbage, but praise God, God loved me unconditionally and Christ died for me and my sins have been forgiven. Yes, I still have a problem with sin; I keep on sinning, but it doesn't matter, because God will forgive me."

Or, have you arrived at a solid conviction that continuing to live like that with known sin is the essence of selfishness?

If it is true that Christ died for me, then it is necessary for me to accept that I died, too; I died to what it was necessary for Christ to die for. So I come to this solid conviction, that I too, must die; I must die to the sins in my life for which Christ died. The consequence of that is that I am no longer free to live for myself. I am free only to live for Christ. I have arrived at this solid conviction: my life is no longer mine, with Jesus Christ only on the periphery. My life is his.

Can you see the difference between being sentimental about Jesus and having conviction about the love of Christ? Let me give you a very simple visual summary. Look at the cross and what do you see? The cross is a great big capital "I," crossed out. No longer I, but Christ who lives in me. The love of Christ hems us into a solid conviction. If One died for all, then all died. Those who live should no longer live for themselves but for him who died and rose again for their sake.

Second, the love of Christ hems us into a *striking conclusion*. Notice the remarkable words in verse 16: "So from now on we regard no one from a worldly point of view. Though we once regarded Christ in this way, we do so no longer." I find these words to be some of the most challenging in Scripture. By the love of Christ, Paul is being hemmed into a striking conclusion from which there is no escape: that he is no longer free to look at human beings from a purely natural point of view. Granted, he says, that he used to look at them that way, but he had to do a radical turnaround.

And he gives us an example. Paul says, "In exactly the same way that I did a radical 180-degree turn in my attitude toward Christ, I've had to do a radical 180-degree turn in my attitude toward people."

Long before he became the apostle Paul, the rabbi Saul of Tarsus knew his Old Testament. The law said, "Cursed is every one who hangs on a tree," and Jesus of Nazareth had hung on a tree. Therefore, Jesus of Nazareth was accursed. But Messiah is not accursed, therefore Jesus could not be Messiah; he was an impostor and his followers had to be exterminated. Saul had it all nailed down and was operating on that basis, when suddenly he had a vision of the risen Jesus and discovered that he had been dead wrong about Jesus. Yes, it was true that every one who hangs on a tree is cursed. Yes, Jesus had been hanged on a tree. Yes, Jesus was accursed. But Saul was wrong in assuming that Messiah could not be accursed. For he hadn't understood that God had sent Jesus as the Messiah into the world, the one who knew no sin, to be made sin for us, to be accursed for us. When Saul realized he was utterly wrong, he did a 180-degree turn. And instead of becoming the great exterminator, he became Paul the great evangelist.

"Because I've had to change my view about Jesus," Paul says, "I am no longer free to look at people from a human point of view, just as I don't look at Christ any longer from a human point of view." What does that mean? It means that when we Christians begin to apply the love of Christ to our lives, we are no longer free to regard people the way we used to.

Take the young man in a premarital class I held who was not very interested. Trying to draw him into the discussion, I said to him, "You've asked this young lady to leave her mother and father, all her family and everything she has known, to become your wife. Look at her and tell me what you see when you look at her."

"Well," he said, "she's a cute little chick."

I said, "That's true. Go on."

"That's about it," he said.

"Come on," I said, "you can do better than that. You've asked her to leave her parents and everything she's known to devote herself to you. She needs to know what you think about her. So come on and tell her."

He said, "She's a cute little chick."

"Would you like to know what I see when I look at her?" I asked.

He said, "If you like."

I said, "I see a piece of divine creation. I see somebody for whom God planned before eternity past. I see somebody whom God loves to distraction. I see somebody for whom Christ died. I see somebody whom the Holy Spirit would love to indwell. I see somebody whom God could use as a means of untold blessing wherever she goes. I see somebody whom God would welcome warmly into heaven. I see somebody of eternal significance.... Would you like me to go on?"

"No, that will do," he said.

Do you see the difference? The love of Christ hems us into the striking conclusion that we are no longer free to look at people the way we used to look at them. So you look at a cute little chick. Do you see a cute little chick or do you see someone for whom Christ died? If you see a big, fat, ugly slob, do you see a big, fat ugly slob or do you see someone whom God loves to distraction? For whom Christ died?

The love of Christ hems me into a solid conviction that I am no longer free to live for myself, but for Christ. It hems me into the striking conclusion that I am no longer free to look at people the way I used to. These two things built into the life of every Christian will utterly transform the church.

Third, the love of Christ hems me into a *serious commitment*. Read the words of the apostle Paul: "All this [that we have been talking about] is from God, who reconciled us to himself through Christ and gave us the ministry of reconciliation: that God was reconciling the world to himself in Christ, not counting men's sins against them. And he has committed to us the message of reconciliation. We are therefore Christ's ambassadors, as though God were making his appeal through us. We implore you on Christ's behalf: Be reconciled to God" (2 Cor. 5:18–20).

If I have arrived at this conviction and if I have come to this conclusion, then I am called upon to make this serious commitment: I will accept the fact that because I have been reconciled to God, I have been recruited as a minister of reconciliation. That doesn't mean that I quit my job and go to seminary. It does mean that whatever my daily life requires me to be and do, in the midst of it and through the means of it, I am a minister of reconciliation. I am to become the means whereby men and women hear the gospel, the call to be reconciled to God. I become the means of reconciling broken relationships, trying to unite that which is fractured and fragmented in my culture through the grace of God. Because I have been reconciled, I have been recruited, and I make this solid commitment. You can call me what you like. You can call me a banker or a physician or a homemaker or a student or a professional athlete. It doesn't matter what you call me. That's secondary. What I am, primarily, is a disciple of Jesus Christ committed to being a minister of reconciliation.

Can you see the possibilities of being hemmed in? Can you see the differences between the people who meander selfishly and sluggishly through life and those who are hemmed in by the love of Christ? If I believe that Christ loved the world, loved me enough to die for me, then I am no longer free to live for myself. That fact becomes a solid conviction. I have no alternative but to arrive at this striking conclusion that I am no longer free to look at people from a purely natural point of view. I have no alternative but to make this serious commitment, that whatever the details of my life might be, I am primarily a minister of reconciliation.

Our world needs such people of depth, drive and direction. Will you be one who is both reconciled and a reconciler? Let Christ's love compel you!

COMMENT

Life is complicated. Popular misconceptions infect not only their immediate subject matter, but other perceptions which are based upon them. There are times in our ministries when, in order to help our congregations answer a crucial question, we have to raise and answer another question first, and maybe even another one before that. Stuart Briscoe's sermon, "When We Are Lacking Direction," is a fine example of handling this kind of situation.

This is a good sermon *theologically* because it recognizes the interconnected nature of our faith. To understand God's direction for our lives, we must understand God's love, and to appreciate that love, we must recognize the depth of our own problem with sin.

This sermon is also distinctive *stylistically* because of a clear, logical presentation that facilitates our following it well, even at considerable length. Briscoe's use of alliterations ("depth, drive and direction", "a Solid Conviction, a Striking Conclusion, and a Serious Commitment") as well as illustrations help to keep his audience with him.

PROBLEM

After an introductory illustration indicating how frequently people have no sense of where they should be going with their lives, Briscoe quickly turns to the subject of his sermon by saying, *"I want to talk about finding a sense of direction."* By saying this, even though he must first handle the topics of God's love and our sin in order to speak about direction for our lives, he helps his listeners keep in mind where he is going. He approaches the problem through a structure which is actually quite common in Scripture: chiasm. This rhetorical structure in the treatment of a subject is characterized by its progress from a beginning point to a middle point, then retracing its steps out to where it began, but now informed by where it has been. Briscoe's logical path in this sermon can be diagrammed like this:

A. Finding a sense of direction.

B. Appreciating God's love for us in Jesus Christ.

C. The depth of the human sin problem.

B'. Understanding God's love, we apply Jesus' death to our personal sin problem.

A'. Appreciating Jesus' sacrifice for us hems us into a life of depth, drive and direction.

Briscoe follows this pattern, no doubt, because it is the one his biblical text follows.

Text

Expository preachers often use the logical structure of their biblical text to provide the framework and construction of their message. Briscoe does that here. But unlike many other preachers, he does it implicitly. The listener doesn't feel forced to follow the subject in the manner prescribed by the logical literary patterns of a first-century Hellenistic Jewish writer. There is no sense of wishing that one's own questions could be considered in a more contemporary way. The text has been so internalized by the preacher that the logic flows smoothly in a modern setting.

Consider the chiastic structure again, slightly expanded, to show how the biblical logic shapes Briscoe's message. The numbers indicate which verses from the text (2 Cor. 5:14–21) are being cited.

14a: "compelled" to a sense of direction

14b: compelled by "Christ's love"

14c: Out of love "Christ died" for us to take care of our sin problem

14d: If Christ "died for all," then that includes me, the listener

15–21: His death for us compels us to live for him with lives marked by:

15. a Solid Conviction: we "no longer live for [our]selves" (depth);

16. a Striking Conclusion: "we regard no one from a worldly point of view" (drive);

17f. a Serious Commitment to our God-given "ministry of reconciliation" (direction).

PROCLAMATION

Robert Henderson, in his book on evangelism, *Joy to the World* (John Knox Press, 1980), suggests that not only are all people deeply concerned with the questions of purpose, acceptance, and their own death, but the Christian faith has unequaled answers for these problems which the world's people need to hear. "When We Are Lacking Direction" shows how God's acceptance of us — by virtue of Christ's death on the cross — not only puts us at peace concerning our own death, but provides for us both a motivation and a rationale for the point of our lives' compass.

Biblical Christians by definition will understand the source of the world's problems differently from those who are informed only by popular or "secular" thought. In the current cultural milieu, sin and personal responsibility are mostly out of favor as explanations for our troubles. But our "new" or "modern" cultural understandings have not effected an improvement in our human condition. By stressing biblical accuracy over political correctness, and by explaining the reality of sin in terms easily understood by his audience, Briscoe urges his listeners to acknowledge that the biblical understanding has much to offer today's society. Because of increased turmoil in both family and society, many people are ready to admit that pop psychology reigns over our civilization's mindset as a naked king. The ability of the Scriptures to shout that the emperor has no clothes can certainly overflow into an increased acceptance of biblical revelation in other areas as well.

Do people really believe God loves them? Do they really know what love is? The perception of God as either cosmic spoilsport or, after C. S. Lewis, a benevolent grandfather who just wants to see a good time had by all — when combined with the prevalent confusion of love with sexual attraction — points to deep disorientation in the human condition. By holding up the sacrificial nature of God's saving act toward us in Jesus Christ, Briscoe goes a long way toward helping us understand love in its truest sense according to this defining, divine example.

Elsewhere in this volume (Neaves, p. 207) the reader will find a sermon based on the question, "Where Are You Headed?" There the subject — important in its own right — is how each person must search to understand the particular way God desires for us to use our talents and gifts to heaven's glory. Briscoe suggests that before we are able to do that, we must first understand any calling in the framework of the love of Christ compelling us into ministries of reconciliation. Some will find their reconciling work identified with their occupations. Others will find their reconciling happening in the workplace or family. Still others will find themselves with the freedom to do their particular ministries because of the occupations. All of life is interconnected.

Response

Briscoe is asking us to respond by changing our understandings. Having become aware that our assumptions regarding sin and God's love need redefinition according to the biblical message, he spends his energy working on our understandings and motivations. The specific responses he solicits are internal: *"God, our Father, is waiting for each of us to come home." "Will you be one who is both reconciled and a reconciler? Let Christ's love compel you!"* Near the end of the message, he brings the listener to particular manifestations of these new orientations: *"I become the means of... trying to unite that which is fractured and fragmented in my culture through the grace of God."* However, Briscoe does not weaken the inner work he is urging by hurriedly calling for specific behaviors. Having proclaimed to his listeners these new understandings, he allows the Holy Spirit to work through the Word in people's lives to translate these biblical truths into a faith that is lived out in the day to day of life.

SUGGESTIONS

- Are there popular misunderstandings standing in the way of your congregation's growing spiritual maturity? Your people may be more interested in addressing those misconceptions if you show how they are inseparably connected to other areas in which they readily admit interest. For example, a Christian cannot rightly understand financial freedom (or church finances) if he or she accepts western materialism uncritically. Or, parents whose children are still maturing may wonder why they have so much trouble getting their children to do what is right. They may need to recognize the biblical mandate for parents to put priority on people over professions. Prayerfully consider your congregation's preconceptions and misconceptions about faith and life as you get to know them. Integrate what you learn into your preaching topics. You will love your people best as you address their real needs and questions along with many of the underlying assumptions in our culture.
- Learn from the structure of this sermon. Do you always have an introduction, three points, an illustration and a conclusion? Do you experiment with different structures? Chiasm allows you to discuss a difficult topic, uncover the underlying components repeatedly until the critical piece of the puzzle has been deciphered, and then return to the topic, enlightened by the new understanding you have all gained together. Consider other structures as well.
- Did you notice the simple power in Briscoe's visual image of the Cross as a big "I" crossed out? Too often we reserve visual aids for children's sermons, when churches of previous centuries utilized them throughout their buildings, in stained glass windows and the architecture itself. Painting more word pictures, or actually using props or multi-media in preaching can keep your proclamation lively and speak to listeners' different learning styles.

Peter J. Smith

Unnatural Compassion

2 CORINTHIANS 5:16–21

REV. DR. MARTIN B. COPENHAVER
THE WELLESLEY CONGREGATIONAL CHURCH
WELLESLEY, MASSACHUSETTS

Rev. Dr. Martin B. Copenhaver

Unnatural Compassion

2 Corinthians 5:16–21, RSV

I.

You are watching your favorite program on television when the host says, "We'll be back after these words from our sponsors." Each week, the words always send you into the kitchen, like Pavlov's dog, looking for food. But as you stand to leave, the image on the screen arrests you. It is a child, looking up with eyes like deep brown pools, his arms as thin as twigs, seemingly stuck into a balloon, which is the child's bloated belly. Flies gather in clusters on his body, but the child seems too weak to brush them away. Perhaps this is a picture of what it is to be four years old and without hope. After the picture has drawn you in, the narrator says that the money we spend on one meal is enough to feed a child like this for many days. He concludes with an appeal to viewers to send funds for a hunger relief agency.

Maybe it is the picture on the screen, that beautiful and innocent child so cruelly battered by the random winds of poverty. (Those eyes! It will be some time before you will forget them, unmistakably the eyes of a child and yet, at the same time, the eyes of an old man who has seen a lifetime of sorrow and disappointment.) Maybe, in part, it is because you were at that moment headed to the refrigerator for food that you do not need and only vaguely desire, so you feel a bit as if you have been caught in the act. In any case, you go past the kitchen straight to the desk where you keep your checkbook. Then and there you write a check to the relief agency for an amount that may not be large for some people but it is for you, and certainly will be to hungry children.

The next time you see the commercial, it touches you again. Those eyes! There is so much in those eyes! You wonder if your friend has seen the commercial. Perhaps you will give her the address so that she, too, can send a check.

The next week there is the child again. And then again. Didn't they play this commercial fifteen minutes ago? It is a good cause, but this is a bit much.

The following week, the host of the program issues the usual announcement: "We'll be right back after these words from our sponsors." Right on cue, you stand to get something to eat. Right on cue, there is the child again. You head out of the room. But before you leave, you press a button and silently, instantly, the child's image disappears.

II.

You stop by the church. There, seated on a bench in the hallway outside the offices is a man who says, "Excuse me, can I ask you something?" You stand frozen. The man says, "Will you sit down because I have a bum leg and I find it hard to stand." You hesitate. It looks like he hasn't shaved in a day or two and his clothes are rumpled. *But this is a church, after all,* you say to yourself. So you sit down next to him.

He begins, "Believe me, I don't like to ask this, but I am really desperate. I came to see one of the ministers, but they tell me that none of them are here. I haven't eaten for two days. I hope you never find out what that's like. I never thought I would. I lost my last job two months ago, and I think I'll be able to start on another one Monday — at least, that's what they tell me. But that means that I still won't be paid for at least another week. I really didn't know where else to turn. So I came to the church. Could you give me five dollars to get some food? I can give it back to you as soon as I get back on my feet."

You want to help. You want to run. As he talks, your mind scampers in different directions: Who knows if his need is real or if this is just a well-rehearsed line? Five dollars. What is five dollars to me? And what would it mean to him? Aren't there places in town where they help people like this? Why did he come to the church? "Blessed are the poor." Seems more like a curse. Poor man. Pathetic. I can't imagine. The only time I've been hungry is when I've overslept.

You reach into your pocket and give him ten dollars. He shakes your hand over and over again, and then leaves. Seeing him walk away on that bad leg, you feel quite sure you did the right thing.

A little later that same day you're running some errands, and as you go into the dry cleaners you spot the same man again, this time backing out of a restaurant, yelling something you can't make out to someone inside. As he turns, you can see that his eyes are ablaze with anger. Did he see you or not? You can't tell. You duck into the shop. You are relieved that you won't have to say anything as you see him hobble away again, this time with the extra wobble of someone who has had too much to drink. You vow to yourself, *This is the last time I help someone like that.*

III.

Most of my early life was spent within the gravitational field of New York City, and I spent a good deal of time in the city itself. On the occasion I want to tell you about, I was going to see a play with a group of friends who were from other parts of the country, and so were less familiar with the city's strange and difficult ways. As we walked to the theater, I had a certain spring in my step. After all, I was with people I enjoyed, the exhilarating rhythms of the city were all around us, and I had in my pocket tickets to the hottest show in town. In short, all seemed right with the world.

To get to the theater we had to walk through a particularly tough neighborhood. "No problem," I assured my companions. "I've done it many times." Conversation flowed. There was much laughter.

Suddenly my companions became silent. Then one said, "Did you see that woman? She looked like a prostitute." Everyone seemed to know who he was talking about. I assured them that it is common to see prostitutes in this part of the city.

"No," one of my friends said, "I mean, did you notice the way she was crying?" Everyone else immediately responded, obviously struck by the same sight.

We walked the next few blocks in silence. But the reason for my silence was different. Though I had seen the woman who so haunted the others, I had barely noticed her. The sight hadn't affected me in the same way it did my friends. And that bothered me. I don't think I am less compassionate than most people. But as I had walked in that neighborhood all those times, I must have left some of my compassion on those streets. It probably lay there on the sidewalk, dry and lifeless, until it was swept up and carried away.

IV.

Or how about this: A woman writes to "Dear Abby," explaining that after she had been married forty years, her husband became afflicted with Alzheimer's disease. It was so difficult to see him struggle to remember the simplest things. Eventually it got to the point that he didn't always know who she was. She cared for him at home for a number of years until it became just too much to handle. He went to a nursing home, but she continued to spend many hours with him each day. She wished that she could take on his disease for a time so he could have at least a momentary release from the agony of confusion. As it was, all she could do was sit at his side, talk to him and repeat herself, reassure him and hold his hand. It was hard. But he had been a good husband, and she wanted to do whatever she could for him.

Then one day, while sorting through some papers in his desk at home, she came across a box of letters. They were letters to her husband from a number of women. As she read them, it became clear that over the years, unbeknownst to her, her husband had had affairs with all of them. She was writing to "Dear Abby" to confess that, since this revelation, the very sight of her husband repelled her, and she wondered if she could be blamed if she never went to see him again.

V.

These stories, as varied as they are, all point in a similar direction. They remind me that, in some circumstances, sympathy can come rather easily to us. Much of the time we don't need to be coaxed into having compassion for those who are in need. Compassion seems easy, almost effortless, as though it is inescapably part of what it is to be a human being.

But when the emotional appeal of the television ad has been made too many times, or we have walked down too many streets of human sorrow; when the one we help disappoints us or takes advantage of us, or shows not the slightest sign of gratitude — then we discover that our compassion is really very limited. At such times compassion no longer seems like a natural human inclination. It no longer seems effortless, for at such times it seems beyond the best human effort.

Many people assume that Christians are supposed to care more deeply and to feel more compassionate than the rest of the world does. And when Christians themselves realize, to their continual frustration, that their feelings of compassion have very real limits and that by nature they are as prone toward self-concern as anyone, they feel as if they have failed.

But Jesus seems remarkably uninterested in how we feel. Instead he enjoins us to act. Jesus does not say that when a person hits you on the cheek you should feel charitably toward that person. Rather, he says that when a person hits you on the cheek, you should forget about your feelings for a moment and *act charitably* by turning to that person your other cheek. Jesus could have said that when a person steals your coat, you should feel all sorts of good things about the thief. But no, Jesus says that if a person steals your coat, offer that person your shirt as well. You may not feel like doing it, you may not have any of the compassionate feelings that we assume are associated with such an act — but do it anyway!

If Jesus were asking us to *feel* compassion, he would be asking something that is not within our control, something that does not follow his teachings, his example, his commands. We simply cannot *feel* on demand. Jesus was wise enough not to ask that of us. Instead he asks us to *act*. Turn your cheek. Give your shirt. Do not refuse those who beg from you. Pray for your enemies. Do not wait until you feel like it. Just do it. (See Matthew 5:38-48.)

You see, Jesus asks us to care for others, to turn our cheek, to give the shirt off our back, to give to those who beg, not because we feel compassion for them, but because God does. We do not care for the poor and pray for our enemies because we are that kind of people, but because our God is that kind of God. That is what God is like. God is kind to the ungrateful and the selfish, makes the sun rise on the good and the bad. When we show compassion, it is not because it is a natural human impulse. Rather, it is because, in Paul's words, "from now on...we regard no one from a human point of view" (2 Cor.5:16).

Someone who works in a shelter for the homeless once told me that he often gets frustrated with the people he encounters there. They can be difficult, surly, contrary, ungrateful — in short, they can act very much like people! Frequently he feels like lashing out, or just giving up. He said that he has found only one way to transcend these natural human impulses. When he encounters a particularly unlovable person, he reminds himself, "Christ died for this person" — *this* person, the one who makes life difficult, the one I can't stand even to look at — this person, of all people! "From now on...we regard no one from a human point of view."

So, we do not care for others because we have compassion on them. That compassion is likely to become thin and easily worn out. Instead, we express the love of God who cares for each one as if he or she is the only one.

We do not turn the other cheek because we have been freed from the human desire for vengeance, but to demonstrate God's forgiveness even for those who turn against us.

We do not give the shirt off our back because we are feeling generous, but because we recognize that God showers gifts upon all of us, even those who are "unworthy" by human standards.

We do not offer help to the poor because they are deserving, but because God's gracious love extends to all, even to those who seem "undeserving."

We do not pray for our enemies in the hope that it might work by making them our friends, but rather because our enemies are God's precious children.

From a human point of view, there are friends and enemies, people who are worthy and people who are unworthy, those who are lovable and those who are unlovable, those who stir our compassion and others who prompt our contempt. But "from now on…we regard no one from a human point of view."

Constant compassion can seem like an impossible task for mere human beings. That is why we don't rely on our own compassion. That is why we have God.

COMMENT

A good sermon makes its point without attracting undue attention to itself or the proclaimer. It invites the hearer to enter into the experience, to interact with its declarations, to identify with its problem, and to lean into its solution.

There are two striking features of this sermon. One is the way Copenhaver has "embodied" a solid exegesis of the text. The other is the artistic skill with which he weaves us as hearers into the problem and leads us toward a final, striking affirmation that is positive and rooted deeply in a fine exegesis of the gospel.

Artistically, Copenhaver's use of different "types" of stories presents the problem to the hearer quite effectively. Notice the four different kinds of stories he uses. The first two are imaginary first-person stories. They are universal experiences that most hearers can identify with — watching an affecting commercial and responding to an approach for help. The third is a true story told in the first person. The fourth is a third-person retelling of a newspaper story.

This variety keeps the interest of the hearers and offers different types of validation. The first two stories appeal to universal experience, the third to personal testimony and the fourth to an objective source.

The stories also vary in their depiction of how sympathy and compassion can be worn away: the first by desensitization, the second and fourth from disillusionment and cynicism, the third by our simple finitude (familiarity may not always breed contempt, but it surely encourages oblivion).

PROBLEM

The four concrete illustrations at the beginning of this sermon frame the problem the sermon seeks to address. The problem, in simple form, is as follows. As Christians we believe that we are to care more about the hurts of others than the rest of the world. Yet we don't. Our compassion has limits. We are subject to the same sins and failings as others. It is therefore easy to feel burdened with guilt and failure.

The form of the sermon is really quite simple — ambiguity, then clarity. Copenhaver begins with an apparent problem, then clarifies it so that we can see a less obvious solution. In other words, the problem seems to be one thing, but as we look at it more carefully it turns out to be something else.

Our misunderstanding is rooted in two difficulties. The first is peculiar to our culture and the second is exegetical. First, we confuse feeling and ethical behavior. Our task in Christian obedience, however, is not that we must *feel* a certain way. In our therapeutic society we have emphasized too much that if our feelings change about something it is the same as changing it.

Naturally, feeling does have its place. The inability to feel *any* empathy for others is a sign of the sociopath! But our feelings have limits. It is possible to behave ethically and justly toward another without necessarily entering into their emotional situation. Instead, we are to *act* in certain ways.

But secondly, we might be overwhelmed by even that. For our capacity to *do* might likewise be overwhelmed. Here is the core of grace in this ethically strenuous sermon. We do what is right, Copenhaver says, not because we possess so much compassion for others, *"but because God does."*

St. Augustine once said that Jesus "loved each one he ever met as if there were none other in the whole world to love, and he loved all as he loved each." It is this love, says Copenhaver, that dwells in us to empower our doing.

What actually changes when we become a Christian? The preacher addresses this question by adopting one of two possible interpretations of a key part of the text, 2 Cor. 5:16–21.

TEXT

How does the interpretation of the text help us to resolve the problem? The answer hinges on verse 17.

In claiming that Christ was raised, Christians mean that the very universe has now been changed. According to Paul in verse 17, Jesus' death had cosmic impact — it brought the possibility of salvation for all people, not just Jesus. In the resurrection, God vindicated Jesus as the Son of God and set loose a transforming power in history.

How are we to understand verse 17? There are two ways to interpret the verse. Both speak to us. And both have their problems. One is the more personal view. I grew up hearing verse 17 this way: "If anyone is in Christ, *he is a new creature,* old things are passed away, all things are become as new."

For hearers steeped in revivalism and moralistic religion, this is familiar turf. This interpretation implies that God changes *us,* whatever the world may do. There are many problems with this interpretation, not the least of which is the reality of human sinfulness, even among Christians. What really changes?

The second interpretation may answer the issue. Christians believe that the resurrection is an "objective" reality — something real that had an impact on all things then and since. Certainly, we could mention the many contributions of Christianity. For example, the modern idea of progress owes much to Christianity. Many wonderful historical changes have happened because of the Christian faith.

Yet this is also a problem. If Christ has risen and everything has changed, as we claim, why are things still as they are? Paul can help us. Modern translations of verse 17 capture the idea better. Paul claims, "If anyone is in Christ, *there is* a new creation" (NRSV). This is more accurate.

This does not discount the new birth, but Paul does have something greater in mind here. Christ has risen and his death and resurrection have accomplished something very tangible, with tangible effects. This world, old and sin-filled and broken, is still here, too. But now we no longer live in one world but two. The two ages, the two realms, existing side by side, like different dimensions, occupy the same space, one dying and defeated, the other growing secretly every day. We can change, because something has *really* changed. Objective and subjective are really one. If Christ is risen, then everything is different, not just my experience, not simply my feelings. Something permanent and eternal and irreversible has occurred that affects each one of us.

PROCLAMATION

Copenhaver has masterfully touched on this tension in the text without caving in to either extreme of interpretation. Something transforming has really happened that enables us to see things differently, respond from another motivating center, and obey when we do not feel like obedience. Yet our humanity is still there. We do not need to do away with it in order to live as Christians. This is a real strength in a world where Christian preaching easily lapses into "You oughta, you should, you must, you don't do enough of this or that...." Copenhaver points us to the real strength and power for a holy life: God alone.

That is why the proclamation in this sermon is so strong. Every person listening can identify with the tension between the need to fulfill the will of God and the sinful discrepancies of human existence. Yet the preacher points us to a possibility in God that frees us from both cynicism and self-deception. Of course we cannot live this life! But we have not been asked to live it without God's assistance. And God in Christ has lived it.

The same living Christ can live it through us as we avail ourselves of that life. This makes the task of moral and spiritual life different from mere conformity to a standard.

Copenhaver's sermon offers us, paradoxically, both a more strenuous demand for holy living and relief from the guilt that results from our inadequacy to do it. The sermon seeks to clarify and to draw us to more foundational truth. The hearer has the opportunity to look at his or her own confused motivations.

The sermon does not lessen the demands of Christ upon us. Rather, Copenhaver asks us to engage in Christian behavior with a different center. We are asked to live the Christian life when we are tired as well as energized, when we are discouraged or angry as well as on a spiritual high. The source for living the Christian life is never within us or within our feelings. Our source and strength for the ethical life is always in God alone. This is good news.

SUGGESTIONS

- See Fred Craddock, "The Formation of a Sermon," chapter 9 in his book *Preaching* (Nashville: Abingdon Press, 1985), pp. 170–93, for a discussion of the selection of a proper form for a text.
- Experiment with a familiar text. Using the list of traditional rhetorical forms Craddock lists on page 177, which of the forms listed (or one that is inherent to the text) best fits this text and its message? Why did you select the one you did? Could more than one form be used to present the message of the same text? How would the selection of a different form affect the message you believe the text to convey?

Gary A. Furr

In a New Light

EXODUS 34:29–35; 2 PETER 1:13–21; LUKE 9:28–36

REV. DR. J. BARRY VAUGHN
ST. STEPHEN'S CHURCH, EUTAW,
AND ALL SAINTS CHURCH,
ALICEVILLE, ALABAMA

Rev. Dr. J. Barry Vaughn

In a New Light

EXODUS 34:29–35; 2 PETER 1:13–21; LUKE 9:28–36

In the beginning God created the heavens and the earth...and God said, 'Let there be light'; and there was light" (Genesis 1:3, RSV).

Have you ever thought about the fact that God created light before God created the stars, the givers of light?

A thread of light connects all three of today's readings.

There was the mysterious light shining from Moses' face that frightened the Israelites.

In 2 Peter the author speaks of the prophetic message he delivers as a "light shining in a dark place, until the day dawns and the morning star rises in your hearts" (1:19, NIV).

Finally, there is the story of the Transfiguration. Jesus journeyed to the top of a high mountain, accompanied by Peter, James, and John. There, the disciples saw Jesus transformed into a being of light: "While he was praying, the appearance of his face changed, and his clothes became dazzling white" (Luke 9:29, REB). They also saw him talking with the ancient prophets Moses and Elijah.

I am inclined to think that the transfiguration of which we speak today was not so much in Jesus as in Peter, James, and John. The light that they saw pouring from Jesus had always been there; they just had not seen it before.

Jesus' life and message had already shed a radically new light on the world. The poor had always been regarded as unloved and unwanted by

God. But in the light that Jesus brought, they came to be seen as special objects of God's favor. "Blessed are you poor, for yours is the kingdom of God" (Luke 6:20, RSV).

Tax collectors and prostitutes were shunned, but Jesus cast an entirely new light on their status when he shared meals with them, causing people to complain that he "receives sinners and eats with them" (Luke 15:2, RSV).

To the learned Pharisee Nicodemus, who came to him by night, Jesus brought light. "Very truly, I tell you [Nicodemus], no one can see the kingdom of God without being born from above" (John 3:3, NRSV). "This is the judgment, that the light has come into the world, and people loved darkness rather than light…" (John 3:19, NRSV). Jesus saw that Nicodemus' real need was not a theological discussion but a radically new way of seeing. And Nicodemus, who arrived in the dark, left amidst God's blazing light.

Then there was the "man blind from birth" (John 9:1) whom Jesus and his disciples encountered in Jerusalem. Here even the disciples were in darkness, for they saw this sightless man as nothing more than a theological dilemma: "Rabbi, who sinned, this man or his parents, that he was born blind?" (John 9:2, NRSV).

Jesus, however, saw the man and his blindness as an opportunity to do the work God has been doing since the beginning of creation: "Neither this man nor his parents sinned; he was born blind so that God's works might be revealed in him" (John 9:3, NRSV). Taking the dust from which God had made Adam, and the water with which God makes the new Adam, Jesus gave the blind man light — God's first creation and first gift to the world.

Today's gospel retells the story of a moment when Peter, James, and John suddenly saw Jesus for who he was — a man filled with the light that God created even before he hurled stars and moons and planets into the inky void.

The New Testament speaks of a world hovering between light and darkness. According to 2 Peter we are in that dim moment just before "the day dawns and the morning star rises" (2 Peter 1:19, NIV).

According to John's Gospel, Jesus is "the light of the world" (John 9:5). The darkness has not overcome the Light, but neither has the Light quite overcome the darkness. There are still those who, like Nicodemus, prefer to do their business by night. There are still those who see, not a great and wondrous miracle when the blind man is healed, but merely a sinner violating the sabbath code. There is darkness in every life. There is an unwillingness to see in each one of us.

The light of which the New Testament speaks is not so much about heavenly bodies or luminous filaments; it is about opening our eyes and stepping out of the shadows. It is about taking the risk of adopting a new perspective.

A child who awakens from a nightmare may see the face of a monster on her wall, but when mother switches on the light, it becomes the laughing face of a clown in a picture.

The Bible tells us of Saul who became Paul. He had seen the followers of Jesus as enemies. But after he was blinded on the road to Damascus by a great light, he suddenly came to see them as brothers and sisters.

Today, August 6, the Feast of the Transfiguration, is also the fiftieth anniversary of the nuclear bombing of Hiroshima. The overwhelming light generated by that nuclear explosion was quite different from the light that shone from Moses' face, or the light of Peter's message, much less the light that frightened Jesus' disciples atop the Mount of Transfiguration.

My father served in the Pacific during World War II, and I am deeply grateful that the destruction of Hiroshima prevented an invasion of Japan in which he would have fought. Even though the bombing of Hiroshima brought a terrible war to a quick end and probably saved the lives of thousands of troops, both Japanese and American, nevertheless it took the lives of thousands of men, women and children.

For over forty years we have seen the world in the light of nuclear destruction. The light that Jesus brought invites us to see the world in a radically different perspective.

Today American veterans of World War II are returning to the sites of many battles, and so are their German and Japanese counterparts. Men who once saw each other as enemies, now see each other as neighbors.

A little over a hundred years ago, many in the South and elsewhere in the United States saw black people as slaves. But now we have learned and are still learning that black and white people alike are "created equal; that they are endowed by their creator with certain unalienable rights...."

According to the Talmud, a Jew must pray at dawn. But when is dawn? It is said that a young student asked his teacher, "Rabbi, when is dawn? Is dawn the moment when the last star fades from the sky, or is it when the sun creeps above the horizon?"

The wise old teacher replied, "No, my son. Dawn is the moment when you can look at the face of another and see not an enemy but a friend."

In the light of Hiroshima we came to see half the world as our enemies, dedicated to our destruction. And we saw ourselves as their enemies, and dedicated ourselves to their destruction.

But in the light of the Transfiguration, God invites us to see the poor as heirs of heaven, to see sickness not as divine punishment but as an opportunity to do God's work, and to see each other as sons and daughters of God.

COMMENT

Sermons come in all kinds of packages. Some are intensive, while others are extensive. Some sermons follow clear outlines which persuade by force of logic. Others are evocative, suggesting images and impressions which linger in the heart and mind long after the worshiper departs. These images become a trigger for further associations. Since people are varied and complex in temperament, this is a positive diversity.

Barry Vaughn's "In a New Light" is an eloquent and simple sermon. The message of the sermon can be easily stated: In Jesus a radically new light has been shed in the world that can transform us and enable us to see others as the children of God rather than as enemies.

Having identified the main theme, however, we do well to dwell on the deceptive simplicity of this sermon, in order that we might penetrate beneath its surface to see its riches. Because of its brevity, its evocative nature and its clear statement of theme, let us look at some outstanding features of the sermon rather than offer a structural analysis.

LECTIONARY PREACHING

First, Vaughn brings the lectionary texts together by seeing their organic unity around the theme of light. For preachers in traditions less familiar with the lectionary, this approach may seem stilted and confining. But good lectionary preaching is really exercising creativity within the bounds of structure.

Few things are as daunting as the task of selecting one's text for the week. By following the three-year cycle of lectionary readings the preacher is able to avoid one of the most terrifying tasks in ministry, which preaching professor Craig Loscalzo calls, "It's Monday, but Sunday's Coming."[1] Far from being confining, the lectionary actually covers a broader range of Scripture texts than the average preacher would choose on his or her own.

Another advantage of lectionary preaching, obviously, is the provision of companion texts which already have some connection to the main text that is selected. This is a positive feature in worship planning. By following a lectionary, one knows well in advance the biblical texts and themes for each week and can plan music and other elements of worship accordingly. In this sermon Vaughn has focused on the theme of light in the Exodus 34, 2 Peter 1 and Luke 9 passages in a way that enables hearers to see this theme throughout Scripture.

SIMPLICITY

Second, this sermon is a fine illustration of the virtue of simplicity. When I began preaching during graduate school, I preached sermons that were, frankly, born in the intellectual atmosphere of attending doctoral seminars. By Sunday I had whittled the great ideas down somewhat, but I still managed to preach sermons that were dense. I imagine that listening to them was like watching a jet fly over at thirty-thousand feet — momentarily interesting, but not relevant to much on the ground!

Simplicity is not the same as simplistic. Simplistic is the statement of the obvious. It elicits the response, "So what?" Simple is more like a compelling testimony by an eyewitness in a murder trial or an announcement by a president in the face of a crisis. Simple truths pierce to the heart of the matter.

Although Vaughn's sermon is both brief and simple, it is full of scriptural stories, images and allusions. Though the entire sermon is less than twelve hundred words, I counted at least fifteen biblical stories or verse quotations in it.

I also like very much the artistry with which Vaughn weaves texts, images and ideas together. He finds the common thread — light — but then enables us to see it through a prism of images. "Light and darkness" is a familiar polarity. Observe how many different pictures of light Vaughn employs:

stars, the givers of light;
Jesus transformed into a being of light;

the light... they saw pouring from Jesus;
a radically new light;
Jesus cast an entirely new light on their status;
a radically new way of seeing;
God's blazing light;
God's first creation and gift to the world;
opening our eyes and stepping out of the shadows;
adopting a new perspective;
when mother switches on the light;
overwhelming light;
see the poor as heirs of heaven;
see each other as sons and daughters of God.

Yet all is not glowing. Vaughn acknowledges the ambivalence of the world in which we live. Hiroshima and the Mount of Transfiguration become two symbols of the profound struggle between two kinds of light, two ways of viewing the world. How is it that in a space of fifty years we could be driving automobiles in the U.S. manufactured by the same company that built the places that bombed Pearl Harbor? Yet here we are, now friends. Transfiguration is a difficult business.

RESPONSE

How are we to respond to such a sermon? Is its purpose to change our mind about the dropping of the atomic bomb on Hiroshima? I don't think so. Hiroshima is given to us as a historical irony. The most powerful blast that human ingenuity ever constructed could not do what the light that Jesus' disciples saw on the Mount of Transfiguration could do — turn enemies into brothers and sisters!

The irony was no doubt heightened when this sermon was delivered, for it was right in the midst of a controversy at the Smithsonian over a display about the dropping of the atomic bomb. Even fifty years later it is difficult to talk about the darkness!

I imagine myself having heard this sermon, and then walking out into the sunlight of a Sunday morning, perhaps to notice its brilliance for the first time. *Things could be different!* I imagine myself musing on the light and dark in myself, my own world, and the world in which I live. The sermon did not last long enough to point it all out. But it did give me cues with which to think about it.

Thinking about a sermon, arguing with a sermon ("Is this really possible?"), disagreeing, praying, wondering and reflecting are just as much responding as are walking the aisle and agreeing. Sometimes even more so. If we recognize that *"there is an unwillingness to see in each one of us,"* then the question is whether we will open *"our eyes and [step] out of the shadows."*

SUGGESTIONS

- Try preaching from the lectionary for a period of time if that is unfamiliar to you. *The Revised Common Lectionary* (1992) is available from Abingdon Press, Nashville. There are many wonderful supplementary resources for lectionary preaching. One I have found especially helpful is Fred Craddock, et. al., *Preaching Through the Christian Year* (Philadelphia: Trinity Press International, three volumes). To get the best sense of the lectionary, I would suggest that you follow it from Advent through Pentecost for one year. You will find the effort rewarding.
- Variation of expression is important. Take a few sermons you have done recently and mark with a highlighter all the ways you described the same central concept. Do you find yourself repeating certain stock phrases or ideas? Now take that list and try to rewrite the phrases so that no phrase is repeated.

Gary A. Furr

Note
1. See Craig Loscalzo, "It's Monday, but Sunday's Coming: Keeping Vitality in Your Preaching," *Review and Expositor* (Summer 1993), pp. 383-390.

Lord, Teach Us to Pray

ISAIAH 42:1–4; LUKE 11:1–13

Rev. Earl Palmer
University Presbyterian Church
Seattle, Washington

REV. EARL PALMER

LORD, TEACH US TO PRAY

ISAIAH 42:1–4; LUKE 11:1–13, NRSV

This is the first in a series of sermons entitled, Lord, Teach Us to Pray.

"[Jesus] was praying in a certain place, and after he had finished, one of his disciples said to him, 'Lord, teach us to pray, as John [the Baptist] taught his disciples'" (Luke 11:1).

The disciples wanted to know how to pray. So do we. They wanted to be sure that they prayed correctly. So do we.

Jesus had probably been a disappointment to his disciples on this account. John the Baptist had taught his disciples special prayers. To do so was expected of all rabbis. We can see this in the Dead Sea Scrolls — most of them contain special prayers for special occasions. Evidently, our Lord had not fulfilled this obligation to his disciples. The disciples wanted to know how to pray properly, so they asked Jesus to teach them. Notice the amazing answer Jesus gives. It must have taken everyone by surprise. First he teaches them only a short prayer, not a great oratorical masterpiece, and then he tells them two parables. The shortened form of the prayer, which we call The Lord's Prayer, is in Luke 11:2–4, "When you pray," Jesus told them, "say:

Father, hallowed be your name.
Your kingdom come.
Give us each day our daily bread.
And forgive us our sins,
for we ourselves forgive everyone indebted to us.
And do not bring us to the time of trial."

Now Jesus tells them the first of two parables. "Suppose one of you has a friend, and you go to him at midnight and say to him, 'Friend, lend me three loaves of bread; for a friend of mine has arrived, and I have nothing to set before him.' And he answers from within, 'Do not bother me; the door has already been locked, and my children are with me in bed; I cannot get up and give you anything.'" What a shock! Our Lord always has a surprise in his parables. We wouldn't expect a friend to say, "I can't give you anything," would we?

What follows is the humorous part of this parable: Jesus says, "I tell you, even though he will not get up and give him anything because he is his friend, at least because of his persistence he will get up and give him whatever he needs." The fact that the first friend keeps knocking on the door and saying, "I know you're in there; please come out and give me some bread for my visitors; I need your help," is what impels the friend to give in to the request.

Our Lord Jesus teaches us two things from this parable. First, that he is a friend. We wouldn't keep on knocking at a stranger's house, because they would certainly call 911. But it is okay to keep knocking at a friend's house. So this is a parable about a friend. But it is also a parable about persistence, about not giving up.

The second parable that Jesus teaches them is the parable of the Good Father. Jesus says, "So I say to you: Ask and it will be given to you; seek and you will find; knock and the door will be opened to you" (Luke 11:9, NIV). Isn't it interesting that our Lord chooses totally secular, nonreligious words to describe prayer? *Ask. Seek. Knock.* They are just earthy, human words that our Lord chooses to teach us about prayer. Then Jesus continued, "For everyone who asks receives, and everyone who searches [seeks] finds; and for everyone who knocks, the door will be opened. Is there any among you who, if your child asks for a fish, will give a snake instead of a fish? Or if the child asks for an egg, will give a scorpion? If you then, who are evil, know how to give good gifts to your children, how much more will the heavenly Father give the Holy Spirit to those who ask him!" (Luke 11:10–12).

The disciples wanted to know how to pray and they wanted to know how to pray correctly. From what we understand of the first-century period, being correct was the most important part of one's prayer life. It is very hard to unlearn that instinct. We, too, always want to do things just right, especially those things that we know are very important. We don't want to make any mistakes on something as important as prayer. Maybe that's because we think of prayer in a ceremonial way. That's what the disciples thought. It's certainly true of the prayers found in the Dead Sea Scrolls. We, too, think of prayer as ceremonial. Prayer is of vital importance to us and our faith, but we tend to consider it a ceremony to be performed in the specified way.

I have some very good news for you, which may come as a big surprise, but which I hope will become wonderfully real for you. My good news can be summed up in two quotations from G. K. Chesterton. The first is one of Chesterton's great one-liners: "The serious business of heaven is joy!" That's a surprise! I would have thought that the serious business of heaven is judgment.

My other quote is also from G. K. Chesterton: "Anything worth doing is worth doing badly." You didn't expect that did you? You expected the Benjamin Franklin quote, "Anything worth doing is worth doing well." But Franklin wasn't as good a philosopher as Chesterton. In the heavenly sense Franklin was wrong. I'm all for doing things well. But anything worth doing, anything really good, is also worth doing badly! It's only the bad things that have to be done well. It's only the really weak things that have to be done really well. Like the car with a lousy engine that has to be really polished up if you want to sell it. A Rolls Royce can be dirty, but that doesn't matter; you'll still sell it. Anything worth doing, is worth our effort, no matter how poorly we may achieve it.

In his parable, Jesus is talking about prayer. You have a friend. You go over to the friend's house and ask for bread. Your friend says, "Sorry, my kids are in bed and we're all asleep." So you keep pounding on the door. Is that doing things well? What kind of friendship do you have? We're not supposed to pound on a friend's door in the middle of the night. But, he comes down, answers the door and says, "What do you want?" You say, "I want three loaves of bread please." "Okay!" says the friend. Anything worth doing, is worth doing badly.

Isaiah 42 teaches that very same thing in a surprising context. Isaiah 42:1–4 is a messianic passage, a so-called "Suffering Servant Song," one of the most famous passages predicting the Messiah. It tells us what the Messiah will be like.

> Here is my servant, whom I uphold,
> > my chosen, in whom my soul delights;
> I have put my spirit upon him;
> > he will bring forth justice to the nations.

[Here comes the surprise]:

> He will not cry or lift up his voice,
> > or make it heard in the street.

The Messiah will be quiet. We don't expect that. We expect him to be a powerful judgment upon the earth. Isaiah means that he will take us by surprise. This is the first hint that he will be a suffering servant. Then comes the best part of all, the next two lines:

> a bruised reed he will not break,
> > and a dimly burning wick he will not quench [extinguish].

That means that when our prayer is so dim, so imperfect and so badly done that we can hardly see the flicker, the Messiah is so good and so caring that he will not extinguish that tiny little flicker of light. When your life feels so bent up, when you are almost breaking and you don't even know how to pray, the good news is that the Messiah is so good, so understanding, that he will not break you, won't put pressure on the bent reed.

When Charles Colson started the Prison Fellowship Ministry, he chose as their symbol a bruised reed and the words from this text, "A bruised reed he will not break." A person in prison is a bent reed. The good news is that God is so good, he will not break that reed. Prison may break you, but God will never break you.

What does this tell us about prayer? Prayer, our relationship with God, the greatest things, the most important things, that are good, real and durable, all these are worth doing badly. Because even when we pray badly, when we mess up, we can't destroy them. Do you have that much confidence in God?

Let me give you an illustration of how this is true in ordinary life. Have you noticed that the best things in life can't be ruined by mistakes made socially? When the union of a boy and girl is so right and good, and the young couple are so happy with each other and others are happy for them, no minister can ruin the wedding ceremony. The service can have lots of mistakes but none will make any difference, because something so good is happening that no minister can destroy it, no florist's error can upset it. I tell young couples who come to me to be married not to overrehearse. Most people overrehearse. "I'll lead you through the wedding," I tell them. "You just come as amateurs. A wedding is an amateur event. Just relax. If there are any mistakes to be made, I'll make them." Weddings are an amateur event, not a professional production. You cannot harm a wedding.

I have good news for you. Prayer is an amateur event. It's for amateurs. Anything worth doing, is worth doing badly.

When should we pray? There are two times when you should pray. One is when you feel like it. The other is when you don't feel like it!

First, when you feel like praying is the time to pray. When you are grateful, or when you are in a grave emergency in which you need help, are two obvious times to pray. Never feel guilty that you are praying in a foxhole. Pray whenever you feel like it. You have the right to, because Jesus Christ is your friend.

Second, pray when you don't feel like it, when you feel dry, when you feel that a friendship has gone cold, maybe on your side. Pray when there is grave emergency that has become chronic and you feel there is no hope.

Pray when you feel like it and pray when you don't feel like it. Prayer is the language of a relationship. That is why our Lord told the disciples the parable of the persistent friend.

Because it is a relationship, prayer is honest. Sometimes it is joyous, sometimes it's frightened. Sometimes it is the language of urgent pleas for help. But always it is amateurish. That's prayer.

There are four kinds of prayer. The first is the prayer of confession. This is prayer in which we are aware of ourselves, who we are and who it is that comes to God. Prayers of confession are honest prayers. Why would we hide anything from our friend? He knows who we are. These are the prayers that focus on the bruised reed and the dimly lit wick. We begin with confession and we ask God for his help. We concentrate on the bruised reed — but not too much! Martin Luther was always confessing his sins. And then he discovered in Romans 8 that God's love was greater than his sins.

The second type of prayer is the prayer of gratitude, the prayer of praise. This is the prayer in which we get to thank God that he is the friend who knows how to heal a bruised reed. In fact, he can and will heal a broken reed. When we are grateful and thank God for both who he is and what he has done for us, those are the prayers of praise. They are a large part of the Bible.

The third type is the prayer of intercession. In intercession we think with God about his work in the world. A great part of prayer vocabulary in both the Old and the New Testaments is thinking, even arguing with God.

The fourth type of prayer is the prayer of meditation. In meditation, we remember everything that God has done. The Bible is full of these great remembering prayers.

How can you pray? How do you pray? Is there a proper way of praying? Hey, anything worth doing is worth doing badly. Prayer is for amateurs!

Sandra and Ray Vanderpole wrote a wonderful article for our church paper about some of the things that they have been through during their time in the United States before they returned to Haiti. Sandra's last paragraph is so moving that it is a wonderful way to end this sermon, and also summarize what this sermon series is all about. Sandra writes:

> I feel Jesus calling us to follow him. We found out that we can trust him. We found out that he will put the pieces together. We found out that he will have breakfast waiting for us when we get to shore. We are confident that he will have breakfast waiting for us. [See John 21:1–14.]

How do you pray? First, you have to make Jesus Christ your friend. Then, when he is your friend, you have the right to barge right in! He wants us just to show up. That's all prayer is, just showing up. Show up as you are, as an amateur. Ask, seek, knock.

COMMENT

Take any introductory journalism class and you can't avoid learning the five "Ws" of good reporting: who, what, where, when, and why. Those are the basic facts every good news story must provide — those are the questions people want answered. Earl Palmer gives his audience the five "Ws" of prayer in his sermon, "Lord, Teach Us to Pray."

Palmer knows the value of teaching. He knows the value of covering the basics. He knows the value of answering the questions in the hearts and minds of those coming to church on Sunday mornings: Who am I to bother God with the particulars of my life? What do I know about prayer? Where do I go to learn to pray? And most importantly, why pray? In less than 2,200 words and perhaps no more than twenty minutes, Palmer delivers "Prayer 101," an introductory class on prayer.

"Lord, Teach Us to Pray" is classic Palmer — straightforward, crisp, clean, uncluttered. With the use of clipped, succinct sentences and a pace that moves quickly through the Lord's Prayer, two parables, and a passage from Isaiah, his preaching is meant to be heard, not read. He preaches to make a point and he makes his point clear. There's no mistaking what the "take away" from this sermon is: *"Prayer is an amateur event."* No matter how long we've been Christians, no matter how little or how much education we have, no matter whether we are laity or clergy, we are all amateurs when it comes to prayer.

THE "WHO" OF PRAYER

"Prayer is an amateur event." This sermon makes it clear that prayer is for everyone — you, me, the person sitting next to us — every individual sitting in the pews. Using the parable of the Friend at Midnight, Palmer teaches that prayer is communication between friends.

The "What" of Prayer

Not only is prayer the common, everyday, unceremonial language of friendship, but prayer is persistent. Palmer says, *"We wouldn't keep knocking at a stranger's house, because they would certainly call 911. But it is okay to keep knocking at a friend's house...it is a parable about persistence, about not giving up."*

Moving into the second parable of the text, the parable of the Good Father, Palmer's clarity is noteworthy. The "what" of prayer is the point Palmer drives homes through quotes by G. K. Chesterton and Isaiah 42:1–4: Anything worth doing is worth doing badly. What is the "what" of prayer? What is the good news? You don't have to be good at prayer to be effective — there is no "right" way to pray, no "wrong" way to pray. Prayer is worth doing, even if done "badly."

The "When" and "Where" of Prayer

The "when" and "where" of prayer are inextricably intertwined and Palmer again makes the point quickly, clearly, concisely: *"There are two times when you should pray. One is when you feel like it. The other is when you don't feel like it."* Any time. Any where. For any reason. For no reason. Again, the strength of Palmer's preaching in this sermon is not profundity — it's practicality.

The "Why" of Prayer

Palmer begins this sermon by stating that it is the first in a series on prayer. An as introductory sermon, Palmer uses his text to establish several important parameters for the sermons to follow. First, he establishes that prayer is not intended to be a professional endeavor. The opening line of Dr. Benjamin Spock's famous book on child care says, *"You know more than you think you do."* That's the message Palmer wants his congregation to hear about prayer.

Second, Palmer establishes that prayer is the *"language of friendship,"* an amateur event, something you do when you feel like it — and when you don't.

Third, as any good teacher does at the beginning of a unit study, Palmer defines the significant terms, the terms which essentially address the "why" of prayer: confession, thanksgiving, intercession, and meditation.

Palmer has set the stage for the weeks to come. He's covered the basics. Who, what, where, when, and why: those are the questions people want answered — those are the questions "Lord, Teach Us to Pray" addresses.

SUGGESTIONS

- When considering a text, particularly a character story or parable, take yourself through the exercise of identifying the five "Ws," who, what, where, when, and why. Your sermon development may take on a new dimension or perspective.
- Use the line from Dr. Benjamin Spock ("You know more than you think you do") or G. K. Chesterton ("Anything worth doing is worth doing badly") as the basis for a sermon on prayer. Many people feel inadequate or unskilled when it comes to prayer. Proclaim the good news — prayer is an amateur event.
- Take a cue from Palmer. We live in a sound-byte culture — clipped phrases and visual images for short attention spans. With this in mind, be intentional in your preaching style in the use of short sentences, repetition, and visual images.

Debra K. Klingsporn

I Believe in Jesus Christ

PHILIPPIANS 2:5–11

Dr. Roberta Hestenes
President, Eastern College
St. Davids, Pennsylvania

DR. ROBERTA HESTENES

I BELIEVE IN JESUS CHRIST

PHILIPPIANS 2:5–11, NIV

About two weeks ago at Eastern College, the Christian school that I serve outside Philadelphia, a group of our students were preparing for a summer internship in Calcutta, working with the Sisters of Charity, among the dying and the poor. It was to be the first time any of them had ever gone on a trip outside of this country, much less all the way to India — particularly to Calcutta.

The students were anxious that all of the preparations be nailed down and firm. So they made a long distance phone call to Calcutta, to the Sisters, where a quiet voice answered the phone. The students asked the kinds of questions that were uppermost on their minds as they prepared for this adventure. What should they wear? How hot would it be? How much spending money should they take? Who would meet them at the airport? What would the living arrangements be? Basically, they were asking, "Will we be taken care of? Will everything be all right?"

The voice on the other end very patiently answered question after question. When all the questions had been asked and answered, the students thought they had better find out to whom they were talking. In case something went wrong they would have the name of a person whom they could go back to. In her most official adult voice, one student said, "Who is it that I am talking to?" The voice on the other end said, "It's Mother

Teresa." The students were surprised and a little embarrassed and then very pleased.

Why were they surprised? They were surprised because they have been brought up in a world, in a culture, that thinks it knows what success looks like and how success behaves. They have been brought up in a world that knows what power looks like, and how power behaves when it makes its way to the top. They have been brought up in a culture that Dr. Daniel Levenson, psychologist at Yale University, identified some years back as "permeated by a pervasive metaphor." The metaphor that permeates our culture is the metaphor of the ladder.

What is life and how is it to be approached? How is it to be dealt with? Dr. Levenson discovered in his research that underneath those questions, for person after person all over the country, was a sense that life is a ladder to be climbed. Somehow you find your way onto a rung and then your task is to climb and climb as far and as fast as you can. Success is reaching the top of the ladder. As you climb, at each stage, and especially as you get to the top, there are perquisites and privileges, there are powers and prerogatives. There are entitlements that belong to you as a right of position and passage, in the way in which the world thinks of you and treats you.

The ladder is such a powerful metaphor, that many times it even shapes the way we in the Christian community think about God and about our faith. Look at the Apostles' Creed. If we are not sensitive to the way in which the culture is constantly coming at us and attempting to shape us, we can read the first clause of the Apostles' Creed in terms of the top of the ladder. Listen to the key words in that clause: "I believe in God, the Father Almighty, Maker of heaven and earth." The images that come from this first line are power and triumph and strength.

But then, we come to the second clause, to the second confession of faith, and we discover a surprising paradox, an astonishing reversal. It is seen not only in this part of the Apostles' Creed but also in our text in Philippians 2:5–11. Here we find the answer to questions people ask about God: "Who is God?" "What is God like?" "How can we come to know and enter into a relationship with God?"

For Christians, from the beginning of the church to this day, there is only one answer to those questions. It comes in the words of the Apostles' Creed in such simple, compressed, tight language. It comes in words that tell a story — a true story. Not words of abstraction and distance or power and privilege, but words that tell the story of Jesus. Listen to them: "who was conceived…born…suffered…was crucified, dead and buried." When you stop and think about those words: *conceived, born, suffered, crucified, dead, buried,* they are words that apply to us, that describe in outline our story. We are born. We know suffering. We face the reality of death and the finality of burial. They are words about us human beings. And yet they are words about Jesus, the Son of God. In the amazing mystery of God, God comes in Jesus, "who, being in very nature God," that is, bearing the very being of God in himself, does not hold onto his "equality with God," in the words of our text, does "not consider [it] something to be grasped." He does not cling to his prerogatives, his perquisites, his entitlements. Rather, he gives them all up and empties himself. He is born as a human being. God, fully God, becomes human like us, fully human, taking on himself all that we endure.

Why? Why does the God of glory, the One present before all things, not only empty himself and take on human flesh but continue to the ultimate emptying — "he humbled himself and became obedient to death"? And death in a particularly awful way, a death which then and even now is an embarrassment, under sentence of execution, death as a criminal. Why, instead of climbing the ladder, this humiliation?

Do you remember a few years ago, when the rains finally came after a long period of drought, and the Los Angeles River once again had water in it? When our family lived in Seattle, we used to drive down to Los Angeles and come in over the Grapevine. It used to catch our fancy that at a certain point on the Grapevine as you drove in from the north, there was a sign on the side of the road reading, "The Los Angeles National Forest." We would always look around and say, "Where are the trees?" Because there is not a tree in sight. Then we'd get to an overpass and there would be a sign on the freeway that read, "The Los Angeles River." The children would say,

"But where is the water?" In that concrete-lined river bed there was no water at all!

That was the state of the Los Angeles River during the long years of drought. But one day the rains came. A young boy who was used to taking his bicycle onto the concrete bed in that river did it again. But he did not realize that since it had rained, the water was coming. The water in the channel was only a trickle as he entered the river, but then very rapidly, unexpectedly, the waters poured down. Suddenly there was a streaming caldron of churning, muddy, debris-laden water. The boy lost his footing on his bicycle and went down into the water. Someone saw him and called 911. The television crews picked up the story and the whole country watched as the boy in the midst of the swirling current was swept from one buttress to the next.

We watched as groups of people came to a place where they could lean over to try to reach out their hands — but they couldn't reach far enough to catch the boy. At the next spot a fire truck had its ladder fully extended and the men were racing to get the ladder out to save him. But it wouldn't reach all the way to where he was. He was swept on down the river.

Helicopters hovered overhead and lowered their dangling rope ladders, but it was not safe to come too far down, so the ladders hung uselessly in the air, the boy's hands reaching up helplessly from below.

A friend of mine was watching all of this on television — the boy being swept along, so many trying in vain to save him — from above — from the side. Suddenly my friend cried out in anguish, "My God, why doesn't somebody get in the water?" There was no other way to save the boy than to get in the water with him — to enter the swift current, to take the risk, to come close enough to grab him with strong arms and drag him to safety.

Friends, that is our reality and our need. In the currents of this world that sweep us along, that claim us, call to us, clutch at us, and leave us beyond our depth, God himself in Jesus entered the raging waters of our struggles, in order to redeem us, to bring us up and out of the floods. Our need was so great that in love and compassion Jesus took no thought for himself, but only for us and for our need. That is why he emptied himself.

When I say the Apostles' Creed, I want to rush quickly past the phrase: "was crucified, dead and buried." When the world wants to know how to find God, it is tempting to let the vague language of religiosity or the search for spirituality in its various forms suffice. But these are not enough. They do not, as the Quakers say, "speak to our condition" — the need that each of us has to be redeemed, to be brought out of the depths by the crucified God. Jesus' death was a scandal. It sounds like foolishness. How can the story of God be the story of a crucified God? Yet, in the mystery of God's love that's what the story is, a story in which each of us is invited to be a participant. Each of us is invited to take hold of the hand that reaches out to take hold of us. Then we are to become part of the work that God is still doing in the world — through his body, the church — to enter into the suffering and pain and sorrow and struggle. So it's good not to rush past the words, "crucified, dead and buried," but to feel their finality, their failure — a failure which then becomes God's victory!

We have a professor at Eastern College whom some of you may know, Tony Campolo. Tony is my favorite preacher. He has a story he has told so often, that at Eastern we have it all memorized. Whenever he starts to tell us that story again, we all know the punchline and can tell it with him. When I think of the greatness and goodness of God, who in love for us was crucified, dead and buried, I remember Tony's story of an old black preacher.

On a Sunday morning, after Tony had preached what he thought was an adequate sermon in an old black church, the old black preacher thought he should get up and let the boy know how preaching really ought to be done.

In that church the old black preacher stood and said,

> There are dark times. There are hard moments in our lives. There are days when the sun is blotted out. There are days in which it's Friday. It may be Friday — but Sunday's a comin'.

There are days when we face the fact that all the strength and energy we were so reliant on are not enough to get us through to the end of the journey. It feels like Friday — but Sunday's a comin'.

There are days in which the children are shot in the schoolyard and evil seems so strong and it's Friday. We know it's Friday and the evil is real — but Sunday's a comin'.

Yes, there are days in which we know our own brokenness, in which we know that our answers in the face of reality are no answers. The dark night comes, the phone call of illness, the child who so bitterly hurts us. In our soul it is Friday. But praise God, as the old preacher said and I invite you to say it with him and me... Because God has come in Christ: *"It may be Friday — but Sunday's a comin'!"* Amen.

COMMENT

Years ago I had the privilege of serving on a seminary committee with Roberta Hestenes. Later, I participated in conferences on small group ministry where she was a respected leader. I was proud to know she was appointed a college president and pleased to see her scholarly and compassionate work in helping draft a Presbyterian statement on sexuality. Now I find that she is returning to the pastoral ministry in California and will be preaching regularly. I envy that lucky congregation!

This sermon is an illustration of Hestenes' gift for communicating a biblically compelling message that is short, sweet, pointed and poignant. I'm not just saying this because I personally like this unusually talented woman. I believe this sermon is a good example of how to take a familiar text, tie it to a familiar creed and apply it in an extraordinary way.

Hestenes teaches and preaches in a gentle, yet compelling manner. In some ways she "sneaks up" on her hearers in this sermon by beginning in one direction, then going in another. At the beginning, we think perhaps she is going to talk about service. But instead, using the biblical text as a springboard, she redirects our attention to an often overlooked dimension of the well-known Apostles' Creed.

THE ISSUE

Hestenes begins with a story of students surprised by having their ordinary questions answered by an extraordinary person — the well-known and respected modern-day saint, Mother Teresa of Calcutta. But rather than directly illustrating her biblical text with this story, Hestenes directs our attention to the assumptions behind the story, pointing out the prevalence of the cultural metaphor of the ladder of success.

The issue Hestenes raises is the biblical appropriateness of this vertical word picture. While the "ladder" may be pervasive in our culture as a measure of success, it does not fit the attitude we are to emulate in Jesus Christ.

As a result of the subtle way our culture conditions our assumptions, we may miss the unique, even astonishing, reversal of that hierarchical metaphor in the confession of our faith.

This is not a sermon on "women's liberation." Hestenes is not raising the issue of gender equality. Rather, she is inviting us to rethink our view of the magnificent paradox of the Incarnation — the "enfleshing" of God in Jesus Christ. And she does so in a way that invites us to rethink many other aspects of our life as disciples of Jesus Christ.

Proclamation

The amazing good news of the Christian gospel is that we are not dealing with a distant deity who expects us to climb some sort of religious ladder to "qualify" for divine favor. Nor are we seeking to appease an impersonal force in order to achieve success in life. Instead, Hestenes proclaims in this sermon that the Creator God became personal, understandable and available for a human relationship. To accomplish this remarkable feat, God had to "humble himself." Both the Servant hymn in Philippians 2 and the Apostles' Creed proclaim this incarnational truth at the center of Christian faith: God became human.

God did not climb down a ladder a few rungs to shout from the rooftops of our world. God *crashed* all the way into the basement of our lives, taking on the form of a servant/slave. Jesus was a man born to die, yet born to initiate life eternal. He was both human and divine. Jesus left behind his divine prerogatives without leaving his divine capacities. And he did so knowing he would have to suffer.

The Creed summarizes the suffering in each word — conception, birth, difficult human existence, crucifixion, death, and burial. We easily overlook the fact that God's suffering did not begin on Good Friday. It began when God emptied himself and became a fertilized cell in young Mary's womb. Observable only to the angels, God's journey to the cross and grave spanned space and time in ways we cannot begin to comprehend. No other religion or human philosophy ever conceived of such an unbelievable notion. The Creator becoming part of the creation in order to communicate his divine love to his creatures is a truth of astounding proportions.

RESPONSE

Hestenes does not elaborate on this central foundation stone of Christian witness. Instead she illustrates the truth of the Incarnation in a way that calls her listeners to respond to the depth of God's self-emptying love. Her story of the drowning boy evokes in us the same anguished cry, "My God, why doesn't somebody get in the water?" Then she ties the illustration to the ancient creed to demonstrate that that is exactly what God did for each of us in our life-threatening condition in need of a savior. God got in the raging waters of our struggles in a "foolish," scandalous way to reach us in love.

Hestenes wraps an invitation into the middle of her explication of the Apostles' Creed when she invites us to "take hold of the hand that reaches out to take hold of us." We are challenged not to rush by the familiar words but to see them in a new light, freed from the cultural definition of success. God's "failure" becomes a victory in exactly the opposite direction from the one we are prone to pursue in our quest for success. Instead of going up the worldly ladder, we are called to become part of what God is still doing in the world by entering into the self-denying life of the disciple. That is a call to suffer for Christ!

Hestenes concludes her sermon by subtly modeling what she is describing. As the president of her college she tells a story often repeated by a colleague in that same school. Instead of drawing attention to herself as the person on top of the "ladder" in academia, she redirects our focus to the well-known phrase made famous by Tony Campolo, "It's Friday, but Sunday's a comin'!" To make a preaching point she quotes her favorite preacher. I like this example of humility. She is not afraid to turn to someone else and give them the credit in order to communicate the truth of the gospel.

SUGGESTIONS

- Reflect on an experience of observing a self-emptying sacrifice when you were growing up or in your more recent experience. What might be a different metaphor or word picture for success instead of a ladder? Where do you struggle to share in God's work in the world? In what ways might Jesus be inviting you to empty yourself to communicate love to someone you know? How could your responses to these questions become part of a future sermon you preach?
- The above or other questions might also be used in a small group Bible study, a sharing group or by individuals looking at the sermon text from Philippians 2. They provide an opportunity to reflect on and apply the biblical principles illustrated in Hestenes' sermon.
- If you haven't done so recently, do a thorough grammatical and exegetical study of Philippians 2:5–11, and begin letting a sermon emerge from your own study and meditation on this great text.
- Take Hestenes' sermon title, "I Believe in Jesus Christ," and begin thinking about preparing a sermon on this subject. What other biblical texts might form the basis for your sermon? How might you develop a sermon series on the Trinity also including "I Believe in God the Father" and "I Believe in the Holy Spirit"?

Gary W. Downing

Martha's Feast and Mary's Portion

GENESIS 18:1–8; LUKE 10:38–42

Rev. Dr. Gilbert R. Friend-Jones
Central Congregational Church (UCC)
Atlanta, Georgia

REV. DR. GILBERT R. FRIEND-JONES

MARTHA'S FEAST AND MARY'S PORTION

GENESIS 18:1–8; LUKE 10:38–42

When Jesus entered the village of Bethany, Martha opened her house to him. In the time-honored traditions of her people, she busied herself to make his stay comfortable. She arranged a room; she drew cool water. She began all the preparations for a feast. She invited many guests from the village and surrounding region. She assembled foods, spices, flowers and beverages. She cleaned and cooked and set the table. The dictates of centuries of hospitality compelled her to incredible busyness. She was honored that the Teacher had consented to stay with her; she wanted this meal to be a memorable occasion for everyone.

All the while she worked, her sister sat with their guest. Mary listened to his stories and engaged him in conversation. With so much work to do, and so little time, Martha grew resentful of Mary's indulgence. Had not both Father Abraham and Mother Sarah jointly prepared the feast for the strangers at Mamre's sacred oaks? Did Mary think she was better than they?

With irritation clearly in her voice, Martha tried to enlist Jesus in her cause. "Good sir," she said, "don't you care that my sister has left me to do all the work? Please, tell her to help me!" How surprised she must have been by his response. "Martha! Martha! You are anxious about many things, but only one thing is necessary. Mary has chosen the better portion, and it will not be taken from her."

Martha was caught in a double bind. To persist in her work would be to choose a "lesser" portion (whatever that meant); but to cease her activity and join the conversation would be to have guests arriving to a meal half-cooked, a house half-cleaned, and decorations half-prepared.

Many commentators, both ancient and modern, fault Martha for not being "spiritual" enough. Mary is seen as the paradigm of the intelligentsia, the patrona of those who value mind over body, spirit over flesh, the contemplative vision over the requirements of practical life. Mary had chosen the "better portion" of conversation, while Martha chose the mundane tasks of preparing the feast.

There is a gloss on this story that comes from the sixth century writings of the Desert Fathers. A visitor once approached the monastery of Abbot Silvanius. When the traveler saw all the brothers working in the fields, he said to them, "Do not labor for bread that perishes. Mary has chosen the better part."

The elder instructed one of the brothers to show the guest to a room. The ninth hour, which was the normal hour for dinner, came and passed and no one came for him. More hours passed. The guest watched the door eagerly, waiting to be summoned to a meal. Finally, he left his room, seeking the abbot. When he found him he asked, "Are the brothers fasting today?"

"Oh, no, they have all eaten."

"Why wasn't I invited?"

"Oh, sir, you are so spiritual. You have no need for bread and material substance. You read and pray all day, and do not need nourishment. You have chosen the better part."

Then the guest prostrated himself: "I beg your pardon, abbot."

The elder pardoned him and then said, "This is how Mary herself stands in need of Martha. It was because of Martha that Mary could receive her praise."

Whatever else Luke's story represents, it is about hospitality. It poses a conundrum for all of us who are Marthas in the world, all of us "practical types," all of us who want to do what is right according to customs and traditions we have learned. But there is no less a conundrum for the Marys among us, all of us who seek some mysterious path to spiritual truth apart from the practical aspects of our lives. The story begs us to ponder the nature of true hospitality, and within that, true spirituality, as well.

Hospitality is one of the universal values that makes us fully human. In every culture, traditions of hospitality run deep. Practices of many kinds have developed to guide us in being proper hosts and proper guests to one another. Sometimes hospitality becomes high ritual, as in the bread-and-salt ceremony of the Ukraine, or the Tea Ceremony in Japan. To knowingly violate the norms of hospitality is to be rude and insulting, and has been known to lead to wars. How a people receives its guests reveals its most fundamental beliefs and values.

The Plains Indians of North America, for example, developed traditions of a generous hospitality that are astonishing to peoples of European descent. (This may reveal why American Indians were so unprepared for what seemed to them the rapacious and callous greed of many European settlers.) The "give-away" is one such Indian custom. At funerals, naming ceremonies, weddings and other major events, but also when there is no special occasion at all, the hosts give away their most prized possessions as a way of honoring their guests. They give away even essential household items. People make beautiful objects such as colorful beadwork and finely woven blankets. They hold competitions to see which are the most beautiful; and then they give them away.

"Things are made to be given," wrote Ella Deloria, expressing a view of the world quite foreign to many of us. The "Give-Away" focuses on "the ultimate need of people to care for each other. Out of that comes all etiquette," explained Lakota artist, Arthur Amiotte. "The idea is that you are a finer person by not having...but by using what you have as a means for ennobling the human spirit. When you give, it becomes an act of love."[1]

I myself have been touched and transformed by the unanticipated hospitality of others. Even in the midst of great scarcity, I have eaten more than my fill from overflowing tables, knowing well the effort and costs to my hosts. Others have invited me, a stranger with no claim on them, into their homes and work places, into the sacred spaces and intimate moments of their lives. So many people of other races, cultures and backgrounds have welcomed me, and shared the substance of their lives with me. They became my tutors, instructing me in the fine art of being human. Were it not for the great kindness and generosity of others, I would be a lesser person.

I always will remember an incident in Saint Petersburg, Russia, then known as Leningrad. It was the Soviet era; people were wary of strangers. New volunteer programs were emerging as part of glasnost. One evening, our group of American volunteers with the Fellowship of Reconciliation were seeking a shelter for homeless people. We were told we would find it in a certain abandoned apartment building. We found our way to the right address, but the building was not abandoned. It obviously was not a shelter. We knocked on an apartment door, and in our limited Russian and English we said, "Homeless…homeless." The woman at the door was very distraught. She did not know where the shelter could be. Then she counted us and threw up her hands. "There are five of you," she said. "I can only take three. Let me call my neighbor."

After she learned that we were not ourselves homeless, she still made a table of foods, vodkas and many sweets. We enjoyed a long evening of limited conversation and much music in the over-heated apartment of this stranger who befriended us. Can you imagine this scene being repeated here?

Our Old Testament text today (Gen. 18:1–8) set the standard for all hospitality. Abraham and Sarah welcomed three strangers in the desert wilderness. Abraham ran to greet them, washed their feet with cool water, and made them rest in the shade of a nearby oak. Although he offered them only a "morsel" of bread, he returned with Sarah to serve a veritable feast. The Hebrew is graphic. In their eagerness, Abraham and Sarah "flung" the food at their guests (v. 8). The *best* cakes, meats and cheeses were spread before their visitors.[2]

Tradition informs us that these three guests really were more than met the eye. Collectively, they were "the Lord" (v. 1).[3] They embodied divinity. By entertaining their guests so lavishly, by pleasing them with good food and drink, Sarah and Abraham unknowingly were entertaining and pleasuring their very God. Encoded in the story, of course, is the message that God expects us to be hospitable. The strangers or guests who come to our door could be "the Lord."

This story represents one of the greatest theological anticipations of ancient times. Already — at the dawn of recorded history — God, the Holy One, the Divine Spirit, comes in neither temple nor totem, but in the flesh and sinews of living people, especially those we call strangers. Jewish tradition is filled with the signs and symbols of hospitality, signaling its importance not just in our communal life, but in our spiritual life as well. It was against this backdrop that Martha and Mary were entertaining Jesus.

This also was the tradition of Jesus. We don't have to strain to recognize the high value of hospitality in his teachings. The observance of ceremonial forms was important to him. On the last night of his life, he knelt before the disciples to wash and dry their feet. He harshly judged members of the privileged class who failed to offer him the proper hospitality prescribed by the etiquette of his culture.

Yet the observance of outward forms was never his central concern. The rules and rituals of hospitality had developed over centuries to facilitate human interaction, but they were merely "outward and visible signs" of an inward and spiritual attitude toward others. Jesus could be as severe toward those who observed the accepted canons as he was of those who didn't. He justified ignoring conventions when circumstances warranted. Not the act itself, but something else, determined its significance.

From his parable of the good Samaritan, to his description of the last judgment, to his last words from the cross, Jesus sharpened and intensified the ancient Semitic affirmation of hospitality. He saw within the universal tradition of a generous welcome a deeper ethical imperative. He advocated a radical hospitality — a hospitality that carries us beyond ethnic, class, political and gender boundaries which continue to divide the human species.

For Jesus, it is not enough to serve those who come to our door. It is not enough to welcome or feed our guests. We must seek out the hungry, the thirsty, the sick. By serving the lonely, the imprisoned and the despairing, we may be serving God.

All of this leads back to our original conundrum. If Jesus so valued hospitality, why did he not acknowledge Martha's selfless generosity on his behalf? What is missing in the story?

Ivan Klima is a contemporary writer whose works were circulated only as forbidden *samizdat* during the Stalinist darkness in what was then Czechoslovakia. Since the collapse of communism, his international reputation is growing as his works are translated. In his *Waiting for the Dark, Waiting for the Light,* he explores how ordinary people dealt with the demands of an oppressive state. He describes how the need to compromise and adapt created a paralysis of the soul, a suspended animation, a spiritual constriction. At one point in his book he asked, "What is tedium?" in the barbed-wire country. He answered: is "time filled with encounters that leave no mark on us." [4]

"Time filled with encounters that leave no mark on us." Martha is at spiritual risk at just this point. She is anxious about many things. She is very busy. She has an abundance of concerns. She is preoccupied. But one thing she is lacking.

She fulfills every conceivable expectation of the generous host. Her guests will be very impressed. They will talk about the Teacher's visit for months, maybe even for years to come. But she is in danger of transforming this *encounter* into an *occasion,* and a potential meeting of minds and hearts into a merely memorable event. After all is over, she will be untouched and unchanged.

Perhaps her generosity is not as selfless as it seems. Unlike Sarah and Abraham, her primary desire is not to serve the Master nor her other guests. In some subtle way, she wants to use his visit to serve her own need for praise and admiration. She will get what she wants. But she will miss much more.

The "better portion" chosen by Mary lies in this and this alone: she remains *present* to her guest. She listens, inquires, reveals, asserts, defends and allows his spirit and hers to engage in mutual transformation. She receives and gives, challenges and appreciates. In this, her spirit grows. This kind of hospitality can never be prescribed, but grows out of wise and caring hearts.

Were this all the evangelist intended, it would be sufficient. How often have we wasted such moments? How often, out of fear or foolishness, have we allowed encounters to become occasions, and forever lost the promise such moments bring? How much tedium have we been willing to bear?

This kind of tedium is the opposite of spiritual fulfillment. This is where the dead bury the dead, where we turn away from life, where, in the words of T. S. Eliot, we put on the "face to meet the faces that [we] meet," and measure out our lives "with coffee spoons."[5] But Christ came to give us life, an abundance of life, an overflowing fullness of life. Christ came to Bethany, bringing the promise of transformation.

"In the Bible," wrote the Latin American theologian, Gustavo Gutierrez, "'to live' always means 'to live with,' 'to live for,' 'to be present to others.'"[6] In other words, to live always involves the fine art of hospitality.

The spiritual challenge for us is not whether we are a Mary or a Martha. We are both — always and inevitably. We are flesh and spirit, mind and body, a union of infinite longing and practical limitations. The challenge is how to be alive, fully alive, in the moments given to us. How can we be open to encounters that bring renewal and transformation?

The key to Luke's story is that Martha's and Mary's visitor is not just another friend, or even a renowned teacher. His role is exactly the same as the three strangers at the oaks of Mamre. He is a "sacred visitor," or more strongly, "the Lord."

We know what the sisters do not: that in this visit, the Word is becoming flesh. The Spirit in this Teacher was present at the beginning of creation, shaping the world and all that is in it. This world belongs to him. It is his Ohana,[7] his home. Though very much a guest at Bethany, he is also Host — the supreme Host who welcomes all. Martha and Mary are as much his guests and he is theirs.

This Jesus bears within himself the image and likeness of God, which is also our true image and likeness. He is the divine messenger, seeking to lead us back to our true divinity. He addresses our true identities, to calling us forth into the fullness of life God intends for us.

If we are both Martha and Mary, we are also, in a terribly important way, "sacred guests." The Lakota believe that we are guests upon the earth. But we are also guests in our era, and guests in our communities. We are both hosts and guests to each other.

What if we practiced being hosts and guests to one another and to everyone whom we meet, even the rudest and most intimidating stranger? What if we invested our better selves in fashioning a welcome to others? What if we conducted our businesses and went about our jobs with the host-and-guest vocation? Would not our politics and economics change dramatically? What if the Bosnian Serbs, Muslims, Croats and others thought of themselves as guests and host to each other? What if Irish Catholics and Irish Protestants assumed responsibility for each other? What if Newt Gingrich and Bill Clinton really tried to live out a tradition of deep hospitality toward one another? Is it not possible to understand "affirmative action" as a kind of radical hospitality?

And on a personal level, what if I am simultaneously host and guest to my partner or my spouse? Or to someone with whom I have a troubled relationship? Or to my child or aging parent? Is not this a way to banish the *tedium* from our lives, and open us to new possibilities for grace and life?

Martha, Mary, and Jesus — each one exists within us and between us. May we be wise enough to choose the better portion.

Notes
1. I call the reader's attention to "Hospitality," *Parabola: The Magazine of Myth and Tradition,* Winter, 1990.
2. Travelers report that such hospitality is still more the norm than the exception among Bedouin peoples in the Middle Eastern deserts.

3. That the three guests embodied one "Lord" was not lost on early Christian theologians, who saw here an anticipation of the Holy Trinity. The famous "Trinity Icon" by Andrei Rublev depicts this very scene.
4. Ivan Klima, *Waiting for the Dark, Waiting for the Light,* trans. Paul Wilson (New York: Grove Press, 1995), quoted in *New York Times Book Review,* March 26, 1995, p. 1.
5. T. S. Eliot, "The Love Song of J. Alfred Prufrock," *Collected Poems 1909–1962* (New York: Harcourt Brace Jovanovich, Publishers, 1970), pp. 3–7.
6. Gustavo Gutierrez, *The God of Life* (Maryknoll, NY: Orbis Books, 1991), p. 11.
7. See Marty Haugen, "One Ohana," the special music for the Sunday this sermon was preached. *Ohana,* meaning "home," comes from the Hawaiian language, meaning "family."

Comment

The old proverb reminds us that "people who live in glass houses shouldn't throw stones," the implication being that public exposure ought to cause one to use discretion when it comes to criticizing others. Visibility and vulnerability are closely linked. Woe to the preacher who fails to heed this truism! If we were to rephrase this aphorism for the church it might sound like this: "Pulpits that are soapboxes soon become slippery indeed." Herein lies one of the great risks of preaching; the honest preacher bares his or her truest self to the congregation on a regular basis and, in doing so, cast convictions upon hazardous waters.

While most of us long to be liked and accepted by everyone, no preacher can afford to let this desire be the determining influence in sermon preparation. As preachers, our integrity depends upon the consistency between our words and our character. Put in popular parlance, "I (meaning who I am as a person) may be the only sermon anyone ever hears." Likewise, as a preacher, I must be aware that any one of my sermons may be all someone ever knows of me. More frightening yet, it may be all anyone ever knows of the gospel.

With the inseparable link between preacher and person in mind, what does the sermon, "Martha's Feast and Mary's Portion," tell us about the preacher? And then, more importantly, what does the sermon tell us about God's character and his call upon our lives?

Preacher & Style

After only one hearing or reading of this sermon, we have a pretty clear idea of the personality and passions of Gilbert R. Friend-Jones. There is an honest transparency here. This is a man who obviously has a love for learning and a deep respect for the diversity of humanity. Throughout the sermon we encounter his fascination with different cultures and traditions, whether it be the ancient Middle Eastern custom of hospitality during Christ's time or the sacred rituals of Native American cultures. The preacher is a learned man and therein we find a level of trust, knowing that we are listening to an avid student of the Bible, of life, and of humanity.

In addition, Friend-Jones is not "preachy." He talks to us as one who lives among us, educating with gentle grace rather than lecturing with platitudes or beating us up with "shoulds and oughts." We sense wisdom in his words, not wrath. One would assume his parishioners come away from worship each week richer in their breadth and depth of understanding of both Scripture and life in general.

Finally, we know that the message emanates from sincere and disciplined study. There's no "winging it" here. Friend-Jones punctuates his sermon with quotes and metaphors gleaned from a discipline of personal study. New preachers take note: Great preachers are not born, they are made from years and years of devoted study. Good sermons are the dividends paid on the preacher's investment of relentless hard work. Friend-Jones' effective sermon is clearly no accident.

PROBLEM

Does this sermon address a real problem in real people's lives? Yes, absolutely. We all live with the tension between directing our energies toward practical action and focusing attention on devotional reflection. In a nutshell, it's the age-old question of works versus faith. Does Mary have *"the better portion,"* while Martha is to be faulted *"for not being 'spiritual' enough"*? Is our Christian faith more a measure of what we *do* than who we *are*?

Friend-Jones, in the character of Martha, finds the personification of this conflict between being and doing. *"Martha was caught in a double bind. To persist in her work would be to choose a 'lesser' portion (whatever that meant); but to cease her activity and join the conversation would be to have guests arriving to a meal half-cooked."* The traditional interpretation of this text depicts Martha as the misguided busy bee who misses out on the blessings that her sister, Mary, discovers in relaxing in Jesus' presence. So it is that workaholics hang our heads in shame and take the gospel's chastisement.

However, Friend-Jones finds something new here, something that may have never occurred to us. Perhaps Martha receives a blessing of her own from spending herself in providing hospitality for her divine guest! Here is a novel notion bound to captivate moderns who are frequently scolded for working too hard, too long, and toward the wrong ends. Could it be that busy work is sometimes commendable? Is there a time and place to step away from sitting adoringly at Christ's feet in order to attend other duties? This sermon suggests there is.

TEXT

Two biblical passages are used as the basis for the sermon: Genesis 18:1–8 (the three heavenly visitors to Abraham and Sarah) and Luke 10:38–42 (Jesus in the home of Martha and Mary). Friend-Jones brings both texts into play, adeptly weaving them throughout his message. The passages are not used to pad the preacher's point but to provide the foundation for a theology of hospitality. No proof-texting here, only a faithful presentation of the role of the host and hostess in the biblical context.

While Friend-Jones utilizes numerous supplemental sources, he consistently returns to the main characters in each of the narratives as models for our own understanding of the role hospitality plays in Christian witness. Many preachers are engagingly anecdotal in style but end up using Scripture as a supplement. Friend-Jones does exactly the opposite. The biblical texts serve as his anchor while he uses periphery anecdotes (i.e., the Desert Fathers story and the Ivan Klima story) as supplements. The well-read preacher has the advantage of an inner file of illustrations. The congregants are the beneficiaries.

PROCLAMATION

In Mary, we find the example of spiritual responsiveness to Jesus' presence in our midst. In Martha, Friend-Jones finds an example of thoughtfulness and hospitality in action. But is there more here? Is there a deeper insight into the relevance of the gospel for our lives? The preacher poses this question for his listeners: *"The story begs us to ponder the nature of true hospitality, and within that, true spirituality, as well."*

Friend-Jones prompts us to move beyond an awareness of the simple grace of providing a warm welcome for our house guests to considering the moral obligation Christians have to care for the hungry and the homeless. Quoting from Ella Deloria, he puts it this way, *"'The ultimate need of people [is] to care for each other. Out of that comes all etiquette.'"* The gospel of Jesus changes our attitude towards all persons at all times. The way of Jesus is to live in a perpetual state of caring for others.

In addition, the stories of Abraham, Sarah, Mary and Martha challenge us to revisit the very nature of God. *"Already — at the dawn of recorded history — God, the Holy One, the Divine Spirit, comes in neither temple nor totem, but in the flesh and sinews of living people, especially those we call strangers...signaling...[hospitality's] importance not just in our communal life, but in our spiritual life as well,"* says Friend-Jones. Thus, hospitality becomes our outward response to the spiritual reality that God welcomes lost souls and attends their deepest needs. In the same way, we demonstrate this theological truth in our treatment of one another, what the preacher calls *"a deeper ethical imperative...radical hospitality."*

Response

The complete sermon is more than an ethical teaching. It is more than a proclamation of truth. It exhorts us to respond. It lifts us to a higher level of spiritual awareness in which our attitudes and behaviors are changed. By this measure, what we have here is a complete sermon. Having made the point that in serving others we are serving God, Friend-Jones takes it one step further. *"For Jesus, it is not enough...to welcome or feed our guests. We must seek out the hungry, the thirsty, the sick."* Our response to the Bible's call to hospitality is more than being ready to serve when called upon. God calls us to actively pursue opportunities to bring grace to others.

Perhaps some of us don't need any help in this area. Maybe we already practice the habit of hospitality in all that we do. No one needs to tell us to perform acts of service. If such persons are in Friend-Jones' congregation, he provides a word of balance. Even though Martha fulfills every expectation of a godly hostess, we cannot know her innermost motivations. However, we need to constantly monitor our own. Generosity is not always *"as selfless as it seems."* Martha is at risk of *"transforming this encounter into an occasion...a potential meeting of minds and hearts into a merely memorable event."* To guard against this, Mary represents the balancing word; she exemplifies the wise and caring heart, in contrast to the functionalism of her sister. With Mary, events are transformed into holy encounters.

Lest this all sounds too high-minded, Friend-Jones is quick to demonstrate where the rubber meets the road. It's not a question of whether one is a Mary or a Martha. In fact, we are both. The real issue is how fully alive we are in the moments of our lives. The preacher focuses on this issue in a series of pointed questions. *"What if we practiced being hosts and guests to one another and to everyone whom we meet, even the rudest and most intimidating stranger?"* Friend-Jones follows with a list of contexts ripe for being transformed into moments of spiritual import — our business dealings, our politics, our economics, in Bosnia or Northern Ireland, and in our own nation's capital. Even closer to home, how about our attitudes and behaviors towards those closest to us, friends and family? Is there a Christlikeness to be found? Are we *"simultaneously host and guest"*? This is the question. What will be our response? The preacher moves the sermon from the pulpit to the pew and leaves it there. Only I, the listener can provide the answer.

SUGGESTIONS

- What does Friend-Jones teach us about good preaching? Several things. First, he is a master at bringing in illustrations from a wide array of sources without appearing elitist in doing so. In this sermon alone we count no fewer than eleven supplementary sources brought in to fill out the biblical lesson. Friend-Jones knows that no reading and no personal experience is wasted on the skillful communicator.

Life is the preacher's library. However, the final measure of success is never the erudition of the speaker; it is how accessible the message is to the audience, and in that way this sermon works. Think about how you use supplementary sources and information in your preaching.

- Notice how naturally Friend-Jones utilizes the primary texts for his sermon. There is no question that the message has been inspired by two specific passages, one from the Old Testament and one from the New. Abraham, Sarah, Mary and Martha remain with us throughout. The frequent use of outside resources might detract from the message were it not for the manner in which it is done, with special attention given by the preacher to the educational level of his congregation. Is the preacher's primary task to familiarize his audience with the biblical text *or* to bring them into a wider arena of awareness, with emphasis on appreciating the culture of other peoples? How this question is answered will largely influence the direction of the sermon. Based on this particular sermon, it would appear Friend-Jones is able to do both, with primacy given to the scriptural lesson.

- As stated at the outset of this Comment, we who preach need to be aware of the transparency of the pulpit. From the lofty perch we betray our deepest passions, our truest character, and, sometimes, even our innermost secrets. Congregants can easily be derailed from tracking with the sermon by the slightest comment taken to be controversial. In this sermon, Friend-Jones chooses to bring in a fleeting reference to "affirmative action," commending it as an expression of godly hospitality. Among certain believers today, such a comment could be most provocative, causing some to turn off and tune out because of their personal opposition to affirmative action. It's hard to keep politics out of the pulpit, even when striving to do so. People will hear what they want to hear, and, unfortunately and just as often, what they *don't* want to hear. Caution should be exercised to assess what issues should or shouldn't be brought into any sermon. If the subject is especially volatile, many will forget everything that's been said before and fall deaf to any subsequent points. The preacher must choose his or her battles carefully, weighing whether igniting potential brush fires will jeopardize the quest for higher ground.

- "Safe" preaching is not necessarily good preaching. If Jesus had colored within the lines, imagine how different his ministry would have been. Sermons that comfort rarely confront, and sermons that confront rarely comfort. Comfortable congregations are stagnant congregations. We would doubt that those who regularly sit under the preaching of Friend-Jones are complacent. We also would have to believe that Friend-Jones has taken his share of criticism. In an era when Christendom is sadly divided between "the liberals and the conservatives," it is especially precarious to stand on the thin edge of the public pulpit. Think about it. How does your preaching comfort? How does it confront?

Richard A. Davis

Crowd Control on Palm Sunday

MATTHEW 21:1–11

Dr. Bruce L. Shelley
Senior Professor of Church History
Denver Seminary
Denver, Colorado

DR. BRUCE L. SHELLEY

CROWD CONTROL ON PALM SUNDAY

MATTHEW 21:1–11, NIV

People in our times are "into" crowds. We eagerly celebrate or protest at the faintest cry. We crowd into stadiums for baseball and football games. We line the streets for parades at Christmas, on St. Patrick's Day or the Fourth of July. We jam arenas for rock concerts and fill orchestra halls for the symphony. We flock to state fairs and art fairs. We storm shopping malls and department stores for special sales and events. We love to be where the action is.

For the most part we love crowds. We think that every crowd is making some sort of statement and we ought to listen. Television reporters and camera people go to the streets and parks because they think that crowds are news. They reflect public opinion, and in this country, as in most western nations, public opinion is king! Or so people think.

Unfortunately in our world big crowds can become big problems. In recent years freedom marches have turned violent and harvest parades bloody. Rock concerts have ended in violence and soccer matches have turned into riots. Political rallies have turned ugly. Why? Because other crowds, new and angry mobs, with a different set of values, want to make their statements or do their thing. Crowds today are often fighting mobs and blood is on the streets.

The problem is not restricted to the steps of city hall. Just move from civic center to the nearest high school campus. School grounds used to be quiet, safe places where kids could learn how to get on with life. But today many high schools are camping grounds for warring tribes, ready to attack their rivals. These crowds are literally destroying young lives, because some of them will give almost anything to belong to the right crowd. Parents are slowly learning that the wrong crowd can destroy their children. Some try to tell their children, "Just say no to the crowd."

That raises a serious question for us in Western countries. In a popular democracy can a crowd be dangerous? Today's Scripture will help us answer that question.

On the Christian calendar, Palm Sunday is about a crowd in the streets a long time ago. Like many of our celebrations, this crowd didn't change much of anything. With all the excitement and shouting in the streets, Jesus did what he had to do, and his enemies in city government did what they were determined to do.

Just five days after the crowds were in the streets, Good Friday came. The skies grew dark. Jesus suffered on Calvary, and God hid his face!

Palm Sunday says to us, "Take crowds seriously, but not too seriously. Listen to the shouts from the streets, but never, never, never sell your soul to a crowd."

This is the way Matthew's Gospel tells the story:

> As they approached Jerusalem and came to Bethphage on the Mount of Olives, Jesus sent two of his disciples, saying to them, "Go to the village ahead of you, and at once you will find a donkey tied there, with her colt by her. Untie them and bring them to me. If anyone says anything to you, tell him that the Lord needs them, and he will send them right away."
>
> This took place to fulfill what was spoken through the prophet:
>
> "Say to the Daughter of Zion,
>   'See, your king comes to you,
> gentle and riding on a donkey,

on a colt, the foal of a donkey.'"

The disciples went and did as Jesus had instructed them. They brought the donkey and the colt, placed their cloaks on them, and Jesus sat on them. A very large crowd spread their cloaks on the road, while others cut branches from the trees and spread them on the road. The crowds that went ahead of him and those that followed shouted,

"Hosanna to the Son of David!"
"Blessed is he who comes in the name of the Lord!"
"Hosanna in the highest!"

When Jesus entered Jerusalem, the whole city was stirred and asked, "Who is this?"

The crowds answered, "This is Jesus, the prophet from Nazareth in Galilee" (Matt. 21:1–11).

Let's make sure we get the picture in focus. Jesus is approaching Jerusalem and the last days of his life. He plans to make a dramatic entry into the city to present himself as the Jewish Messiah — but not the kind of Messiah public opinion polls supported.

As the Feast of Passover was drawing near, all male Jews who lived within twenty-five miles of Jerusalem were expected to attend the feast. But throngs of pilgrims from many countries were also streaming into the city. The city looked for a million people during this greatest event on the Jewish calendar. Jesus could have chosen no better time to present himself with a public symbol to his people, but he was fully aware that the minds of the religious leaders were set against him. He had no reason to expect anything but hostility from them.

Near Bethphage, a crossroads two miles from the city, he had arranged for a donkey and her colt to be brought to him. When they arrived, his disciples laid their garments across the colt as a makeshift saddle for Jesus. On the colt he headed for the city. That is where he met the crowds.

I say "crowds," plural, because according to Matthew's account of the events at least three distinguishable groups responded to Jesus' appearance at the feast. There was a crowd primarily from Galilee, a second, angry crowd from Jerusalem, and a third, somewhat hidden crowd that I'm going to call "the crowd of Jesus."

Palm Sunday itself is mostly about the crowd from Galilee. This is the throng on the road just outside the city who spread their cloaks in Jesus' path and cut palm branches from the trees and spread them on the road.

This is the crowd that cried, "Hosanna! Hail to the Son of David. Blessed is he who comes in the name of the Lord."

These Galileans lining the road into Jerusalem were welcoming their local hero, much as small towns everywhere form a parade for their state champions or war heroes. This crowd was a lot like people in our own society who find it easy to cheer for a popular hero in the open air.

At a certain level in their personal lives, those who made up this Galilean crowd had a deep respect for Jesus. They would have been offended, as many of us are today, when some religious fanatic in Los Angeles or Waco, Texas, claims to be a messiah. These Galileans were just run-of-the-mill common folk who respected Jesus and on rare occasions went to religious services to praise him. They represent popular religious crowds of all sorts. Not fanatics, mind you, not extremists, just good folks who are willing, some of them even eager, to wave a few palm branches for Jesus when it is convenient and in style.

With all the bad press religious extremists have managed to muster in recent years, most common folk still feel good about religion and God. Most of them believe that God loves them and that they are going to heaven when they die. They don't think of angels as messengers of judgment. No, angels, it seems, always surround us tenderly, in mercy.

I have no doubt that most of the people in this crowd waving palm branches on Sunday were unspeakably distressed when they heard that Jesus was crucified on Friday. But when the deed was done where were they? I imagine them asleep in their beds. Their high praises were missing in the hour of crisis. By the time they got up and began to stir about, Jesus was already on the cross!

Don't you think we ought to be just a bit guarded in listening to the voice from the crowd of popularity? This crowd pursues the celebrity, like the popular hero, does the popular thing. But the "popular" is often so superficial, so fleeting, so deceptive. If everybody is for it, if everybody is doing it, if everybody says, "It's okay, you won't get caught," it probably isn't something a real follower of Jesus will want to endorse.

Someone has said, "Fame is written in ice and eventually the sun comes out." It was Jesus himself who said, "The road to destruction is broad and crowded. The road to life is narrow and few people find it." It is enough to make you stop and think about what crowds and public opinion are doing to us.

When Jesus entered Jerusalem, he met another crowd. Verse 10 says, "The whole city was stirred and asked, 'Who is this?'" Jesus' plan worked! Just as Billy Graham does today, Jesus announced to the city, "This is the hour of decision!" Many responded by asking, "Who is this?"

That is the central question for Palm Sunday. Is Jesus the popular prophet from Galilee, the gentle teacher who gives common people hope and meets their needs? Or is he a troublemaker who has come to the temple to spoil our celebration? Has he come to Jerusalem to interfere with our lives and question our favorite religious practices?

You see, within the bustling city there was another crowd, the people who feared Jesus. They saw him as a troublemaker. Some of these people would cry out on Friday morning, "Crucify him!" And by midday they would watch him die and scoff at his claims: "He saved others. Now let him save himself. Come down from the cross!"

The gospel story will not let us forget that mob before Pilate crying, "Crucify!" Undisciplined crowds can be vicious things. Think about that the next time you hear, "Everybody else is doing it," and remember that ten thousand people telling a lie do not make it the truth!

When the Nazi war machine crumbled and peace returned to Europe after World War II, American authorities tried to understand the thinking of the German people. They circulated a questionnaire in the areas they occupied, asking 150 typical Germans to answer a set of questions, promising absolute secrecy. One of the questions was this:

"Who do you think was responsible for the outbreak of the war?

1. The German High Command;
2. The Nazi party leaders;
3. The German people as a whole;
4. The Allies."

Out of 145 answers, 20 said, "The German High Command"; 123 said, "The Nazi party leaders"; 1 said, "The German people as a whole"; 1 said, "The Allies."

The respondents were saying, "Not me! It wasn't me!"

Do you see why I say, "Listen to the crowds in your life but never, never, never sell your soul to them"? You are responsible for your life to God, not to a popular or an angry crowd.

We are here this Palm Sunday, however, not to celebrate with the "popular crowd" or the "angry crowd." We are here to find ourselves in the "hidden crowd."

You have to listen to the story carefully to hear from this hidden crowd. Notice the Bible says that Jesus prepared for the ride into Jerusalem by arranging with someone for the donkey and colt ahead of time. He planned for this celebration, and he apparently had help in planning it. Notice too, that Matthew tells us this took place to fulfill prophecy. God had a hand in both the ecstasy and the agony of these events.

The crowd that we really ought to join this morning is that little company that began to gather a week later when they discovered that their Friend who had died so shamefully on Friday was alive on Sunday. The hidden crowd in this story starts as a small gathering but grows in only seven weeks to a company of thousands, when they hear that the crucified prophet from Galilee was in fact the "Lord of heaven and earth."

Palm Sunday should mean to us, deep within our souls, that Jesus is Lord! He rides into our lives humbly on a colt, sometimes with exciting shouts and sometimes in quiet solitude, but he rides into our lives to take charge.

Being a Christian who follows Jesus through the streets means listening to the crowds but never, never, never selling your soul to them. Your soul belongs to God — through faith in the Lord Jesus Christ.

Let me tell you a story to show you what I mean. You probably have never heard of Dr. Bracket. Neither had I until pastor Will Sangster told his story some years ago. Bracket was one of those dedicated doctors in a small town in West Texas or New Mexico. He specialized in serving poor people. He would get up on the coldest night and drive for miles to help some needy soul out in the country. Everybody for miles around knew his office. It was on Main Street over a clothing store, and there was a brass plate on the door.

Doc Bracket never married. Early on he fell in love, but on the day of the wedding he was called out to the birth of a Mexican child, and his bride-to-be gave him up. She said that a man who would fail to show up for his own wedding for the sake of a Mexican child was not any good as a husband.

After forty years in that town, Dr. Bracket died. He was over seventy. His funeral was the biggest the town had ever seen. But people soon began arguing about a fitting memorial stone and what should be put on it. Months passed and nothing was done. The only people who seemed to worry about it was that family where the child had been delivered on Dr. Bracket's wedding day.

In the end they were the ones who settled the matter of the memorial. It was the undertaker who discovered what they had done. The family couldn't afford a proper monument, so they took one from the doctor's office door, his brass plate. And there, passing through the cemetery, the undertaker saw it. In a mass of flowers was the sign:

Dr. Bracket

Office Upstairs

People in the hidden crowd will get the message.

COMMENT

While listening to a sermon, one listens for an authentic voice that enriches life in community. The preacher has an obligation to do justice both to the sacred text and to the human situation. This, as James Crenshaw explains, must foster a skeptical disposition on the part of the hearer, a critical attitude due, in part, to the perceived disparity between one's own experience and the one the preacher envisions for humankind. So with one foot "firmly planted in the modern age and the other tentatively feeling for a toehold in the biblical period,"[1] the preacher must attempt to link the two distinct worlds by constructing a window through which to peer into the biblical world. In this way the preacher can help persons examine themselves in the light of what they learn from looking through the many colored windowpanes of the biblical text.

Bruce Shelley selects from the text the windowpane of "the crowd" on this distinct Sunday of the church year in which a crowd is significant. Palm Sunday sermons usually assume the crowd's welcoming attitude. But Shelley stops to examine the crowd. While remaining faithful to the biblical record, Shelley's use of creative imagination provides a reflective sermon which helps listeners examine their own religious commitment and encourages a stronger sense of the call for sacrifice and perseverance in living the Christian life.

PROBLEM

The sermon begins by describing a fairly normal experience of the hearer and affirms that, generally, people in our times are "into" crowds. After describing the importance given by media to finding public opinion expressed by crowds, Shelley cites the explosive potential of crowds, which can erupt into something dangerous, effectively building within the listener some skepticism toward crowds. By pointing out the possibility that the crowd a teenager joins may adversely affect their life's direction, the sermon makes hearers — especially parents, aware of the influence of certain potentially harmful groups. So what was seen as safe, even pleasurable, is now presented as a threat. By the time the question is posed, "Can a crowd be dangerous?" the hearer is prepared to answer in the affirmative.

Pointing out the dangers of following what is popular upsets our equilibrium and helps us take a critical look at the makeup of the Palm Sunday crowd. By considering the future action, or nonaction, of the crowd five days later on Good Friday, Shelley identifies three distinct groups which, by inference from the larger Gospel narrative, appear to make up the crowd in the present text. Initially, the hearer is likely to recognize their identification with the Palm Sunday crowd. The sermon likens this crowd to groups which espouse a popular form of culturally bound Christianity, using an entirely appropriate analogy of those who cheer a champion's return at a hometown parade. Yet the sermon points out the spiritual vulnerability of this crowd which found itself "asleep in their beds" when needed in the crisis on Friday. Their lack of support for Jesus in his time of need moves the congregation away from what might have been their initial identification with this crowd. The sermon thus identifies the key problem of following the crowd, a metaphor for a Christian's tendency to follow Christ only as long as it is popular to do so.

TEXT

As any preacher knows, making a sermon fresh and meaningful while dealing with overly familiar texts can be a challenge. While the central idea of the text of the Palm Sunday entry into Jerusalem is about the inauguration of Holy Week, the passage is so well-known that it easily succumbs to merely a sentimentalized treatment of a triumphal entry. To fashion an unexpectedly engaging sermon, Shelley uncovers the identity of the crowd to reveal a message buried within the Palm Sunday text. Thoughtful analysis of the crowd, an element which is rarely if ever given serious consideration, provides a new window through which the congregation can critically evaluate their own faithfulness to Christ in light of the biblical setting.

Shelley includes a stylistic device which effectively expresses the crowd's diversity, by making the singular "crowd" plural — "crowds." By taking into account the whole biblical story, it is appropriate to read between the lines to assume the diversity of the crowd. In this situation, most of the crowd that cheered Jesus could not be counted on when it became unpopular to support him.

The levels of commitment of the three crowds act as metaphors for helping the congregation consider their own level of Christian commitment. Shelley draws parallels to contemporary crowds to distinguish these groups. For instance, the main crowd gathered on Palm Sunday is likened to the people who find it easy to rally round a local hero, while shying away from religious extremists. They are, for example, people who would reject *"some religious fanatic in Los Angeles or Waco, Texas."* And he compares the skeptics of Jesus to those who do not respond to "The Hour of Decision" with Billy Graham. Such images also help the hearer see the relevance of the biblical text to the contemporary religious context.

The sermon continues to drive home the reality that the popular crowd of Palm Sunday did not change what would occur on Good Friday. Examination of the crowd provokes an admonition to live according to something deeper and more trustworthy, namely, God. In the events of Holy Week, Shelley notes how Jesus could not trust the crowd but instead took the narrow path. This is a fitting metaphor, one Jesus had used for following God no matter how unpopular that might be.

Proclamation

The authentic call to follow the narrow path echoes throughout this sermon. Shelley's reflection about three distinct groups helps us to examine ourselves and to ascertain which crowd would define our own religious commitment. The exploration of the crowds encourages us to be wary of the popular crowds around us. Just as Jesus could not count on the crowd's support on the following Friday, we should not put our faith in crowds, but in God.

The memorable saying, *"Never, never, never sell your soul to a crowd,"* is a very effective rhetorical device that appears three times in the sermon. Instead of sounding parental or authoritarian, given its negative overtones, Shelley manages to use this formula as a kind of moral wisdom, a biblically inspired message which emerges from the experience Jesus had with crowds in his last week on earth. The first time the formula is used, it directly precedes the reading of the biblical passage. Placing it here alerts the congregation to listen for the references to the crowd during the reading of the text. The second use of this saying follows a dramatic illustration of crowd apathy demonstrated in the widespread denial by German people of their responsibility for the outbreak of World War II. The third repetition serves as a powerful capstone to the climax of how Jesus now rides, not into Jerusalem, but *"into our lives."* We are to follow Jesus through the streets, listening to the crowds, *"but never, never, never selling your soul to them."* This final repetition emphasizes the gospel as a call to follow Jesus and no other, no matter how prominent or well-respected an individual, idea or mass movement may be. The call is personal and there is an immediacy to Shelley's warning.

The sermon, crystal clear in its tight focus on crowds, concludes with a long story. The story, while fairly complex, drives home the thrust of the sermon. Its ending is a clever one with double meanings. Shelley points out that it is a type of riddle and allows us to complete the meaning, which serves to deepen its impact for us.

RESPONSE

This sermon deals with our tendency in mass society to follow the crowd without caring or thinking deeply about what it is we are following. Shelley calls us to examine our own depth of commitment to Jesus in comparison to the Palm Sunday crowds. The sermon causes us to ask ourselves whether we will be present at times when we are needed, whether we will be swayed by what is popular or will follow what our soul knows is right. The definition of these three distinct crowds provides a fresh window through which we may reflect on our own depth of faith. The sermon calls us to a new consecration of our lives to Christ, to follow "the narrow path."

Shelley's use of the first-person plural also emphasizes the inclusive nature of the reflection taking place. He is not setting himself above the congregation; rather, he participates in the sermonic event by placing himself in the position of hearer as well as proclaimer. There is a kinship with the listener and a sense of humility and sincerity elicited by his use of the first-person plural, giving the subliminal message that the preacher himself sits alongside those in the pews. Together, then, we consider which crowd we might be in if Palm Sunday took place today and the events of the coming week depended upon our response to Jesus.

SUGGESTIONS

- Try announcing a key theme with distinctive stylistic elements, as Shelley does in the statement, "Never, never, never sell your soul to a crowd." Repeat it where appropriate, each time following a section which underscores a unique dimension of its message. However, take care that an admonition does not become authoritarian.
- Examine the often glossed-over elements within a familiar text, such as the crowd in this Palm Sunday text. Play with the word, do biblical word studies, and consider its meaning for then and now. How might this "windowpane" from the text stimulate refreshing perspectives for faith? The Holy Spirit can breathe new life into dry bones by courageously reflecting upon what is often assumed by readers.
- Shelley's closing story about the doctor allows the hearers to draw their own conclusions. When using an illustration, take care to allow the congregation to think for themselves, to make connections and draw meaning for themselves, rather than explaining it and, thereby, deflating its impact.

Dixie Brachlow

Note
1. James L. Crenshaw, *Trembling at the Threshold of a Biblical Text* (Grand Rapids, MI: William B. Eerdmans, 1994), p. 5.

Can I Sing When the Going Gets Tough?

PSALM 137

Rev. Dr. William Powell Tuck
First Baptist Church
Lumberton, North Carolina

REV. DR. WILLIAM POWELL TUCK

CAN I SING WHEN THE GOING GETS TOUGH?

PSALM 137

Picture the scene. The year is 586 B.C. A temple musician from Jerusalem has been deported and made a slave by the Babylonians. He is in a strange city, in a strange country, hundreds of miles from his homeland. He is frightened and his faith is fragile. The God whom he thought would sustain him, he believed had let him down. He belonged to the chosen nation that, he believed, could never be despoiled or taken into captivity. Now he sits beside the canals of Babylon, where his captors taunt him and say: "Sing to me some of your religious songs about your great God, his power, and how you are his special people. Sing to us some of those religious songs and play on your harp now, holy man. Tell us of your great God."

Hurt and lonely, the psalmist had reached the lowest moment of his life. His only possession was his harp; his only asset was hope, and there was not much of that left. His writing is filled with grief and anger, frustration and vindictiveness, patriotism and hatred, homesickness and torment, love of Jerusalem and loathing of Babylon.

What are we to make of such a psalm as this, where the writer even calls down the curse of God upon small children and pleads that their heads be dashed against rocks? I believe we can find two major lessons in this psalm.

First, notice that the psalm calls us to *remember*. The psalmist began to remember his home. Filled with homesickness and nostalgia, he wanted to go home again. He longed for the hills of Judea, the temple of Jerusalem, good times, familiar streets, friendly companions, home, family, security, hope and love. But all were gone.

Who of us has not been in some strange place and has not longed to go home again? But few of us have had the experience of being removed so quickly and drastically from his home as he was. During World War II, however, some other Jewish people suffered that same kind of experience. They, too, were ripped from their homeland and thrust into concentration camps. They, too, wondered where God was. "Where is God now that I am in Dachau...in Auschwitz?" they asked. "Where is God? Where is God in this moment of my captivity?"

In the eighteenth and nineteenth centuries blacks from Africa asked the same questions when they were snatched from their homeland, taken to foreign countries and sold as slaves. They, too, wondered where God was during those desperate moments of their lives. Many of the Palestinians and the displaced persons in Bosnia have raised their voices wondering where God was in their time of need. The starving people in Somalia, in the inner cities, in the remote mountain regions of our own country have often raised the same cry.

During this time of suffering, the psalmist drew upon his memory. He obeyed the bidding of another psalmist to "forget not all God's benefits." And so he remembered the God who was with him in Jerusalem. Remembering his God gave him hope. Memory can give us hope; it can give us encouragement.

Memory is most effective when it enables us to sense the presence of God in this present moment as well as in the past. The psalmist remembered the God who had been with him in the past. But if he were to survive at all, he had to discover the God who was with him in Babylon. The true believer is one who remembers a former meeting with God and finds it sustaining in the present. Abraham never forgot God's call to him to go look for a city without foundations. Sarah never forgot how God gave her a son in her old age. Jacob never forgot his experience of wrestling with God in a riverbed. Moses never forgot his encounter with the power of God in a bush that burned but was not burned up. Isaiah never forgot his vision in the temple, where he saw God high and lifted up. Peter never forgot how Jesus forgave him after he had denied his Lord three times. Mary Magdalene never forgot meeting the risen Lord in a cemetery. Paul never forgot his vision of the risen Christ on the Damascus road. A true believer is one who remembers a former meeting with God and is sustained by it.

Somewhere in the past you may have met God. Now you can be sustained by that experience. On a bright beautiful spring day, perhaps, you felt the power of God penetrate your life and you were reborn. In a Christmas Eve service, God's Spirit silently moved into your presence and transformed you. Or on a cold wintry night, God moved into your life in an experience of worship, and you were transformed. Remember the experience and be sustained by it. When you hit the low moments and the valleys, the recollection of a meeting with God in some other place or at some other time can sustain you in the present difficulty. The psalmist remembered God, and he was sustained. So can you be and so can I.

Frederick Buechner recounts a dream of being in a hotel where he was staying in a lovely room which seemed to meet his every need. In the room he felt happy and at peace. He left the room and the hotel and wandered off, looking at and doing other things. When he came back to the hotel, he found himself in another room, one that seemed dark and cramped, and not as good as the one he had before. He didn't enjoy it and felt dark and cramped. When he went down and complained, the clerk told him there would be no problem. He could give him the same room he had before. All he had to do was to ask for it by name. "What is the name of the room?"

"The name of the room," Buechner said, "is 'Remember.'" At that, Buechner woke up instantly. The answer had shocked him awake.[1]

"Remember" is a room into which you and I can return again and again. We can enter the room of memory, and in reliving past experiences with God find that the memories help to sustain us. Our rich moments with God in the church, with friends, will nourish our lives as we remember them.

It is true that memory can be destructive as well as constructive, negative as well as positive. But if we will open our lives to the room of memory, we will be reminded of the reality of God's presence even in times when God seems so far from us. The psalmist in Babylon remembered the God who had sustained him in Jerusalem and asked that his life be cursed if he dared to forget God. Remembering helped him in his time of need.

Second, notice that though the psalmist is commanded by his captives to sing, he would not. We don't know if he ever sang, but he certainly didn't want to. We don't know what kind of songs they demanded, but he was certainly not going to sing his holy songs for heathen. He was not going to cast his pearls before swine, or throw what was holy to dogs. He believed that the sacred should not be profaned. He refused to make a mockery of his faith for his captors.

What about us? Aren't we too often willing to take holy things and profane them to entertain the secular world? What should be reserved for holy moments before God has been profaned by using it to entertain the heathen. This psalmist, however, will not profane his holy songs before those who want to use them for unholy purposes.

The psalm tells us that during times when we cannot sing, when we are in the wintertime of our lives, it is wrong for others to try to make us sing. At some time or another, we will all experience dark, stormy winter nights of anxiety, stress, sorrow, pain, frustration, suffering, doubts, fears, or some other negative feeling.

Unfortunately, some Christians refuse to acknowledge the negative, or to experience the pain. They want only to live in the summertime of life. They seem to express praise to the Lord every moment, and be always bursting with sunlight and joy. I wonder if these persons have ever encountered any of the winters of life. Do you remember the black musical, *The Wiz*? One song in that movie says, "Don't give me no bad news!" Many of us want to go through life telling others, "Don't tell me any bad news, I just want all good stuff." We want to experience only summertime religion.

In his book *A Cry of Absence,* which he wrote following the death of his wife, Martin Marty noted, "Not every believer can move easily into the rhythms of country-and-western Christianity with its foot-stomping, exuberant styles."[2] Not everyone can always be a summertime Christian, because there are north winds that chill us with the cold agony of pain, the reality of grief and suffering. There are times when the winter chill of depression, the agony of defeat, the reality of twenty thousand people killed by a volcano permeate our being. We cannot close our hearts to the tragedy of thousands dying of starvation, or killed in accidents; we cannot close our eyes to crime, like the awful murder of a young Indiana teenager by several of her peers.

When the darkness of life, the voices of loneliness, the emptiness of doubt, the despair of disbelief flood our mind, when the winter storms of life beat down upon us, summertime Christianity seems unreal. You can't sing songs when your life is in the pits. It's easy to sing when life is jubilant, sunny and joyful. But when the storms beat down upon us, it is difficult to sing. Unfortunately, all of life is not made up of springtime and summer. When people are in the winter and fall of life, it is difficult, even impossible for them to sing.

But if we don't sing, do we curse? That is what happened to the psalmist in the despair and bitter agony of defeat and rejection. He reached out and asked God to curse his enemies. "They have mocked your people, O God; now you curse them. Dash their babies' heads against the rocks. Destroy them. Let your power not be mocked. Show them that you are still in control."

It is easy to stand back and condemn those who curse when they are in the pits. But if you were among the millions of Jews and others who were thrown into Nazi concentration camps during World War II, or were one of the thousands killed or injured in Bosnia, would you have found it easy not to be bitter? When we face the agony and frustrations of life, it isn't easy to keep from cursing.

How awful it was, we say, for the psalmist to talk about dashing the heads of small children against rocks. Yet, in Vietnam our American troops killed children, women and whole villages of people. We dropped bombs on villages and destroyed thousands of lives. Yet we claim to be more civilized than these ancient people whom we consider to be primitive. It makes you wonder, doesn't it?

So what are we to make of the psalmist's curse here? For one thing, it is true that these people did respond primitively to their enemies. During times of war, ancient people destroyed all of their enemies. After they captured a village, if they did not take slaves, they simply killed all of the men, women and children. But before we are too harsh in our judgments on them, remember our own bombings, our own killings in war, our own devastation, as well as the potential for complete destruction which any nuclear war brings.

For another thing, we should remember that these people expressed their emotions very freely. In this psalm we hear the cry of oppressed people for justice. Their plea for retribution was a plea for the assurance of God's presence. In the pit of despair, they cursed their enemies for what they had done to them, and asked God to punish their captors. They didn't hold back their feelings, or cover them with a veneer of niceness. They openly cursed their enemies for what they had done to them. Here is bitter nationalism at its worst.

We also need to remember that though all the Scriptures are inspired, they are not all on the same level of being profitable or inspiring to us. There is no way that this passage of Scripture is on the same level with the record in the Gospels where Jesus says, "Do to others as you would have them do to you," or "Love your enemies" (Matt. 7:12, 5:44, NRSV). This passage of Scripture is pre-cross; it was written before Christ. Christ has called us not to hate but to love, not to scorn but to gentleness, not to injury but to love, not to demand vindictiveness but grace.

It is human to want to curse. But remember the old saying, "It is better to light a candle than to curse the darkness." Perhaps we could rephrase it to say, "It is better to sing a song in the darkness than to curse it." So the psalm sets us a demanding challenge: Can we sing when the going gets tough? The dark storms of trouble, difficulty, pain, or suffering can make us bitter or better, exasperated or enriched, battered or blessed, hateful or humble, depending on whether we curse or sing, doubt God or depend more on God.

Does the psalmist eventually learn to sing in Babylon? We don't know. Perhaps he never did sing for his captors, but I'd like to think he survived because he sang within his own soul. He sang within his religious circle. He sang in his solitude. He sang his songs about Zion. He sang his songs about the reality and presence of God. He kept his faith without a building, without a religious system, without a political system, because he had a song in his soul. His song enabled him to have the reality of the presence of God with him. There is plenty of evidence that Israel even in captivity continued to worship God and to know God's presence through it all.

That kind of song has sustained Christians down through the years. Even when they could not sing, the song was still there. They might not have been able to sing it, but it echoed and vibrated within their being. Jesus sang a song in the upper room with his disciples the night he was betrayed. Right after that he went out with his disciples to Gethsemane and to the cross. At midnight, locked in the stocks in a jail at Philippi, Paul and Silas expressed their faith by singing hymns. In the next few centuries, Christians would sing a song together before they were led to their death. In the darkest moments of life, we can still sing. Even if the words are not verbalized but remain deep down within the recesses of our being, the song is still there, and it echoes, rebounds, and assures us of hope and God. Even when the pain or ache is so severe that we cannot voice the words, the Spirit will sing them through our groans and aches. Christ's commission in Acts 1:8 calls us to take our songs, our witness to Christ, to the ends of the earth.

A teacher who was an atheist wrote on the blackboard the words, "God is nowhere." After a break the students returned to find that someone had moved one letter. Instead of reading, "God is nowhere," the sentence now read, "God is now here." Even when you are in a strange land and God seems nowhere, remember that you can still sing because God is now here. Never forget that. Let the truth sustain you in your high moments. But most of all remember it in your low moments. So you will always be able to sing the Lord's song, even in the strangest of lands.

Notes
1. Frederick Buechner, *A Room Called Remember* (San Francisco: Harper & Row, 1984), pp. 1–3.
2. Martin E. Marty, *A Cry of Absence* (San Francisco: Harper & Row, 1983), p. 5.

COMMENT

Understandably, the lament psalms rarely find a home in Sunday morning preaching. What is the good news to be found in a passage such as "Happy shall they be who take your little ones and dash them against the rock!" (Psalm 137:9)? Most people attending Sunday morning services don't eagerly embrace the frustration, grief, torment, and occasional curses found in the psalms of darkness.

Considering the time constraints most ministers face on Sunday mornings, only a brave and daring soul would be so bold (or ill-advised!?) as to tackle Psalm 137. This is not a comforting text. It's not prophetic. It's not a passage destined to encourage spiritual growth. This psalm is a lament, a passage filled with a community's sorrow, confusion, and spiritual questioning.

Yet entire books have been written on the psalms of lament. Scholars have given years of specialized study to this literary genre. For centuries the church has wrestled with the words of anger, grief, hopelessness, and hatred found in the laments. These psalms need to be heard when the community of faith gathers, because they are a significant part of our biblical legacy and an important expression of our faith experience.

William Powell Tuck deserves credit for tackling what has to be one of the most difficult challenges of being faithful to the biblical canon: preaching from the lament psalms. And he does so by tackling it head-on. No tap dancing around the difficult realities of words which sting with anger, hatred, and nationalism. No tap dancing around pain and suffering, injustice and oppression. This sermon is as real as Auschwitz, Vietnam, and Bosnia.

TACKLING A DIFFICULT TEXT

One cannot reflect on "Can I Sing When the Going Gets Tough?" without giving special attention to the text itself. In his commentary, *The Message of the Psalms*, Old Testament scholar Walter Brueggemann writes:

> I think that serious religious use of the lament psalms has been minimal because we have believed that faith does not mean to acknowledge and embrace negativity....It is no wonder that the church has intuitively avoided these psalms. They lead us into dangerous acknowledgment of how life really is. They lead us into the presence of God where everything is not polite and civil. They cause us to think unthinkable thoughts and utter unutterable words.[1]

Brueggemann goes on to say that use of these psalms of darkness is a "bold act of faith." In looking to the psalms of lament for his text, Tuck acts boldly, and builds his sermon around two valuable lessons from these words of travail.

Where Remembering Takes Us

Brueggemann says, "It is hard for complacent bourgeois folk who have suffered little to understand the tenacity of affronted memory among the brutalized."

Tuck recognizes that most of his listeners need a "refresher" course in how consistently the dark side of human nature has prevailed throughout history. Cruelty, oppression, injustice, and racial vendettas aren't something consigned to ancient Babylon. These realities are a common thread throughout history. From the Jews during the Holocaust or blacks in eighteenth-century Africa, to Palestinians and Bosnians on the nightly newscast, Tuck traces that thread. A brief walk through history, without resorting to melodrama, makes the point simply, but effectively.

Tuck doesn't try to elevate the psalmist to a level of spiritual superiority by casting him as a defender of God's enemies. He paints the picture of a very human, very real person struggling with the events that have shredded the fabric of Israel's life.

The first lesson Psalm 137 teaches us is that memory can take us one of two places. Memory can take us into the presence of God and sustain us in the present — or memory can be negative and destructive.

Yet perhaps the most grace-filled point that Tuck makes in this sermon is the lesson to be learned from the negative, impassioned emotions of grief and anger found in the lines of this psalm. Powerful negative emotions are not incongruent with profound faith.

In *A Theological Introduction to the Book of Psalms,* J. Clinton McCann writes:

> The structure of Psalm 137 teaches us that the crucial act of remembering is energized by the strong and inseparable emotions of grief and anger....In the face of monstrous evil, the worst possible response is to feel *nothing*. What *must* be felt is grief, rage, outrage. In their absence, evil becomes an acceptable commonplace. To forget is to submit to evil, to wither and die, to remember is to resist, be faithful, and live again.[2]

First Tuck establishes the call to remember. Then he uses the psalmist's refusal to sing as the springboard to give his listeners permission to feel their pain. He says, *"The psalm tells us that...when we are in the wintertime of our lives, it is wrong for others to try to make us sing....You can't sing songs when your life is in the pits."* This is the heart of the good news: even when we are in such pain that we curse the darkness — or the perpetrators of that darkness — God is present. People of faith can ultimately sing of the presence and sustaining grace of God even in the dark times.

Teaching in Tandem with Proclamation

Tuck draws two lessons from Psalm 137, but he goes one step further than proclamation in this sermon. He uses the most offensive words in the psalm — the curse in verse 9 — as an opportunity for theological education. And again, he does so by dealing with the psalmist's curse head-on. Tuck refuses to tap dance around sensitive issues. If any strict inerrantists were present in the congregation, Tuck surely challenged their tightly constructed presuppositions by saying, *"Though all Scriptures are inspired, they are not all on the same level of being profitable or inspiring to us."* Tuck not only preaches the lessons of the psalms, he teaches his congregation to be discerning in their study of Scripture.

We could safely assume that Psalm 137 is probably not on William Tuck's list of top ten favorite texts. Preaching from the lament psalms is challenging, but Tuck's sermon is a responsible, truthful — and ultimately encouraging — response to the challenge.

SUGGESTIONS

- The most obvious suggestion? Preach a sermon or series from the psalms of lament. When was the last time you preached using a lament as the text? Brueggemann says the psalms are "the most reliable theological, pastoral, and liturgical resource given us in the biblical tradition."[3] They deserve to be heard in their entirety — not selectively.
- Tuck deals with the power of memory in biblical faith: *"Memory can give us hope; it can give us encouragement."* Do a study of the theme of "remembering" in the Bible, and preach a sermon or series on the importance of memory. Read Buechner's sermon, "A Room Called Remember," cited by Tuck.
- If you were to preach a sermon next week on Psalm 137, how would you apply this psalm in your congregation?

Debra K. Klingsporn

Notes
1. Walter Brueggemann, *The Message of the Psalms: A Theological Commentary* (Minneapolis: Augsburg Publishing House, 1984), pp. 52-53.
2. J. Clinton McCann, Jr., *A Theological Introduction to the Book of Psalms* (Nashville: Abingdon Press, 1993), p. 119.
3. Brueggemann, p. 15.

How "User-Friendly Churches" Get Used

1 CORINTHIANS 11:23–26

Dr. William H. Willimon, Dean of the Chapel
and Professor of Christian Ministry
Duke University
Durham, North Carolina

Dr. William H. Willimon

How "User-Friendly Churches" Get Used

1 CORINTHIANS 11:23–26, NRSV

"For as often as you eat this bread and drink the cup, you proclaim the Lord's death until he comes" (1 Cor. 11:26).

Odd for you to come to this dark place at noon on such a bright day. Not many of you have come. Perhaps that is as it should be, considering that for which you have come. You have come to hear the proclamation of the Lord's death.

If you're here again tonight, we shall offer you wine and call it Jesus' blood. We shall break off a piece of bread and call it his broken body. We shall proclaim, in a world clinging to life, Jesus' death.

This proclamation is in stark contrast to the spirit of the age. Gary Trudeau, in one cartoon, depicts a hurt Yuppie couple leaving a suburban church after the pastor has slipped up and used the word "sin." They explain their exit to the pastor, "We're looking for a church which meets our needs."

Such a church is sometimes called "user-friendly," a place where anyone can walk in off the sidewalk and feel good, where all is dumbed down to the comprehensible and the comfortably accessible.

Last week, I saw an advertisement entitled, "CAPPUCCINO AND CHRIST." Under a coffee mug the ad read: "Sleep a little later, throw on some jeans, have a hot cup of Joe, listen to some great music and get together for some wonderful fellowship. _____ Church invites you to join us for a unique service that offers an alternative. No pressures, no commitments, no hassle. All we ask is that you give us forty-five minutes of your Sunday."

This is the "user-friendly church." This is the church which is proving to be useful in a grimly optimistic, willfully evasive contemporary world. We use everything we touch for our own devices and desires. Why not use the church as well?

But this is *not* the church of Maundy Thursday, the church which "proclaims the Lord's death" into a death-dealing yet a death-denying world. To a world seeking glory, success, power, we preach Christ and him crucified. And yet, in an odd sense, this *is* what we need, so proclaims the church which proclaims the death of Christ.

Last spring we had a wonderful evening with the popular spirituality writer, Thomas Moore. He was a kind, gentle man, with a warm, generous philosophy, though somewhat akin to *Mr. Rogers' Neighborhood*. Not long after, I was talking to a woman whom I had seen at the Thomas Moore evening. "How did you like it?" I asked.

"Fine," she said, "as far as it goes."

"As far as it goes? What does that mean?"

"He was fine, for those who don't need more. I think I need more."

"Explain that," I said.

"Well, his spirituality seems fine for folks who are relatively well fixed. But it's no match for the really difficult aspects of life, I think."

She could sense my desire to hear more.

She continued, "You see, I was raped when I was a teenager, by a family friend. So I'm glad that we're moving into Lent, where we'll talk about the cross, and innocent suffering, injustice, evil, and blood. Makes you grateful to be a Christian, don't you think?"

I am grateful that the poor old compromised church still is able to proclaim the Lord's death, the cross, innocent suffering, injustice, evil, and blood.

Catholic theologian Karl Rahner speaks of the non-user-friendly word of the cross as Christianity's greatest contribution:

> A Christian sees reality as it is. Christianity does not oblige [the Christian] to see the reality of the...historical experience of life in an optimistic light. On the contrary, it obliges [us] to see this existence as dark and bitter and hard, and as an unfathomable and radical risk.[1]

Note
1. Karl Rahner, *Foundations of Christian Faith*, trans. William V. Dych (New York: Crossroads, 1978), p. 403.

COMMENT

The irony of a small number of worshipers gathered on Maundy Thursday at noon to remember and worship the suffering and dying Jesus, becomes for William Willimon an opportunity to say a very brief but challenging word regarding an important issue in the contemporary church.

PROBLEM

Using several well-turned provocative phrases, Willimon presses an issue that is only implied: the appropriateness or authenticity of "user-friendly churches." The style and methodology of these churches seems incongruous with a genuine biblical understanding of the church that celebrates and worships a suffering and dying Savior. The "user-friendly church" movement wants to make Christianity convenient and enjoyable. It blends church with upbeat, cheerful lifestyles and caters to people's needs and desires. This, Willimon suggests, is in sharp contrast with the hard realities of a faith that proclaims a dying Savior and a lifestyle of sacrificial commitment.

This issue seems to relate to the contemporary church as a whole, more than the needs of the individuals to whom it is addressed. At the same time, however, Willimon's sermon produces for me, and for others with whom I shared it, a greater appreciation of and gratitude to God for Jesus' suffering and death. It spoke to my need for spiritual depth and renewal.

TEXT & PROCLAMATION

The biblical text from 1 Corinthians 11:26 is an effective reminder of the core of the Christian message and the essence of the church as the gathered Christian community. It also is an interesting connecting thread between the occasion for the sermon (Maundy Thursday noon) and the worship that would be celebrated later that evening in Holy Communion.

Like the problem Willimon addresses, the proclamation of the good news in this sermon is implied as much as it is directly stated. Willimon intensifies the irony of the setting and the message by affirming the broken body and poured out cup — the suffering and death of Jesus — as the "good news" the church proclaims and offers. The "good news" is set in the context of some not-so-good-news: a very small group of people worshiping indoors on a day that is bright outdoors. They are celebrating a dying Lord and reflecting on innocent suffering, injustice and evil.

The good news of the gospel that concludes this sermon in the quote from Karl Rahner, is that Christianity proclaims reality in contrast to the unreality of much of the death-denying, wishful-thinking, *"grimly optimistic, willfully evasive contemporary world."* According to Rahner we are called to see the world, *"as dark and bitter and hard, and as an unfathomable and radical risk."*

While I appreciated and was challenged by the Rahner quote, and by this brief meditation as a whole, I would have liked the biblical word of "good news" to have been more explicit, more extended, and with additional application. The end seems a bit abrupt and leaves me wanting more. This is obviously intentional and has a dramatic impact on the listener. Leaving a sermon wanting more is always better, I think, than leaving a sermon wanting less! But Willimon's approach here raises the interesting question: Is the good news of the gospel elaborated enough in this sermon for most audiences? The answer may depend largely on one's preaching context.

Response

This sermon does not directly call for a response. Although some listeners could leave thinking, "Hmh, interesting," "So, what?" or "What am I to do?" I did find that it challenged me to respond with a desire to be more deeply committed to the understanding and proclamation of the "realistic" Christ, the suffering innocent Christ who identifies with and relates to the suffering innocents of ordinary life. And, it led me to a greater appreciation and love for Christ.

STYLE

I found this sermon contemporary and thought provoking. I wanted more. It reflects a preacher who is very aware of contemporary culture, especially as viewed from the perspective of the literate, reflective Christian that I assume participates in a Duke University Chapel congregation. The sermon reveals a preacher who knows the heart of the Christian message in its profound simplicity. Provocative phrases abound:

- *"we shall proclaim, in a world clinging to life, Jesus' death";*
- *"where all is dumbed down to the comprehensible and the comfortably accessible";*
- *"in a grimly optimistic, willfully evasive contemporary world";*
- *"into a death-dealing, yet death-denying world."*

These expressions effectively stimulate our reflection on Willimon's analysis of our society, the contemporary church, and the importance of proclaiming the Lord's death.

Willimon's conversation with the woman eager for Lent is effective, first, in introducing his main point — the need for the church to continue to proclaim Christ's suffering and death even if it doesn't fit well with a consumer culture; and, second, bringing the issue into a concrete, "life-as-it-really-is" setting.

I appreciate Willimon's reference to Gary Trudeau and *Doonesberry*, the ad regarding "Cappuccino and Christ," and the reference to a familiar campus event from the previous year. These illustrations place the message into the life experience of the listeners. Perhaps one could argue, however, that those popular and contemporary references are themselves "user-friendly."

Two concerns arise. First, I wonder how appropriate it is to refer to Thomas Moore's philosophy as being *"somewhat akin to* Mr. Rogers' Neighborhood." It seems a bit pejorative and condescending in this setting. Second and more importantly, this message makes a helpful prophetic statement about the contrast between the suffering Christ (and therefore the suffering church) and the "user-friendly church." But I wonder if it misunderstands and understates something of the purpose and value of the "user-friendly church." Perhaps before a contemporary world can hear, understand, and appreciate the message of a suffering Savior, a relationship of openness needs to be developed. This is what Dr. John MacKay called "winning the right to be heard."

Having reflected on Willimon's message for several weeks, I am aware of how much I was impacted by this message. Its prophetic word has gently haunted and encouraged me. And, I suspect its simple and profound image will stick with and inform me for years to come. I appreciated and was challenged by this brief sermon. It made me think. Effective preaching always does!

SUGGESTIONS

- We can benefit from some of the literature coming out of the user-friendly-church movement, such as George Barna's *User Friendly Churches* (Regal, 1991), Mike Regele's *The Death of the Church* (Zondervan), or from another perspective, Loren Mead's *The Once and Future Church* (Alban Institute, 1991). If you haven't done so, gather and study the variety of literature available on this subject and evaluate the issues in terms of your own theological perspective and understanding of ministry.
- The subject of this sermon could be expanded into a sermon series or a class on the nature and style of the church in contemporary culture. Most churches and their leaders are wrestling with whether or not to be more "user-friendly, and what that means in relation to more traditional understandings of the church. Develop a class, discussion group or series of sermons on the subject, "The Church in Contemporary Culture."
- Building on the stark contrast between hot contemporary topics such as, "user-friendly churches," and the events of Jesus' life and ministry,

one might think of other dramatic contrasts. Making these contrasts can bring greater emphasis or support to the gospel message (i.e., the Rich Young Ruler who keeps all the commandments, but misses the Kingdom of God), or Jesus' teaching that the one who would be great must be servant, in contrast to modern notions of power and influence.

- Notice again how short this sermon is and how suddenly it comes to a close. Its brevity and stark conclusion are part of its effectiveness. Can you occasionally preach a sermon of this length? Experiment with some short sermons. What did you feel you could learn from Willimon's conclusion to this sermon?

David Williamson

Peace for the Journey

EXODUS 17:1–7; JOHN 4:5–42; ROMANS 5:1–11

Rev. Dr. David C. Fisher
Colonial Church
Edina, Minnesota

Rev. Dr. David C. Fisher

Peace for the Journey

EXODUS 17:1–7; JOHN 4:5–42; ROMANS 5:1–11, NRSV

It was high noon and hot. Across the shimmering, parched earth a woman trudged toward the well outside town. She was alone. The other women had been to the well already. They came together in the cool of the morning to fill pots with water for the needs of the day.

It seems she was alone a lot those days. She was an outcast in her village, maybe even in her family. She'd been married five times and was living with a man who wasn't her husband. Small towns often have even smaller hearts; and very religious people — well you know how they treat social deviants. Her reputation was shot and, no doubt, her heart was maimed. Her soul? Who knows? Maybe she felt like a woman I know who told me, "I'm twenty-eight years old and I'm all used up."

She carried a heavy pot through the heat toward that well. She carried a larger burden in her soul. She hadn't expected her life to turn out this way. Of course. None of us does. Whether her life was the result of her own bad choices or a series of bad men or just sheer bad luck, she came to the well that day with a dry and empty soul.

Like the children of Israel in the Old Testament lesson for this Sunday (Ex. 17:1–17), she lived in a dry and barren wilderness. The journey had started with such high hopes and glad songs. Most journeys do. Who starts off any chapter of life expecting to wander in the wilderness? Israel didn't.

The long brutal slave days were over and they were on the march toward God's promised land. But then came reality. Contrary to all their expectations, a long, difficult and dangerous journey lay between them and the promised land. In fact, most of them would die in that foreboding wilderness.

This woman at the well knew all too well that life can be like that fearsome desert. Hopes and dreams too easily fade in the heat of realities that empty the heart and parch the soul. We start so many chapters of life with high hopes too soon dashed on the rocks of reality. Our hopes and dreams seem like a mirage: they appear much better than they are.

More than anything we want our journey to be a good one. But it seems as though joy, satisfaction, happiness, call it what you may, though real, is all too temporary and seldom more than partial. Even at its best, the journey is long, difficult and unpredictable. Twenty years ago, O. J. Simpson told a reporter from *Newsweek*, "Fame is a vapor, popularity an accident and money takes wings." What do you suppose he'd say today?

At its worst, life can be hell. Eric Clapton, a rock-and-roll legend, richer than his wildest dreams, gifted beyond belief, writes in his song "Lonely Stranger" that his quest for fulfillment, for satisfaction of his hungers and thirst, is "sure to end in tears."

Even good things, very good things, often turn to dust. Ask the Samaritan woman. Love, God's greatest gift, broke her heart and damaged her soul. If we could just find the right person, we think, or another person, we'd be in the promised land of life. But then…reality. In fact, all of God's gifts easily become heartbreaking realities. This world is a barren desert, a punishing, even lethal place to live, and we need help.

And I must say it. Religion, even the Christian faith, can become just a dry hole that empties the soul. I know! I work for God! I think leading the church is the most satisfying work possible. After all, pastors are an integral part of the prayer, "Thy kingdom come. Thy will be done on earth…," in people's lives. We live it! But I also know full well that religious demands, well-meaning religious people and religious institutions can break your heart and empty your soul. That's life.

You see, we think *things,* or *doing things,* all this human stuff, can somehow satisfy the deepest part of us, our soul. We really believe that we can determine our own fulfillment. So we run from place to place, from experience to experience, from store to store or mall to mall, from love to love, from person to person, from career to career, from one success to another, looking for something to feed our souls. And sometimes it works — for a while. But none of this human stuff, not even all the good stuff, not even all the stuff on earth put together, can form a heart in the shape of God's heart. Nor will it fill a human soul with the peace of God.

The Israelites asked a powerful question. Did you hear it at the end of the reading? "Is the Lord among us or not?" (Exodus 17:7). Is God here or not? The question wasn't about God's power the previous week or the previous month. After all, they'd just walked out of Egyptian slavery under the hand of God. They didn't ask, "Was God *there?*" They knew the answer to that question. Rather, their question, and our question, too, is more profound: "Is God here, in this desert, in my life, here and now?"

It's the right question because it asks another question: Can we determine our own fulfillment? In this life, on this planet, with our gifts, abilities and powers, can we feed the center spot of our own existence, our souls? Or must we look beyond ourselves to something or someone else?

At Sychar the woman who came to the well in the noontime heat got the surprise of her life. In fact, she came face to face with the barren wilderness her life had become. There, sitting at the well waiting for her, was a man — a Jewish man. Against all her expectations he spoke to her. That was shocking enough. In that world Jews avoided Samaritans like the worst kind of plague. Samaritans were considered worse than dogs, and most self-respecting Jews would not even set foot on Samaritan soil.

Her shock went even deeper. Jewish rabbis commanded men never to speak or even to greet a woman, not even their own wives, in public, for fear of gossip. So to hold a conversation alone with a woman was a shocking breach of conventional morality. Later, when Jesus' disciples showed up at the well, they seemed surprised and a bit upset that Jesus was talking to a woman.

You know the story. Jesus moved the conversation from the physical water in that well to the dry soul of this sad woman. He told her he had enough water to nourish her parched soul forever. To be sure, life is a long, dry and difficult journey. She couldn't change that, and Jesus didn't offer to change her barren world. He offered to change *her*.

John's Gospel later records Jesus' trip to Jerusalem at the Feast of Tabernacles, when he stood in the temple and cried out, "Let anyone who is thirsty come to me, and let the one who believes in me drink. As the scripture has said, 'Out of the believer's heart shall flow rivers of living water'" (John 7:37–38). That last sentence is a very mild translation for a powerful metaphor in the Greek. Try this: "Out of their belly shall flow rivers of living water."

Like all of us, this poor woman had spent her life and energy trying to feed her soul from the outside in. She had failed to realize that she needed soul food to feed her soul. The spirit is fed by the spirit. When you think about it, that makes sense!

In fact, that's the point of the story. Jesus' disciples went off to the store to buy lunch, while Jesus waited at the well for this woman to show up. By the time they got back she knew more than they did about soul food. She had drunk some of the water Jesus offered her and raced back to town to tell everyone where to come to get a real drink of life.

Meanwhile the disciples were worried about Jesus' reputation and his lunch — in that order. They'd walked up on a life-transformation and all they saw was a possible scandal, a loaf of bread and their next ministry assignment. While they talked about their next meal, the woman was back in Sychar telling everyone about living water.

The disciples' souls were dulled by common realities. Jesus had to tell them he had some bread they couldn't even imagine. He'd just led a soul-starved woman to new life.

The story ends wonderfully. Jesus is having his "bread" talk with the disciples when, wonder of wonders, a whole chorus of men from Sychar, friends of this woman, come running from town crying out, "This is the Savior of the world." They believed in Jesus for five minutes and already had a better sense of the soul than the twelve apostles. They knew from experience that the human soul must be fed from the inside out.

I don't know what wilderness experience you bring to this Lord's Day in Lent, 1996. I do know we're part of a long, difficult and dangerous journey. And I know the deep and desperate hunger that is too often part of the journey.

The good news I bring you this day is this: There is One who sits by the well waiting for you. He joins us on the journey, every dry and dusty step of it, and offers us food and drink for our souls. The woman at the well came face to face not just with the wilderness reality of her sad journey but, miracle of miracles, with the One who transforms every life open to him. He is the One sent from God to make the desert place in your soul blossom like a rose. The woman at the well believed. Do you?

Several years ago, Mother Teresa was lecturing at an American university. She told of her religious "social work" among the poor of Calcutta where she brings love, joy and hope to the sad and hopeless. During the question-and-answer session that followed, a young man studying to be a social worker thanked her for her talk and the transforming work she and her community contribute to the poor of Calcutta and the world.

"But," he continued, "I am bothered by your constant references to Jesus. We live in a pluralistic, even secular world. I want to do the work you do, but I don't want to do it with Jesus."

"How old are you?" Mother Teresa asked.

"Twenty-one," the student answered.

"I'm seventy-six," Mother Teresa said. "When you are as old as I am and have done what I have done, you come and tell me how you've done this work without Jesus."

The epistle reading for this Sunday (Rom. 5:1–11) helps us understand the power and mystery of this life-transforming water that springs up in the soul. There Paul says those who trust in Christ know the *peace* of God in their soul, have access to an amazing *grace* and live in *hope*. What bigger and better words are there in any human language? Indeed, peace, hope, and grace are the living water that springs up in the Christian soul.

Why? Because, the apostle declares, God pours out his love in our hearts. There's the source of living water for your soul. Here is the foundation of the moral universe and the center of the Christian faith. We've made a desert of this world and our own lives. It hurts us and we hurt each other. The end of it all is a shriveled soul and darkness.

But God, rich in mercy and boundless in compassion, pours out his love in our hearts. That is the issue in life and in death. Will we receive the love of God?

But there's more. This is a church text. Jesus led the woman from living water in her soul to living worship in the house of God. She left the well a lone believer in the Messiah and came back with a church full of singing men. By its very nature the Christian faith is communal. After all, our faith is about the love of God poured out in us. You can't have love by yourself. Love takes more than one person — it takes people.

The love of God puts on skin and lives in our midst. First Jesus. Now the church. The church at its most basic is a community of people trying to drink out of the fire hydrant of God's love. Naturally, the love of God spills out of our hearts and splashes on each other. God's love is real, palpable, personal. It is made visible in the people of God.

Down the journey of my life, from a little church in the Northwest to this large church in the Midwest, God's people have laid hands on my soul and I'll never be the same. If you think about it, that's your story too. We're a bunch of God's children on a journey led by Jesus who pours out God's love in our hearts. The journey is long and difficult, even painful. But it is good. Because the One sits by the well, and he's waiting.

Why I Did What I Did
David C. Fisher

I came to this text with a bit of fear and trembling. I've avoided John's Gospel for years. This Gospel's theological depth and literary richness intimidated me. But the lectionary overpowered me (one good reason for lectionary preaching!). This text in John 4 was the first of three straight Gospel lections from John in Lent, 1996. I took a deep homiletical breath followed by a great leap of faith into John's Gospel.

My guides through the Johannine forest were exceptionally helpful. Alan Culpepper's *Anatomy of the Fourth Gospel* (Fortress, 1983) unlocked structure and themes for me. George Beasley-Murray was my exegetical guide. His commentary *John* in the World Biblical Commentary series (Vol. 36) and its companion volume, *Gospel of Life* (Hendrickson, 1991), were both helpful. Paul Duke's *Irony in the Fourth Gospel* (John Knox, 1985) is a brilliant piece of literary analysis and theological insight. Duke not only took me deep into the Johannine Gospel but also prompted my homiletical instincts. And, of course, all students of John's Gospel stand in debt to C. H. Dodd, whose magisterial *Interpretation of the Fourth Gospel* is a never-ending source of information and stimulation.

Early in the week, I made an exegetical journey through the text. It seemed clear to me that this story illustrates what is probably the main theme of John's Gospel: *life*. Jesus came to bring this life and it has the quality of eternity. It is "life eternal." The Samaritan woman, the heroine of the story, discovered at that well that her life was a poor substitute for the new life Jesus gave her.

Along the way, I discovered this story also contains other Johannine themes. Water is very important in John's Gospel. Earlier, in chapter 2, Jesus' first "sign" is to turn water into wine. Water, in John's Gospel, means something more than ordinary water. In chapter 3, Jesus tells Nicodemus he needs to be born from above, a birth of water and Spirit (3:5). Now a woman comes to a well for water and Jesus tells her of another kind of water that will feed her soul. Later in the Gospel Jesus promises that anyone who believes in him will have this divine water flood their heart (7:38).

Another important theme that looms large in this story is the dullness of the disciples. They stand in the presence of the light of the world, yet they perceive so little. With great irony, this story contrasts the disciples' inability to see beyond lunch bread with the clear insight of this Samaritan woman, a religious outsider who quickly perceived that life is much more than human food and drink.

But as every preacher knows, it's one thing to discover what a text means and quite another to put that meaning into sermonic form that serves the text and the listening church well. The "aha" of interpretation must be followed by a second homiletical "aha." And that is, in my opinion, where the difficult work begins. This second "aha" is the creative moment when we discover the sermon "package" in which we deliver the biblical message.

During Lent and Advent, I have wonderful homiletical help. Colonial Church's teaching pastor and I conduct a Wednesday night Bible study featuring the lectionary readings for the following Sunday. We try to tie the lessons together and give introductory commentary on them. I discuss the text on which the sermon will be based (usually the Gospel lesson). I've never yet had my second "aha" by Wednesday night!

This week, as usual, I had very little homiletical direction and simply told the Bible study members what I'd learned so far. Then we opened the class up for discussion and questions. During these study sessions I listen intensely to the discussion. After all, these are some of the folks I'll be preaching to on Sunday. At the very least, talking through the text out loud is illuminating. I often have a few minor "ahas" while I talk. Listening to and answering questions is also very illuminating.

During the week I was preparing for this sermon, the Wednesday night discussion centered on the theme of water and the wilderness setting of the Old Testament lesson (Ex. 17:1–7) along with the wearying noonday heat of the Gospel lesson. The epistle lesson (Rom. 5:1–11) uses the interesting verb "poured out" to describe our experience of the love of God. As I talked, I received the second "aha" in primitive form. If these biblical stories are also our stories, then Jesus is waiting for us in the wilderness of our lives.

I am convinced that the biblical narratives carry inherent power. So, when I preach from narrative texts, I want to retell the story but not get in the way of the story's inherent power. I want to engage my hearers in the story without altering the character of the story itself. After all, it's their story too.

So, my next task was to determine the structure the sermon would take. For some time now, I've thought of sermonic structure as a trajectory. It's an arc through a series of ideas or thoughts aimed at a well-defined target. My target this week was Jesus sitting in the wilderness of my congregation waiting for them. The structural question was the trajectory of the homiletical journey that would get us all there.

I determined to retell the story and engage my hearers early and often. Already in the second and third paragraphs I brought my hearers into the story. I wanted to be sure all of us were in the dry and barren wilderness with the Samaritan woman. It's not a long journey. All I needed to do was look around at the world and look across the congregation gathering that Sunday.

A few telling illustrations and quotations took us all to the wilderness. I also looked for powerful words and metaphors that would drive us deeper into the desert. I listed words, phrases and metaphors that would assist the biblical story. These are some of the phrases I listed: "I'm all used up," "fearsome desert," "empty the heart and parch the soul," "dashed on the rocks of reality," "mirage," "turn to dust," "lethal place," "dry hole in the soul." In the original sermon I quoted an entire verse of Eric Clapton's "Lonely Stranger" which cannot be reproduced in this volume for copyright reasons. When I finished the quote, you could have heard a pin drop. I thought if nothing else moved the people toward the wilderness, the familiar lyrics of a rock-and-roll song would.

Along the way I wanted to refer to the Old Testament lesson since it illustrates life in the wilderness so well and because it ends with the powerful question, "Is God here?" — in this desert? That is the question we all ask all the time.

All of this was to move the "plot" of the sermon toward the moment which the biblical text highlights: Jesus is waiting in your wilderness to change your life. This is the good news. The grace of God was the target of this sermon. The entire trajectory of the message moved toward this moment. To make my point clear, I used a phrase I often use at this point in a sermon: *"The good news I bring you...."* I think some form of gospel or grace must be the target of any genuinely Christian sermon.

With Eugene Lowry, I think sermons are best structured to create in the hearer some form of tension that is relieved only toward the end of the sermon in this moment of the grace of God (*The Homiletical Plot,* John Knox, 1980).

I added the story of Mother Teresa near the end of the sermon to illustrate the power of Christ to change lives, and perhaps to drive the point home for any who may have missed it. I also added the epistle lesson here to complete the thought and give objective form to the life-changing power of Christ. God's love poured into our hearts is a graphic metaphor that gives a certain gospel shape to faith that is no mere idea but takes objective form in the church.

In the final paragraph of the sermon I sought to drive the point home one more time. My own story is, in fact, the story of the people of God pouring the love of God into my heart. The last sentence is, in fact, an invitation to faith: "Because the One sits by the well, and he's waiting." It's short and, in a sense, incomplete. The hearer's response completes the sermon.

Pilgrim People, Pilgrim Faith

HEBREWS 11:1–2, 8–16

Rev. Dr. Stephen Brachlow
Professor of Church History
and Christian Spirituality
North American Baptist Seminary
Sioux Falls, South Dakota

REV. DR. STEPHEN BRACHLOW

PILGRIM PEOPLE, PILGRIM FAITH

HEBREWS 11:1-2, 8-16, RSV

Next week, Thursday, is Thanksgiving, a national holiday. It's a day off for most Americans, as it will be for us as a seminary community. It is also something of a bonanza for commercial interests, sandwiched as the holiday is between Wednesday, one of the busiest travel days of the year for the airline industry, and Friday, the busiest shopping day of the year for retailers, when the Christmas shopping season is officially inaugurated at shopping malls that now seem to stretch across this great land of ours from "sea to shining sea."

Hidden and almost completely lost in all this consumerism is the celebration of Thanksgiving that occurs in many American churches, a day of offering thanks to God for the provisions of life and for the grace extended to us in Christ Jesus. The roots of this religious celebration run deep in the New England soil of early seventeenth-century Puritan life, especially in the celebrated story of those Puritan *Mayflower* Pilgrims who arrived on the shores of this continent in 1620.

The reputation of the Puritans has, of course, fallen on rather hard times these days. They have become perhaps the preeminent symbol of a Eurocentric, imperialist Calvinism bent on destroying native culture and denigrating the land for commercial purposes. Recently, things have gotten even worse. Those very same Puritans were put in the unenviable position of having to accuse Demi Moore of adultery and branding her with a big red "A" in the recent movie version of Hawthorne's *The Scarlet Letter*. This is not very helpful as a public relations strategy should the Puritans ever wish to gain sympathy in American popular culture!

Whatever we may think of the Puritans, and whatever their sins (like us, I'm sure they had many), the actual story of the people who lived the *Mayflower* adventure still holds the potential, I believe, of offering us a rich and meaningful metaphor for what it may mean to be pilgrim people in our own day.

The epic journey of the *Mayflower* Pilgrims began in 1620 when they set out from the city of Leyden in Holland. Leyden had been their home for more than twelve years. There they had lived as exiles of conscience, having fled persecution as Puritans in their native England under "ye Dread King James I."

Their voyage that fall across the stormy North Atlantic, while packed in the hold of the tiny *Mayflower,* was a harrowing experience. The ship bobbed like a cork in the furious ocean for seven long weeks until on November 11, they found themselves deposited at Cape Cod, far to the north of their intended destination of warm and sunny Virginia. They found themselves on the shores of a vast and, for them, unexplored continent. They had landed on the edge of the Massachusetts wilderness at the worst possible time of year, when, as the Pilgrim governor William Bradford wrote in his *History of the Plymouth Plantation*, "all things stand upon them with a weatherbeaten face, and the whole country, full of woods and thickets, represented a wild and savage hue."[1]

Within a few weeks of dropping anchor, winter storms descended upon them with a vengeance. Icy winds and heavy snows swept through the large cracks of their hastily constructed cottages. The food they brought with them proved inadequate and soon turned stale. Then the epidemic set in. By the end of that first winter, only half the original company of 101 were still alive. Four entire families had been wiped out. Only three married couples survived. Spouses walked away from the fresh graves of those they loved. Many remarried. Then they gathered the orphans and welcomed them into their homes as their own.

The Pilgrims had embarked on this journey, according to Bradford, as "an adventure almost desperate." But what they encountered that first winter was something they had never imagined. The experience was so overwhelming that one member of the party committed suicide; it was Bradford's own wife, Dorothy, whom historians suspect took her own life by jumping into the frigid waters of the Cape. The brutal conditions of the wilderness were simply too much for her to bear.

Many years later, Bradford remembered, with evident pain at the thought of it, the feeling of complete devastation and helplessness upon their arrival. "What," he wrote, "could now sustain them but the Spirit of God and His Grace?"[2]

Like Abraham, in our text from Hebrews 11, the Pilgrims came to understand that they were but poor strangers and exiles on this earth. But somehow, through their faith in God, they found courage to face the pain and the enormous hardships. How that faith remained alive in the midst of their adversity is a great mystery. It is the mystery of the Spirit of God who provides, as the text in Hebrews says, the "assurance of things hoped for, the conviction of things not seen."

When the Pilgrims left Holland for the New World, Bradford recalled their grief at the departure from the friends and family members who stayed behind. He wrote:

> ...truly doleful was the sight of that sad and mournful parting, to see what sighs and sobs did sound amongst them, what tears did gush from every eye, and pithy speeches pierced each heart.... But they knew they were pilgrims [Bradford wrote in what must be his most famous words], and so looked not much on those things, but lift up their eyes to the heavens, their dearest country, and quieted their spirits.[3]

These are the closing days of November, when the harvest has been gathered in, farm fields lie fallow, and trees stand leafless and lonely against gray skies — skies that are laden with the promise of another long winter. In this season of the *Mayflower* Pilgrims, we discover again that we, too, have been called, along with all of those who have gone before us in faith, to seek a better country, our true homeland, that "new heaven and new earth," which is our hope in Christ.

The story of the Pilgrims is, in part, a metaphor of the strange truth about faith. It is a pilgrim faith. Once we have encountered the call of Christ in our lives, once Christ's sometimes disturbing and always disarming Spirit has penetrated the defenses of our lives and we have glimpsed the hope of heaven, we will never again be content with our old securities. Pilgrim faith awakens a restlessness within us, so that we can no longer be complacent about our life or the needs of others around us, never fully content with the world as it is and with our place in it.

At the same time, pilgrim faith recognizes that the sustaining presence of God is often to be found in the most difficult challenges we face. This is always hard for us to accept. We avoid pain and adversity as much as possible. We so want life to be comfortable, and wonderful, and full of happy and fulfilling things.

But the truth is that God is often to be discovered afresh in those disturbing, "wilderness" experiences of life. And, as we all know from each of our own experiences in this and other seminaries, theological education can become such a wilderness. Coming to seminary can be like finding oneself washed up on the shores of a seemingly vast, unexplored continent of ideas that appear as forbidding and impenetrable as any wilderness encountered by the *Mayflower* Pilgrims. This is perhaps especially the case these days when there is seldom any clearly recognized theological consensus to guide us, when so many new paradigms of faith tend to confound or challenge all the old familiar ones, and when changes — or lack of change — in language about God in public worship can cause discomfort and profound feelings of alienation.

Finding oneself in such a wilderness, however uncomfortable, is also often the precondition of grace. Martin Luther discovered this when he went on pilgrimage into new theological territory in the sixteenth century. We too easily forget that such a venture was full of great risk and considerable turmoil for him. Yet, it was precisely at that point, when Luther was willing to let go of his old securities, that he discovered God's sustaining presence in ways he had never dreamed. "No one," Luther wrote about his own pilgrimage, "is taught through much reading and thinking. There is a much higher school where one learns God's Word. One must go into the wilderness, then Christ comes, and one becomes able to judge the world."[4]

This the Pilgrims of Plymouth were to realize so clearly in their most challenging moments that first winter. As this frail, stricken company hung on precariously for life, while winter storms blew in off the coast, and disease took its high toll, Bradford wrote in this King James, seventeenth-century idiom:

> What could now sustain them but the Spirit of God and His Grace? May not and ought not the children of these fathers rightly say: "Our fathers were Englishmen which came over this great ocean, and were ready to perish in this wilderness; but they cried unto the Lord and He heard their voice and looked on their adversity."[5]

Pilgrim faith is a restless thing that discovers in the wilderness of life the sustaining presence of God. Somewhere near the end of his own life, when Plymouth Colony had prospered, William Bradford scribbled this little poem in the margin of one of the books he owned:

> From my years young in days of youth,
> God did make known to me his truth,
> And called me from my native place
> For to enjoy the means of grace.
> In wilderness he did me guide,
> And in strange lands for me provide.
> In fears and wants, through weal and woe,
> A pilgrim passed I to and fro.[6]

This is pilgrim faith. It is ours to live out in our own wayfaring pilgrimage of life wherever — and through whatever — that journey of faith may take us. Amen.

Notes
1. William Bradford, *Of Plymouth Plantation,* Samuel Eliot Morison, ed. (New York: Alfred A. Knopf, 1979), p. 62.
2. Ibid., pp. 62-63.
3. Ibid., p. 47.
4. Quoted in Roland H. Bainton, *Here I Stand: A Life of Martin Luther* (New York: Abingdon Press, 1950), p. 224.
5. Bradford, *Of Plymouth Plantation,* pp. 62-63.
6. Ibid., pp. xxvi-xxvii.

COMMENT

"To have faith is to remember," says Frederick Buechner.[1] In his sermon, "Pilgrim People, Pilgrim Faith," Stephen Brachlow helps us do a lot of remembering. We remember the origins of Thanksgiving. We remember the *Mayflower* and the Pilgrims. We remember Plymouth and that first winter. We remember Martin Luther's journey into "the wilderness." And we remember Abraham, our ancestor in the faith, setting out on a journey, not knowing where he was going.

Remembering those who have gone before us, Brachlow urges us to consider that their story is our story. The story of the *Mayflower* Pilgrims in particular *"still holds the potential…of offering us a rich and meaningful metaphor for what it may mean to be pilgrim people in our own day."* They were pilgrims on a journey. Theirs was a pilgrim faith. To remember their story is to encounter the true meaning of faith.

Brachlow's sermon is distinctive for the way in which it effectively relates the past to our present and our future in the faith. This sermon is a beautiful and tightly woven tapestry. There is nothing extraneous. Here "history" is vivid and powerful. "Their story" becomes our story. We see ourselves in the tapestry.

It's not easy to preach this kind of "historical sermon." One must be careful with history. But it can be done, and it must be done, without idealizing the past or engaging in reductionism. Brachlow is careful with his use of history in this sermon. He goes to the core of the Pilgrim story to lift up one idea: the "pilgrim" metaphor and its implications for us as "pilgrim people" in our own day. This sermon proclaims in a powerful way that to have faith, to discover the meaning of faith, is to remember the past.

PROBLEM

The problem is that we are prone to forget. It's not simply that we forget the past. It's that we easily forget the true nature of faith. In a consumer culture, we forget the true meaning of Thanksgiving. Clinging to our old securities, we forget that faith is about the unseen and unknown. Comfortable where we are, we forget that faith is a journey. In a culture of complacency, we forget that faith is a restless longing that the world around us might be a different place. In the face of adversity, we easily forget that God is present in the most difficult challenges we face.

So we need to be reminded of the true nature and meaning of faith. That's the problem and the point of the sermon. Faith is a journey. Faith is about the wilderness places of life. Faith is about discontent with the world as it is. Faith is about God's presence in our lives, especially in the most difficult times. But part of the problem is that this is hard for us to accept. *"We avoid pain and adversity as much as possible,"* Brachlow says. *"We so want life to be comfortable, and wonderful, and full of happy and fulfilling things."* But it's not. Bradford and the Pilgrims knew it. So did Luther and Abraham. Brachlow knows it. And you and I know it.

There is a realism in this sermon that draw us into the wilderness places of life and helps us to see that it is precisely there that God's grace and presence are most fully known. The story of the Pilgrims exemplifies this truth. Note Brachlow's vivid descriptions:

- *"Bradford recalled their grief at the departure from the friends and family members who stayed behind."*
- *"Their voyage...was a harrowing experience."*
- *"Winter storms descended upon them with a vengeance."*
- *"The food they brought with them proved inadequate and soon turned stale."*
- *"Then the epidemic set in."*
- *"By the end of that first winter, only half the original company of 101 were still alive."*
- *"the brutal conditions of the wilderness...."*
- *"Bradford remembered...the feeling of complete devastation and helplessness upon their arrival."*

As the sermon develops, almost without realizing it, these descriptions become metaphors for the wilderness experiences in our lives. We are called to reflect on our own lives and the challenges we face as people of faith: our grief, our harrowing experiences, the storms of our lives, our hungers, the epidemics among us, the brutal conditions of our world, the helplessness and devastation we experience. The problem is the wilderness. We all share the Pilgrim "wilderness."

But there is good news. We also can share the pilgrim faith: *"In wilderness [God] did me guide,"* wrote Bradford, *"and in strange lands for me provide."* This is the heart of pilgrim faith and ultimately the good news proclaimed in this sermon.

Proclamation

Brachlow states his theme in one simple sentence: *"Pilgrim faith is a restless thing that discovers in the wilderness of life the sustaining presence of God."* There is much good news here. "Pilgrim faith" itself is good news. By it, Brachlow means that like those who have gone before us, we, too, are called *"to seek a better country, our true homeland, that 'new heaven and new earth' which is our hope in Christ."* This faith is a journey in response to the call of Christ, who provides for us along the way and offers us ultimate hope.

Such faith that endures in the face of pain and enormous hardship is a gift from God: *"It is the mystery of the Spirit of God who provides…the 'assurance of things hoped for, the conviction of things not seen.'"* Here the preacher reminds us of an important theological point. Faith is not something *we* do. Faith is always a gift from God.

But there's more good news. *"Pilgrim faith,"* Brachlow says, *"recognizes that the sustaining presence of God is often to be found in the most difficult challenges we face….God is often to be discovered afresh in those disturbing, 'wilderness' experiences of life."* In fact, *"finding oneself in such a wilderness, however uncomfortable, is also often the precondition of grace."* In Luther's words, "One must go into the wilderness, then Christ comes." The good news here is that even in the wilderness, or perhaps *especially in the wilderness,* when we must let go of our old securities and embrace risk and hardship, we often discover the sustaining presence of God in new and deeper ways.

Text

One is struck by how sparingly Brachlow draws directly upon the biblical text in this sermon. The passage (Heb. 11:1–2, 8–16) was presumably read before the sermon was preached. At first glance, the text seems to provide only a backdrop for the sermon and is directly introduced at only one key point. On closer consideration, however, any listener familiar with the great eleventh chapter of Hebrews can hear the text speaking throughout the sermon.

Brachlow's sparing use of the biblical text actually increases the impact of the text. Halfway through the sermon he says, *"Like Abraham, in our text from Hebrews 11, the Pilgrims came to understand that they were but poor strangers and exiles on this earth."* Here the preacher effectively connects the Pilgrims to the biblical text and to Abraham. Then he describes the Pilgrims' faith and Abraham's faith in the words of Hebrews 11:1 — "the assurance of things hoped for, the conviction of things not seen." This is all the preacher needs to say. He has defined "pilgrim faith" as biblical faith. We have the connection. We hear the remainder of the sermon with the biblical text echoing through the lines.

Less is often more when using the biblical text in a sermon. It's good to let the hearer make the connections. This sermon was originally preached in a seminary chapel context, so we can assume that the listeners were very familiar with the text from Hebrews 11. It is good to note, however, that in other preaching contexts, where listeners may be less familiar with the content of biblical texts, it may be important to give greater elaboration or explanation to the text. But even in other contexts, in certain types of sermons it is often most effective to employ minimal but precise use of the text.

Response

This sermon invites us to understand and live out our faith in a certain way. We are called to a pilgrim-faith journey which recognizes the restlessness of faith: *"We can no longer be complacent about our life or the needs of others around us, never fully content with the world as it is and with our place in it."*

We are also called to see the sustaining presence of God in the wilderness places of our lives. The closing lines of the sermon offer the call to respond: *"This is pilgrim faith. It is ours to live out in our own wayfaring pilgrimage,"* wherever that journey takes us.

This sermon is good news and effective proclamation. It calls us to a new kind of faith — a faith that remembers the past and moves us toward the future. *To have faith is to remember.* To remember the goodness of God. To remember those who have gone before us. To remember our own lives. To remember the times and places where we have seen glimpses of God. And when we remember, there is hope. Faith becomes more real, the journey possible, the wilderness bearable — because of our awareness of the sustaining presence of God.

Suggestions

- Do a study on the theme of "journey" or "pilgrimage" as a metaphor for faith arising out of the Scriptures. Then develop a series of sermons or a class around this theme.
- Study the theme of "the wilderness" in the Scriptures and develop sermon material on this theme. Be sure to include the people of Israel in the wilderness in Exodus and Numbers; images of the wilderness in Isaiah 40-55 at the time of the exile; and the role of the wilderness in Jesus' ministry in the Gospels. What is your understanding of "wilderness" as a metaphor in Scripture? How can this metaphor speak to your congregation?
- "God is often to be discovered afresh in those disturbing, 'wilderness' experiences of life." How have you personally experienced this? How have members of your congregation experienced it? Address this theme in a future sermon, using your story or stories of people in your congregation.

Gary W. Klingsporn

Note
1. Frederick Buechner, *A Room Called Remember* (San Francisco: Harper & Row, 1984), pp. 1-12.

JESUS
THE WORD

JOHN 1:1–18

REV. DR. MARK D. ROBERTS
IRVINE PRESBYTERIAN CHURCH
IRVINE, CALIFORNIA

REV. DR. MARK D. ROBERTS

JESUS THE WORD

JOHN 1:1–18, NRSV

My friend Jim was alone in New York one evening at dinnertime. He stepped into a restaurant, sat at the counter, and ordered his meal. As he ate, he began to chat with the man sitting next to him at the counter. The man seemed vaguely familiar, but Jim couldn't place him. As it turned out, this man, who identified himself as Gordon, had many interests in common with Jim. So they hit it off and continued their conversation for a couple of hours over several cups of coffee.

Gordon, Jim learned, was a musician — singer, actually. Since most New Yorkers who identify themselves as musicians or actors usually fall into the "aspiring and unemployed" category, Jim didn't press too hard to find out what Gordon had done in his chosen profession. He didn't want to put his new friend in the awkward position of apologizing for his vocational failures. Instead they talked about art in general, about politics, and other shared curiosities.

Finally Gordon said that he had to leave for an appointment. Much to Jim's surprise, Gordon picked up the tab for dinner as he departed. "He must not be hurting too much financially," Jim surmised. As he readied himself to leave, the restaurant manager came over to speak with him.

"So are you guys friends?" the manager asked.

"No," Jim responded. "We just met tonight. An interesting man, that Gordon. Says he's a singer."

The manager looked puzzled. Finally he said, "You don't know who that was, do you?"

"Sure. That was Gordon Sumner. Who do you think it was?"

The manager laughed. "Yes, that is Gordon Sumner. That's his real name. But he goes by another name professionally — Sting. You had dinner with the rock star Sting tonight!" (For those of you in generations that don't know Sting, for rock fans he has the stature of Neil Diamond or Frank Sinatra in earlier eras.)

I wonder if our relationship with Jesus isn't something like Jim's encounter with Gordon Sumner, a.k.a. Sting. Many of us have come to know Jesus personally. He is our friend, our companion, our encourager, our counselor. Yet we don't know who he really is. We don't see him in his glory. We completely miss the majesty of the One we call our friend. I don't mean to imply that Jesus is not our friend. Indeed, he calls us his "friends" (John 15:14–15). But that isn't the whole picture. Even as Gordon Sumner, the pleasant dinner companion, is also Sting, the world-renowned rock star, so Jesus our friend is also the very Word of God Incarnate. We don't know Jesus fully until we know him in both ways.

Today we examine Jesus' title "Word." What did it mean when early Christians acclaimed Jesus as the "Word"? How should we relate to him today as the "Word"?

WHAT IS "THE WORD"?

Before turning to our text from John 1, we must first look at the background which will help us to understand what it means for Jesus to be the Word. The Greek term translated "word" is *logos,* from which we get words like *logic* and *theology. Logos* had a great variety of meanings in ancient Greek, including "a word," "something spoken," "a speech," "thought," "reason," "rationality." Many Greek philosophers believed that the *logos* was the ordering principle of all creation, that which set the world in motion and kept it running according to plan. Human beings, with their capacity for rational thought, had tiny seeds of the cosmic *logos* planted within them.[1] This allowed humankind to rise above the animals and to understand the deeper *logos* of the universe.

Although Greek philosophy may have influenced early Christian understanding of Jesus as the Word, Judaism provides a more direct and relevant background for the prologue to the Gospel of John. In the Hebrew scriptures the word of God creates. Genesis records that heaven and earth came from God's word; God spoke all things into existence. As Psalm 33:6 summarizes, "By the word of the Lord the heavens were made, and all their host by the breath of his mouth." Creation demonstrates the power of God's word.

Moreover, *the word of God reveals*. One hundred and nine times the Old Testament says that "the word of the Lord came" to someone to reveal the purpose of God to or through that person. (See, for example, Jeremiah 1:1–4.) The great Hebrew prophets spoke as the word of God inspired them. Because the word reveals, it is known to be true.

Jewish scholars who majored in God's wisdom merged the word and the wisdom of God. In Proverbs 8, for example, the wisdom of God, here pictured as a woman, says that when God created the universe she "was beside him, like a master worker" (Prov. 8:29–30). In the Wisdom of Solomon, a Jewish writing from the Old Testament Apocrypha, the word of God active in creation is equated with the wisdom of God (Wisdom 9:1–2).

Jewish hymns to God's wisdom sound very similar to what we read in John 1. Listen to this excerpt from Proverbs:

> [Wisdom speaks.] The Lord created me at the beginning of
>   his work,
> the first of his acts of long ago.
> Ages ago I was set up,
>   at the first, before the beginning of the earth....
> When he established the heavens, I was there,...
>   when he marked out the foundations of the earth,

then I was beside him, like a master worker;
and I was daily his delight,
rejoicing before him always,… (Prov. 8:22–23, 27–30).

A similar hymn to wisdom is found in the Wisdom of Solomon:

[Wisdom] is a reflection of eternal light,
a spotless mirror of the working of God,
and an image of his goodness…
She reaches mightily from one end of the earth to the other,
and she orders all things well…
She glorifies her noble birth by living with God,
and the Lord of all loves her.
For she is an initiate in the knowledge of God,
and an associate in his works (Wisdom 7:26, 8:1, 3–4).[2]

Who Is "The Word"?

Now listen again to the beginning of John's Gospel:

In the beginning was the Word, and the Word was with God, and the Word was God. He was in the beginning with God. All things came into being through him, and without him not one thing came into being. What has come into being in him was life, and the life was the light of all people. The light shines in the darkness, and the darkness did not overcome it (1:1–5).

We can hear the similarities between John's "hymn" to the word of God and the Jewish praise of wisdom. Just as God's wisdom is his associate in creation, so is the word of God. As God's wisdom is light, so is the word. Like the Jewish sages before him, John melds together the wisdom and the word of God. The word of creation is also the word of revelation. The same word that inspired the Jewish prophets now reveals "grace and truth" (1:17), but in a unique way (1:18).

Although John's hymn to the Word has been influenced by previous

Jewish reflection on the word and wisdom of God, John makes a move that was completely unprecedented in Judaism (or in Greek philosophy, for that matter). He says: "the Word became flesh and lived among us" (1:14). Some Jews believed that wisdom came to Israel in the form of the Mosaic law (Sirach 24:1, 23; Baruch 3:37–4:1). Certain Greek philosophers believed that little bits of the *logos* formed the human soul. But neither Jew nor Greek would have made the outrageous claim that the divine Word, the very *logos* of the universe, had "become flesh and lived among us."

We who are familiar with Christianity can hear this line as saying something ordinary. We generally respond with such nonchalance to the miracle of the Incarnation, the Word becoming flesh. We should, in fact, be blown out of our chairs. We should be shocked, amazed, dumbfounded. The Word of God made flesh? The Word through whom God created all things has become a human being? The very source of life and light in the cosmos dwelling among us? Unbelievable! Incredible!

Notice what else John says about the Word made flesh. He shines with the very glory of God (1:14). He offers "grace upon grace" (1:16) and brings "grace and truth" (1:17). The Word who is the only Son of God, who is even identified as God, he alone has seen God and revealed God to us (1:18).

Because the Word of God Incarnate reveals God and offers grace and truth, through him we have the opportunity to know God and to become God's children (1:12). Although many rejected the Word, even his own Jewish kinspeople, we have the chance to receive him and thus be adopted by God the Father.

Who Is "The Word" To You?

The prologue to John's Gospel makes clear what our response to Jesus the Word made flesh must be: we are to receive him, not reject him. How do we receive him? First, we receive him by believing in his name, by believing that Jesus is, indeed, the Word of God Incarnate. Although we can see evidence of this reality in Jesus' unique life and ministry, we come to affirm the Incarnation through faith, as the Spirit of God leads our hearts. The Holy Spirit helps us to believe what the Scripture teaches — that our Savior and Friend, Jesus the Messiah, is in fact the eternal Word of God. This, by the way, is not a belief we master and control. It continues to stretch us, to challenge us to greater reflection and meditation.

Second, we receive Jesus as the Word of God Incarnate by accepting what he gives us. John says that from him we receive "grace upon grace" (1:16). Grace is God's unmerited, undeserved kindness. Grace means that God loves and forgives us even though we do not deserve it. From Jesus the Word we receive, not just grace, but "grace upon grace" — endless grace, limitless grace.

Moreover, through grace, the Word Incarnate gives us knowledge of God the Father. No person has ever seen God except the Word, identified in verse 18 as God's Son. The Word, who has seen God and is close to the Father's heart, "has made him known" (1:18). Later in the Gospel of John, Philip the disciple asks Jesus how he can see God: "Lord, show us the Father, and we will be satisfied" (14:8). Jesus answers: "Have I been with you all this time, Philip, and you still do not know me? Whoever has seen me has seen the Father" (14:9). As the divine Word made flesh, Jesus reveals God the Father to us in a unique way. In Jesus alone we may truly see God. So if we want to respond rightly to Jesus the Word Incarnate, then we will allow him to show us the Father.

Knowing God Through "The Word"

In the life and teaching of Jesus we learn what God is like. In his person and character we see a clear reflection of God. In the death and resurrection of Jesus we perceive and receive God's gracious love. We who are searching for God need look no further than Jesus. Jesus, as the Word of God Incarnate, reveals God to us.

Knowing God through Jesus is both intellectual and relational. Our culture teaches us to value the second much more than the first, to prize experience and feeling over rationality. No matter how important relational knowledge of God is, exclusive emphasis on this aspect of faith fails to take seriously Jesus as the Word of God. Remember that "word" in Greek is *logos*. It means "reason" or "rationality." Jesus, as Word Incarnate, teaches us to think rationally about God, to have right *theology*. You may know that the word *theology* comes from the Greek word for "God," *theos*, and the word *logos*.

Jesus the divine *logos* helps us to know God with our minds. He calls us to think theologically. That call pertains not only to those of us who do theology as a profession but to all Christians. My friends, we who know Christ personally have a great need to know him intellectually as well. In a culture that tends to devalue thinking, we must respond to Christ the *logos* of God by developing a rational, biblical, Christ-centered theology. Because we know Christ first through faith, faith informs and lays a foundation for our theology. The best theology or philosophy is, in the words of the medieval philosopher Anselm, "faith seeking understanding."[3]

I realize that I may have lost some of you in this discussion of theology. But my point is really quite simple: part of our response to Jesus the Word is to develop our God-given reason in thinking rightly about God. My concern for you as your pastor is also simple: many of you have come to know God personally, but you have a great need to know him intellectually as well. Because Jesus is the Word of God, I would call you to a new commitment to theology, to thinking about God as revealed through the Incarnate Word of God.

Knowing God Personally

Some of us, however, get so wrapped up in knowing God intellectually that we fail to know God relationally. Jesus the Word Incarnate not only helps us think rightly about God; he gives us the "power to become children of God" (1:12). In response to Jesus the Word, not only should we develop right theology; we should also grow in an intimate, personal, deep relationship with our heavenly Father. Through Jesus the Word we know about God in truth, and we know God truly, as a child knows a loving father.

My daughter Kara is just five months old. She doesn't know too much about me. She doesn't know my name, my history, or what I do for a living. But Kara knows me personally. Her face lights up when I come into the room. She squeals with delight when I pick her up and give her a big kiss. She truly knows her father.

Jesus has come as Word Incarnate so that we would know God as his beloved children, in the way my daughter knows me. Jesus helps us to know about God in truth, and to know God intimately in love.

Rena Ingraham never knew her father personally. Growing up, she knew just a little about him: that he had been married to her mother; that he left home in 1940 to find a better job to support his family; that he never returned. She'd ask her relatives: "Do you know my daddy? Where's my daddy? Tell me about my daddy." But answers never came.

When she was in her twenties, during the early 1960s, a relative found some letters from her daddy, Marvin Clark. In these letters Clark professed his love for Rena and her mother, Vergie Lee, and his hope to be reunited with them. Rena then discovered the painful truth that her mother's relatives, who didn't like her father, had kept these letters from her mother. In fact, Rena later discovered, the relatives had sent letters to Marvin Clark supposedly from Vergie Lee. These fake "Dear John" letters told Marvin that Vergie Lee had gotten remarried, and that he should just get lost. And so he did, though never giving up his love for his wife and his daughter.

Through her daddy's letters, Rena began to learn the truth about him: that he was a man of integrity, of faithfulness, of abiding love. She learned how much he still wanted to have a relationship with his family. The more Rena knew about her father, the more she wanted to know him personally. The facts weren't sufficient. So thirty-five years ago she made a valiant effort to find her daddy, but to no avail. She knew he was somewhere in Virginia, but could never make contact. Sadly, she gave up the search.

Last August Rena Ingraham's daughter, Margaret, moved from South Florida to Virginia. Before she left, she promised her mother that she would look for Marvin Clark. For months Margaret searched through nursing homes, cemeteries, and old phone books, but without success. She asked members of her church to help. Finally one church member realized that she had a "Marvin Clark" living in her apartment building. Sure enough, he was the right Marvin Clark. Margaret found her seventy-five-year-old grandfather — still waiting, still hoping to find his family.

As Rena Ingraham stood by gate F12 of the Fort Lauderdale-Hollywood Airport in south Florida, she waited to meet this man she knew about, but never really knew in person. She scanned the passengers exiting from the plane, looking for someone who could be her daddy. Finally a stocky man with a cane hobbled through the gate and headed toward her, with a dozen roses in his hand.

As he approached his daughter for the first time in fifty-five years, Marvin Clark said, "It's been a long time since I held you in my arms." Then he embraced her.

Finally Rena was able to know her father deeply, intimately, personally. "This is the most beautiful day of my life," she said. "I feel like I've been born again."[4]

Not a bad turn of phrase, actually. Through Jesus, the Word made flesh, we can be born again to know about God in truth and to know God personally in love. We aren't limited to reading his love letters to us. Jesus the Word gives us power to become the children of God, to know God as our heavenly Father. Through Jesus we can know God's embrace, even if we have never known him before. And if once we did know God's love but have wandered far away, like Marvin Clark, he says to us, "It's been a long time since I held you in my arms," and then embraces us.

Dear friends, we have a heavenly Father who wants us to know him fully. He has never given up on us. As John says in his Gospel, "For God so loved the world that he gave his only Son" (3:16). Jesus, the Son of God, the Word of God, came in human flesh so that we might know God. Jesus wants to guide us into true thinking about God. Jesus wants to give us the power to become and to live as God's beloved children.

How will you respond to Jesus the Word?

Will you receive him today?

Will you believe on his name?

Will you accept him as the very Word of God Incarnate?

Will you allow Jesus to reveal God to you?

Will you receive his grace, grace upon grace?

Will you allow Jesus to give you the power to know God and to be embraced by God as his beloved children?

My friends, that's what it means to respond to Jesus, the Word of God!

Notes

1. J.N.D. Kelly, *Early Christian Doctrines* (New York: Harper & Row, 1978), pp. 17–19. See also *The New International Dictionary of New Testament Theology,* edited by Colin Brown (Grand Rapids, MI: Zondervan/Regency, 1978), s.v. "Word," 3:1084.
2. I do not have time to explore the relationship between Philo and John 1. The Jewish philosopher, Philo of Alexandria, who lived during the time of early Christianity, brought together Greek philosophical speculation about the *logos* with Old Testament images of the word of God. The *logos* becomes God's intermediary, through which God created the world. Many scholars see a close connection between Philo and John 1.
3. Anselm, "Proslogion," chapter 1.
4. Tony Pugh, "Family Finds Missing Dad After 55 Years," Knight Ridder News Service, March 2, 1995. Retrieved through San Jose *Mercury News.*

COMMENT

A well-known Christian educator once tried to argue for a change in the way seminaries train their students. In an exhaustive volume, he made his case for theological training to be more relational and less cerebral. At the end of every chapter in his book, he suggested that his readers pursue the possibilities he was raising by reading further or writing a research paper of their own. But his ideas never found much fertile ground of acceptance. While making the case intellectually for a change to a more balanced approach, he modeled a continuation of the old one-sided model.

By contrast, in "Jesus the Word" Mark Roberts models what he wants his congregation to do with their faith. On the one hand, he appeals to the intellectual aspects of faith with an argument that is both reasoned and well-researched. On the other hand, he shares very human illustrations which emphasize the importance of personal relationship. So he gives a living example of a Christianity balanced between the logical and the emotional.

Roberts also works hard to communicate effectively while delving into the often ignored area of rational instruction in the faith. To paraphrase G. K. Chesterton's comment on the Christian faith in general, teaching theology in the local church at the end of the twentieth century has not been tried and found wanting. Rather, it has been found difficult and left untried. Roberts seeks to bridge this gap by allowing his own excitement about the implications of his message to come through in his delivery, particularly during the application-focused third paragraph in his section on Jesus, the Word, in John 1 — "Who Is 'The Word'?" By his strong language (*"Neither Jew nor Greek would have made [that] outrageous claim"*), and even his punctuation (the repeated use of question and exclamation marks), we are compelled to reflect on the impact of Jesus' being the very Word of God. He also breaks from the argument to speak directly to the congregation: "My friends, we who know Christ personally have a great need to know him intellectually as well," and, "I realize I may have lost some of you in this discussion...But *my point is really quite simple."* Such breaks into the heady flow of logic actually draw back into the dialogue of preaching those who may have mentally wandered away.

Problem

By focusing on the question of what it means that Jesus is the "Word," Roberts is also addressing a greater problem introduced by his opening illustration: How can we have a full knowledge of Jesus that is not one-sided in its focus? He assumes that many in his congregation *"have come to know Jesus personally";* therefore he emphasizes strengthening his listeners' *theological* knowledge of Jesus. However, he returns to his greater concern for a rich, well-balanced knowledge of Jesus just before his closing illustration, when he warns against getting *"so wrapped up in knowing God intellectually that we fail to know God relationally."*

Roberts, then, focuses his efforts particularly on those who focus on Jesus as their friend and counselor. He does this by careful exegesis of his text.

Text

There is perhaps no New Testament passage with more undercurrents of intentional intercultural appeal than John 1:1–18. Roberts takes us through the biblical writer's purposes by quickly summarizing what *logos* meant to the ancient Greek culture as *"the ordering principle of all creation."* We learn how, in Psalms and Jeremiah, the Word of God both creates and reveals what is *true.* The sermon then briefly explores a stylistic comparison between the text and Jewish thought at the time as demonstrated in both Proverbs and the apocryphal Wisdom of Solomon.

What is wonderful stylistically at this point is the balance Roberts maintains in speaking to both the intellectually and the relationally oriented people in his congregation. While he makes the defensible assumption that most of his listeners tend to focus on the relational, his own skill as an exegete would certainly tempt him to show some academic flourish here, and indulge the smaller portion of his audience who love to feast on scholarship. But instead, he keeps the needs and abilities of the congregation he serves at the forefront of his concerns and intellectually stretches them *just enough,* while showing how John's prologue demonstrates that Jesus not only satisfies both Greek and Jewish longings, but goes beyond!

PROCLAMATION

One Sunday, a small ensemble in a Midwest church presented "What the World Needs Now Is Love, Sweet Love" as the musical offering in the morning worship service. To its pastor, this was the last straw. The next week he preached on "Why Jesus is not our 'Buddy'!" To a society that has lost sight of the holy and its significance, Roberts' sermon proclaims the important message that Jesus brings us the opportunity for relationship and reconciliation with God not simply because he is loving, but because he is the very Word of God. If Jesus were not the agent of Creation, its ordering principle, and the actual revelation to the world of who God is, then the relationship with God he offers would not only be weakened, but impossible.

Recognizing the built-in spiritual need within each person, Roberts makes it clear that *"we who are searching for God need look no further than Jesus."* But because we must look at him intently, as a lover does his or her beloved, we hear that *"knowing God is both intellectual and relational."* As always, a good illustration furthers the preacher's purpose. Because we have already learned that *"Gordon Sumner, the pleasant dinner companion, is also Sting, the world-renowned rock star,"* we know that *"Jesus our friend is also the very Word of God Incarnate,"* and are ready to believe that our lives will be the richer when we intentionally explore the question of who Jesus is. Roberts has argued that *"we don't know Jesus fully until we know him both ways."*

Roberts makes this point passionately. It is crucial to his intent to convince his listeners that all Christians, not only the professionals, must be led by their theologically grounded understanding of God: *"My friends, we who know Christ personally have a great need to know him intellectually as well."* At this point, the majority of listeners, who may be caught up in the anti-intellectual spirit of our times, need to be convinced: Why? Why do I need to bother to know Jesus intellectually?

Roberts applies this proclamation to the human situation through the final illustration, which also addresses the listener's need to be convinced of the importance of Christology. Marvin Clark was important to Rena Ingraham because of *who* he was. We can understand Rena's personal need to know her human father: there was an incompleteness to her identity, and a longing for relationship. Roberts uses this story to drive home his point: *"Through her daddy's letters, Rena began to learn the truth about him...The more Rena knew about her father, the more she wanted to know him personally."* In the same way, growing in our theological understanding of God will not dampen our enthusiasm to know God but rather intensify it and make the relationship even more satisfying. There is a winsome evangelistic appeal in his sentence, *"Through Jesus we can know God's embrace, even if we have never known him before."*

Notice that Roberts mentions the particular airport and gate where the reunion took place. What is left unsaid is the theological significance of such true stories. This was a miraculous reunion, particularly in that *the* Marvin Clark was living in the same apartment building as a church friend of Rena's daughter, when all they had known was that he was somewhere in the same state. Pastorally, we must remember that our people need reassurance that God's power to make our lives "work out" is real, and is manifested today. We should never lose sight of the power of the particular in driving home the reality of the story.

Response

Roberts calls for specific responses throughout this sermon, but before he finishes, he reiterates the points of application. He invites his listeners to respond by receiving and not rejecting Jesus, the Word of God. What is more, he says to them that they are to do this by believing in his name, by allowing Jesus to reveal God to them, by accepting what he gives — his endless grace, and by allowing *"Jesus to give you the power to know God and to be embraced by God as his beloved children."* Through his plea for theological growth among Christians, Roberts has made it clear that part of our response to Jesus' identity as the Word is to develop our own God-given reason, by thinking rightly about God. Such intentional emphasis on the need for response insures that his hearers will walk away with more than just a heartwarming story. They will leave with the tools they need to allow God to work powerful, positive, personal change in their lives as they believe on the name of Jesus the Word and receive from him grace upon grace.

SUGGESTIONS

- How much emphasis do you place on exhorting/teaching your congregation to think on all of life Christianly? Do you teach on doctrine? Do you explain its significance in terms the congregation can understand? Do you yourself understand its relevance to them? Talk to them about it in your visitation. Look at local and cultural human predicaments with an eye to uncovering some of the poor theology that contributes to the pain of your people. Address these issues in your preaching.
- Writers like Os Guinness *(The Dust of Death)* and David Wells *(No Place for Truth)* plead for a return to intellectual depth in Christendom. Their books may help your efforts to bring out the same in your congregation.

Peter J. Smith

FINDING PEACE

ISAIAH 2:1–5; MATTHEW 1:18–25

REV. DR. GARY A. FURR
VESTAVIA HILLS BAPTIST CHURCH
BIRMINGHAM, ALABAMA

Rev. Dr. Gary A. Furr

Finding Peace

ISAIAH 2:1–5; MATTHEW 1:18–25

To bring about the reconciliation of opposites requires not an act of the intellect but a leap of the imagination. For in order to find peace, we must find some way to bring together two things that normally cannot go together, to fit a square peg into a round hole, to make 2+2 equal something more than the sum of its parts. Peace is the reconciliation of opposites.

Peace in the world of nations is often a plodding process in which diplomats sit for hours or days among coffee cups and briefcases at a conference table, exchanging ideas, arguing differences, stating cases. But if there is ever to be peace in reality, the unthinkable has to happen: enemies have to shake hands; stereotypes must be surrendered. For peace to come, there must be what news commentators almost always call "a breakthrough." And only the realm of God, the unseen world of dreams and imagination, can give us a breakthrough.

The world of nations is a perilous world, full of danger and threat. How we know that right now, as thousands of our troops head into a place full of death and hatred in the hopes of giving fragile peace a chance in Bosnia! Such peace will not come about with calculators and charts. It will happen in our dreams first. It is in our dreams, in our imaginings, that we can meet the terrifying and exciting call of God.

We tend to think of peace as a place where struggle and fear are absent. As a result we abdicate courage, we cease striving, we avoid confronting the uncontrollable and we stop taking risks in life. So our life moves along, safe but boring. The problem is that the risks find us anyway. Our handy little moral systems and hackneyed proverbs for guaranteed living fall aside. For life serves us situations fraught with danger and hard decisions, where there are not always clear answers. There is only our faith in God, leading us into the unknown.

In our Gospel reading today, Joseph finds himself in such a situation, one that was more complex than we realize. At that time there were two steps in marriage. First a formal exchange of consent took place before witnesses. Then the groom took his bride to his home to meet his family. "Consent" usually occurred when the girl was between twelve and thirteen years old. From this time forward, the man had rights over the girl. She was henceforth his wife (even though the New Revised Version uses the word "engaged"). Any infringement on his rights could be punished as adultery. The girl, however, continued to live at her home for a year. After the year was up, the formal transfer took place, the ceremony in which the bride moved permanently to the groom's home.

Joseph's problem? Mary was expecting and it was not his child! Verse 19 says that Joseph was a *diakaios,* translated variously as "righteous," "just," "upright." This is a favorite Matthean word. One interpretation is that because he was an upright man, he was therefore not willing to expose her publicly. However, the words can also mean that he was an upright man *but* not willing to expose her publicly. The reference is to Deuteronomy 22:13, 20–21, the case of a young woman brought to her husband's home and found not to be a virgin. She was required by law to be stoned as an adulteress. In a less severe interpretation of the law, she could simply be put away in a divorce. Only this interpretation assumes that Joseph believed Mary to have been unfaithful.

What was the moral thing for Joseph to do? What was the right thing?

Trying too hard to be a moral person can, on rare occasions, get in the way of doing what is right. And, on the other hand, listening to God can get us into trouble. For we may find, to our disappointment, that religious institutions are more institution than religious. And religious people are more people than they wish to acknowledge.

The solution for Joseph comes to him in his sleep, as a dream.

Dreams can be a threat to the culture because they represent the unfettered imagination. In our society, there is a long tradition of rejecting persons of genius and invention: poets, scientists, artists, people whose imaginations often cause them to leap far ahead of the capacity of the rest of us to see where they are going. The result, sadly, is that we heap rejection and misunderstanding on them before they are given the accolades of acceptance and appreciation.

In the same way, Christianity is often a threat to the status quo when properly introduced, because it questions the order of things and undermines inherited traditions. Though we are a society that prizes individuality, this prizing is constantly threatened—witness our constant pressures for censorship, restrictions of liberty, suppression of rights for the sake of order. Dreams teach us that the way that is rejected by most may be the future for all.

This same conflict also occurs in our inner world. We are called on to confront things in ourselves that threaten the whole order of our existence—feelings we cannot manage, fears we cannot conquer but try to ignore or suppress, hurts we try to forget, intuitions that do not fit our normal way of life. Dreams often represent these despised or neglected parts of our lives. So we must listen to our dreams, not only to get in touch with the hurts of the past but also to lead us into the future, despite our fears of the unknown, and no matter the cost. For obeying our dreams may require suffering, but in suffering we learn to be open to hope.

As we confront our own brokenness, how do we keep from being crushed under its burden? There is no easy answer. But one thing I know, the evidence of suffering, like a scar, is a map of the past. Scars tell about the real us. Scars are badges, reminders of pain that we have survived. They tell others that we have faced some tests and passed (even if we only made a D minus). They are evidence of grace and strength.

Suffering deepens us. There is a shallowness of soul and heart in people who have never been wounded. For without wounds we cannot love. Our dreams point the way. So we must be open to our dreams.

Joseph followed his dreams. He gave up his rights in order to listen to God. But I think he also desired to love Mary. He was willing to be misunderstood, to suffer derision and ridicule, in order to obey God, but perhaps also for the love of a woman.

How do scars and suffering lead to transformation? I don't know how. I only know this: God is with us. That is the assurance the angel brought to Joseph in his dream. Leave the past behind and go with God into this unknown future, obeying the dream, and the rewards will surpass everything you have known.

As we go with God, we will find our peace, not so much as the lack of turmoil or the absence of pain, but in the joy of discovering the wholeness God has for us.

Dreams can lead us into that future because they come from beyond the everyday, they arise out of our unguarded depths, beyond the reach of a censorious society. They take us beyond the strictures of the status quo, the limitations of space and time. Think about this: Joseph almost rejected Mary and the baby Jesus in trying to do what he thought was "the right thing." So may we, in the name of some provincial "right," reject the call of God.

Victor Frankl once observed that the mental patients he treated would not talk about their religious experiences and beliefs for fear that they would not be taken seriously or believed. How could God be there, they questioned, in a psychiatric ward? But God, he found, *is* in the psychiatric wards.

So this raises a possibility. If there are religious people called upon to go into "the world" to follow the will of God, consider also the possibility that there are "worldly" people who are leading deeply spiritual lives, but without always being able to name the One who is in the midst of their search. There, in the brokenness, in the heartache, in the rough and tumble of a family crisis or a shameful failure, is the provident God calmly and mysteriously at work.

In fact, I might go so far as to say that often I have observed more signs of God's life "out there" than at a thousand organized pep rallies for Jesus, or a hundred civil-religious-self-celebrations whose message is, finally, "Behold what manner of men and women we are!"

We are called upon to hear this deeper truth all the time in our relationships: to look beyond the immediate to the unknown. Frank Tupper has said of this passage, "Families are ragged things. Yet within the realism of ongoing family life, Matthew's infancy narrative says that scandal, public or private, does not in itself destroy the providential work of God."[1]

Do we see what a terribly threatening idea this is? That God works through us, with us, in spite of us and, at times, utterly without us. But God works anyway. We are fearful of being pushed to the outer circle of importance. Or of losing control. Or that morality and decency will be watered down and washed away. But there is a terrifying and wonderful possibility as well: that God continues to work and bless even if we do not have it together, if our families do not have it together.

Let me sketch an imaginary situation for you—but it's one that happens all the time. A mother and son talk one day and the mother is stunned to discover that her son thinks he is gay and is "coming out." Over the months to come, this mother must come to terms with her pain, her ignorance, the condemnation of the Christian community and her own deepest convictions about "how it is supposed to be." But these must also be weighed against the memory of this son when he lay in her arms at birth, how she loved him then and loves him still.

This mother must believe, somehow, that though her convictions remain, she cannot listen to the simplistic caterwauling of TV preachers any more. She still believes in God and the Bible. And she still believes in her son. Somehow there will be a way. Because God is with her.

So don't be afraid. Listen to your heart and your imagination. You may stand today at the edge of some dark and fearful choice whose outcomes are not clear to you. You may face the need to reconcile two loves that cannot be brought together. You may stand between two poles in a conflict that you are certain will tear you apart. You may be caught between your head and heart, or between a love and a truth. You see no way. But the declaration of

Advent is not, "Jesus solves all the problems before they happen." The good news is rather a name: Immanuel — "God is with us." God is with us as we enter into the fearful depths to heed his call.

At the end of his Gospel, Matthew records another dream. It comes during the trial of Jesus. Pilate's wife sends word to him about a terrible dream she has had, and she warns Pilate, "Have nothing to do with that holy man"(Matt. 27:19). God was speaking, even then, even in the trial of Jesus. God was in Christ, as Paul said, reconciling all those things which cannot be reconciled. Reconciling the world unto himself (2 Cor. 5:18–19).

Note
1. E. Frank Tupper, *A Scandalous Providence: The Jesus Story of the Compassion of God* (Macon, GA: Mercer University Press, 1995), p. 110.

COMMENT

Gary Furr had two strikes against him when he sat down to write an Advent sermon. The first strike was one of the seasonal themes: peace. What can one pastor say about peace that hasn't been said before? The second strike was the text: the story of Mary and Joseph. How do you come up with something fresh? Something that will break through the numbed familiarity many adults bring to the Christmas story?

You know what they say: three strikes, you're out. Pastors preparing sermons for Advent Sundays could easily adopt the popular saying "been there, done that" as their seasonal refrain. But Furr didn't strike out—he hit a home run.

Short of plagiarizing his sermon, how can we do what he did? What does this sermon model that can break through our own familiarity and indifference to the birth narrative? How many times have we read these passages? Or heard the story preached? Or watched the story enacted by children wearing bathrobes and sheets? What can we learn from yet another sermon based on the Christmas story?

THE STRUCTURAL CHOICE

When approaching any writing or speaking task, an individual has to choose whether he or she is going to go from the general to the specific or from the specific to the general. A sermon that begins with an illustrative story or the text itself often goes from the specific to the general, like a symphony that begins with a single instrument playing an isolated melody, and is gradually joined by the full complement of the orchestra. The function of moving from specific to general is one of leading the hearer along, broadening the appeal, reaching a wider audience, creating a structural "envelope" that wraps around your audience. This inductive approach is usually a more effective method of hooking the interest of the intended audience.

Gary Furr does the opposite here. He begins with the general (the topic of peace and reconciliation) and moves into the specific (the Christmas story). Why? And more importantly, why does it work?

Moving from the general to the specific is the first technique Furr uses to break through the auto-response "ignore mode" of adult listeners. In essence he comes in the back door. If he had followed the rules and gone from specific to general (birth narrative to peace/reconciliation) his listeners would have already tuned out. He would have lost the attention of half his congregation.

Furr could have easily titled his sermon "Mission Impossible," because that's the set-up he creates with his opening. He names the impossibility of peace in his opening paragraphs when he says, *"If there is ever to be peace in reality, the unthinkable has to happen."*

Once you've opened a sermon with the admission that what follows addresses an irrefutable impossibility, you've got your congregation's attention. Then he moves the issue of peace from "out there" in the world of diplomats and briefcases to "right here," in *our* world when he says, *"life serves us situations fraught with…hard decisions, where there are not always clear answers."*

The bat cracks as the ball is hit and Furr is on his way to first base. The deductive movement from general to specific continues with his next line: he introduces the text.

Juxtaposing the Unrelated

What does the story of Mary and Joseph have to do with world peace? What does a teenage pregnancy two thousand years ago have to do with our lives today, making "right" choices, or healing our hurts? What do we have in common with the distant world of a Jewish carpenter and a young girl engaged before she wore her first training bra?

The second technique Furr employs in "Finding Peace" is that of juxtaposing two seemingly unrelated or conflicting issues, concepts, or visual images. He pairs the inherent conflict of Joseph's dilemma with our assumptions that "doing the right thing" and "being a moral person" are one and the same. He challenges our comfort zones in this sermon, ever-so-respectfully pricking and probing at our carefully constructed moral systems.

This sermon is replete with juxtaposed contradictions:
- *"What was the moral thing for Joseph to do? What was the right thing?"* Implied question: Is there a difference between the two?
- *"Trying too hard to be a moral person can, on rare occasions, get in the way of doing what is right. And on the other hand, listening to God can get us into trouble."* And this is good news?
- *"Joseph almost rejected Mary and the baby Jesus in trying to do what he thought was 'the right thing.'"* How can doing the "right" thing be the "wrong" thing? And how can we know the difference?

These are only a few examples of Furr's juxtaposing inherent contradictions. They are midsermon wake-up calls, statements not easily ignored, statements designed to call back wandering minds — and they work.

Finding Your Personal Passion

The third technique we can learn from Furr's sermon is at the heart of effective preaching. He proclaims the good news from the perspective that has the greatest personal significance for him and for us. He calls us to listen to our imaginings, the voice of God that comes to us when we are least resistant: our dreams.

The statement he makes in his opening paragraphs is carried through the sermon: *"It is in our dreams, in our imaginings, that we can meet the terrifying and exciting call of God."* The sermon is literally punctuated by the phrases that bring us back to the truth.

This sermon is from a series of Advent sermons titled, "The Dreams of Christmas," inspired by the book, *A Scandalous Providence: The Jesus Story of the Compassion of God*, by E. Frank Tupper, which Furr quotes in the sermon. The intersection between Furr's personal passion for listening to the inner voice of God and the impossible mission of peace and reconciliation is where the good news of the gospel is met: *"That God works through us, with us, in spite of us and, at times, utterly without us. But God works anyway."*

Continuing the movement from the general to the specific, Furr brings the sermon home with that statement and the quotation from Tupper's book. He's now talking specifically to the person in the pew: to the ragged family struggling with private shame, to the individual bearing the wounds of imperfect love, to the Christian facing a decision in which no choice is a good one.

Furr's closing words are worth reading again:

So don't be afraid. Listen to your heart and your imagination. You may stand today at the edge of some dark and fearful choice whose outcomes are not clear to you. You may face the need to reconcile two loves that cannot be brought together. You may stand between two poles in a conflict that you are certain will tear you apart. You may be caught between your head and heart, or between a love and a truth. You see no way. But the declaration of Advent is not, "Jesus solves all the problems before they happen." The good news is rather a name: Immanuel — "God is with us." God is with us as we enter into the fearful depths to heed his call.

When a home run is hit, even the distracted fans in the stand take notice. Furr hits a home run; even the distracted, the distraught, or the dismayed hear their own story in the message of hope in this sermon: the assurance of God's presence in our lives no matter how "ragged" our circumstances.

SUGGESTIONS

- Which of the techniques used in this sermon was the most compelling to you? The three techniques were 1) moving from general to specific (also called a deductive progression); 2) juxtaposing unrelated or conflicting concepts; 3) preaching from a personal passion. As you read through this comment, which technique triggered

thoughts, ideas, musings for possible sermon ideas? Those musings are the voice of your "imaginings." Jot the ideas down, spend some time reflecting on those ideas and let a sermon evolve from those possibilities.
- Read the book by Frank Tupper, *A Scandalous Providence,* for sermon ideas or develop a sermon around the phrase "Families are ragged things."
- Do a study of the function of dreams in the Old and New Testaments, and consider developing some sermons on them.
- Have you ever used one of your dreams to illustrate or form the core of a sermon? Be bold. Try it.

Debra K. Klingsporn

THE POWER OF YOUR STORY

JOHN 9:1–25

REV. DR. SCOTT WALKER
FIRST BAPTIST CHURCH
WACO, TEXAS

REV. DR. SCOTT WALKER

THE POWER OF YOUR STORY

JOHN 9:1–25, NAS

My father was a Baptist minister. He has been dead now for over thirty years, but I treasure my hazy childhood memories of him. I can still see him standing in a pulpit on a sizzling hot Sunday in South Carolina, preaching as if the fate of the world rested on the passion of his appeal. Dressed in a white suit, white shoes, with a red rose in his lapel, he looked like a young, flushed Colonel Sanders. I guess the bleached cotton cloth kept folks cool in an age before air conditioning.

Dad was prone to the dramatic and loved to recite poetry. I don't recall a single sermon title of his, though I do remember a high energy moment when, with all of the appropriate gestures and vocal modulations, he recited a poem about a man being chased through a forest by a ferocious, frothing hunting dog. The vivid scene lodged secure in my five-year-old memory.

Several years ago, I stumbled across a poem in an anthology and realized that my father had been quoting from "The Hound of Heaven" by Francis Thompson. Depicting God as a relentless hound forever in pursuit of the wayward soul, Thompson writes of his own attempt to escape from God:

> I fled Him, down the nights and down the days;
>   I fled Him, down the arches of the years;
> I fled Him, down the labyrinthine ways
>   Of my own mind; and in the mist of tears
> I hid from Him, and under running laughter.
>   Up vistaed hopes, I sped;
>   And shot, precipitated,
> Adown Titanic glooms or chasmèd fears,
> From those strong Feet that followed, followed after.

After discovering the poem, I felt compelled to read up on the life of Francis Thompson. I discovered "the story behind the story."

Francis Thompson was born in England in 1859. Raised a Roman Catholic, he intended to be a priest. However, when his school master decreed that his temperament was too unruly and reckless for future ordination, his physician father sent him to Manchester to study medicine.

Thompson flunked his medical board examinations three times, then dropped out of medical school and escaped to London. Adrift without purpose or job, he slid into poverty, illness, and opium addiction. He was finally reduced to selling newspapers and matches on the streets, while spending most of his nights in a drugged stupor on the squalid sidewalks of Covent Garden market.

In sober moments, Thompson began to write poetry. On the verge of suicide, he submitted some poetry to Wilfred Meynell, editor of the magazine, *Merry England.* Meynell, a devout Christian, took an interest in the derelict youth, and invited him to stay in his home.

Through the love and witness of Wilfred Meynell and his wife Alice, Francis Thompson became a Christian and a noted writer. He died prematurely at the age of forty-eight, but his printed words continue to bear witness, as evidenced in my own life.

Several months ago, my wife and I had an opportunity to reflect again on Thompson's epic story. On holiday in London, we had been to a theater near Covent Garden and were walking to a restaurant. Amidst the nightly throng of theater patrons and gawking tourists, a man's voice shouted above the din of the crowd, the cadence clearly the rhyme and rhythm of a street preacher. I quickly spotted a young man nearby, microphone in hand, drawing a curious flock to him.

Normally, I would have paid little attention. But there was something about this fellow that riveted me. Edging closer, I could see that he was handsome, clean cut, winsome, articulate — most likely a college student. He was using a flip-chart and marker to present a very theological and propositional approach to Christianity. He sounded like an animated gospel tract, a theology lecture in process.

As I intently watched his expressive face, his words seemed to fade away. "Who are you?" I asked in silence. "How did you get here? What convinced you to become a Christian? What motivates you to preach on the streets? Tell me your story! Come on, tell me your story!"

But instead of his story, I was hearing words dripping in the language of Zion, phrases like "the blood of the Lamb" and "died for your sins" and "Jesus is Lord!" Of course, I know what these phrases mean, and I revere their truth. But for the uninitiated, indeed, for most of this young man's audience, these theological terms sounded like the clichés of a cult; words both antiquated and nonsensical.

As the crowd slowly drifted away, I wanted to scream, "Why don't you tell us your story? Share your story and how Jesus changed your life. We came to listen to *you!*"

Standing in the very place where Francis Thompson heard the Hound of Heaven breathing down his neck a century ago, I realized that the power of the gospel is always biographical; it is always best told through the story of flesh and blood and human passion.

Isn't this scripturally true? When God chose to reveal himself ultimately to this world, he did not send a theology, or a philosophy, or even a sacred scroll or holy book. What he sent to us was a man named Jesus who through his life, thought, personality, example, death and resurrection showed us what God is like. It is revelation through flesh and blood. It is biography. And it is a very human story that has never lost its gripping power.

In John 9:1–25 we read the account of a man who was blind until he bumped into Jesus. When Jesus touched his eyes, suddenly the man was able to see. The healing caused quite a stir among Jesus' critics. The poor man was hauled before the angry Sanhedrin, where he was cross-examined and pressed to explain how his vision had been restored. Unable to present a logical or a theological explanation, he finally blurted, "One thing I do know, that, whereas I was blind, now I see" (v. 25). The Pharisees and the Sadducees came nose to nose with the fact that the one thing that you cannot refute is the evidence of a changed life. And the strongest argument for Christianity will always be the power of the human story…the story of blind people made to see and young derelicts seized by the unrelenting love of the Hound of Heaven.

Today, you must see that your primary task as a Christian is to tell your story. Your conversion may not be as dramatic as that of Francis Thompson. But your story is just as vital, just as important. Aided by the Holy Spirit, there is nothing more effective than the telling of your unique story to those who are lost without faith or hope.

Go and tell someone how the Hound of Heaven caught up with you. Go and testify to the skeptics of this world that once you were blind, but now you can see. Give God the chance to speak through your story.

COMMENT

Not only is the contemporary American novelist Pat Conroy alive and well, he is apparently living in Waco, Texas, and moonlighting as a Baptist preacher under the pseudonym "Dr. Scott Walker." At least one might think so after reading the sermon, "The Power of Your Story." Walker employs classic Conroy form (a la *The Great Santini* and *The Lords of Discipline*) in communicating the gospel. Maybe it's because they're both from South Carolina. Must be the drinking water. Whatever it is, it works. This is a laudable example of the power of story in proclaiming the faith — no coincidence in light of the sermon's title and theme. This is a well-told story about the power of telling stories well.

Walker's sermon demonstrates not only the power of story but also the richness of the diversity that exists in the preaching of God's truths. No one style or method is better than any other. Great sermons come in many forms. Good communication is good communication. Here we find a short but poignant presentation of a simple truth: *"the power of the gospel is always biographical."* (More particularly, we might say "autobiographical.") And Walker's story works. Why? Because he practices what he preaches even while he preaches. You can imagine how his message might be extinguished in the hands of a less skilled communicator, someone who smothers the message under a barrage of platitudes or of scholarly analysis. Heaven forbid!

PROBLEM

The problem addressed by the sermon is personified in the young street evangelist at Covent Garden. How often have well-intentioned proselytizers shot themselves in the foot by failing to draw upon their most powerful tool, their own story. On the surface, it's confounding. Why do we not talk about the very thing we know the best? Ourselves. We do it in so many other arenas of life. Why not also in the enterprise of sharing the gospel of Jesus Christ?

Seminary education, packaged evangelism programs, countless books on the shelves of Christian bookstores — all of these try to equip the Christian for the effective spreading of the Word. But is it working? Never in history have so many had so much information and done so little. Why is this? Walker suggests it's because we're doing everything except that which should come so easily and naturally to us: telling our own story.

TEXT

The point of reference for Walker's message is John 9:1–25, the story of the blind man healed by Jesus at the pool of Siloam. Notice how one point is drawn from the text and clearly presented. Rather than complicating his sermon with a lengthy discourse on the story's first-century context or the minutiae of the original Greek, Walker focuses on this single point: Without being able to explain the who, what, where, why, and how of his healing, the newly sighted man does know that *"whereas I was blind, now I see!"* Here is the bottom line when it comes to telling others about Jesus. Just speak out what you know for sure. That's it! God will do the rest.

PROCLAMATION

Walker engages his audience immediately in his first few words. *"My father was a Baptist minister."* Interested? Either he's about to regale us with tales of his wayward and rebellious past growing up as a "PK," or else he's going to shed new light on what it's like to share a home with a fundamentalist father. But before we can guess where this might go, he shows his hand. *"He has been dead now for over thirty years, but I treasure my hazy childhood memories of him."*

It's hard to imagine a pew-sitter so jaded that she or he doesn't feel at least a small pang of emotion when someone shares about a relationship with a parent. This is the fabric of life. In only a couple of sentences, Walker has captured our attention. Then he begins his narrative with a vivid description of his preacher-father in the white suit. *"[He] looked like a young, flushed Colonel Sanders."* The details help to set the stage for the recitation of a poem which will guide us into the heart of the sermon.

In the prosaic style of all good storytellers, Walker introduces us to Francis Thompson, the nineteenth-century English poet whose life was a classic tale of redemption — from great expectations, to the gutter, to God. In hearing Thompson's story, we are impressed by his witness to Jesus Christ. It's yet another example of the power of one person's story.

From Thompson, we move on to Walker and his wife making a sojourn back to the very streets where the poet had been a derelict a hundred years earlier. The clever segue is not lost on us, as it provides a smooth transition into the story of the modern street preacher. Each piece falls into place with an economy of words. The sermon progresses like a poem itself, each anecdote serving as a stepping stone to the next, until, in the end Walker leaves us standing before the very Hound of Heaven, who now beckons us to become his next witness.

Response

With that persevering yet patient Hound on our heels, it remains for us either to join God's band of biographers or sit silently nearby, keeping our story on the shelf. Walker's sermon leaves no room for excuse, as he builds his case on three basic assumptions:

1) every believer has a story to tell;
2) telling our faith story is our *"primary task"*;
3) *"aided by the Holy Spirit,"* our story will be evangelistically effective.

Nothing complicated here. However, simple truths are not simplistic. Jesus is God's personal story in the flesh. John's blind man is Jesus' story revealed in power. Francis Thompson is the story of God's redemption through the witness of Wilfrid and Alice Meynell. And what is our story? Well...? It's left for us to fill in the blanks.

Suggestions

- Never underestimate the power of sincerity and vulnerability. Walker speaks as one who has been impacted by the love of others and, because of that, he brings his love for the congregation into the pulpit. There's no doubt that too much candor in preaching can become self-indulgent or even manipulative. (Have you ever sat through a sermon where it feels as though the preacher is holding a personal therapy session?) Done wisely, a sermon with flesh on it has universal appeal. On the other hand, behind every dead church is dry preaching.
- Notice how brief but effective Walker's message is. Why do so many preachers think they have to fill a set amount of time every week? Why not vary the length of the sermon according to the nature of the subject? In this case, giving twelve points to effective witnessing would have been counterproductive. The message would have been lost in a pile of platitudes. While briefer is not always better, remember we're dealing with a generation raised on sound bytes. The average person's attention span is three seconds! Is it the pastor's duty to single-handedly extend that span to forty-five minutes? Walker knows better, which is one of the secrets of his effectiveness.
- Reread the sermon with an eye for structure and style. Take special note of the length of Walker's sentences and paragraphs. They are short and carry a punch, evidence that the message is written for the ear rather than the eye. The best preachers understand this difference. A sermon may make a great read but be a lousy listen. This sermon is a great listen. As an added bonus, it also ends up reading well. Such is the power of a story well told.

Richard A. Davis

WHERE ARE YOU HEADED?

MARK 10:32–34, 11:1–10

REV. DR. NORMAN NEAVES
CHURCH OF THE SERVANT
OKLAHOMA CITY, OKLAHOMA

Rev. Dr. Norman Neaves

Where Are You Headed?

MARK 10:32–34, 11:1–10, NEB

A few years ago, a neat movie came out that caught the imagination of many who saw it. *City Slickers,* starring Billy Crystal and Jack Palance among others, was about three middle-aged, upper-class guys who decided to work out some of their midlife crises by going to a dude ranch out West for a couple of weeks.

One of the three was Billy Crystal. While he and his friends were on a cattle drive, he struck up a conversation with an old cowboy, played by Jack Palance. This is the way the conversation went.

Palance said, "Yeah, you guys come out here every summer at about the same age and you have the very same problems. You spend fifty weeks out of each year getting knots in your ropes, and then you think that two weeks out here will untie them for you. None of you get it." He pauses a long time and then says, "Do you know what the secret of life is?"

Billy Crystal says, "No, what is it?"

Palance holds up one finger, his index finger, and says, "This."

"Your finger?" exclaims Crystal.

Palance replies, "One thing, just one thing. You stick to that and everything else doesn't mean a thing."

"One thing?" Crystal says, "Well, that's great, but what is that one thing?"

Palance throws his head back and laughs out loud and then says with a little wry smile, "That's what you've got to figure out."

I'm not sure that "one thing" is the same thing for everybody at all. In one sense it's a very different thing for each one of us. Yet, when you look below the surface, the "one thing" is the same for each of us after all. What is it, this one thing we've all got to figure out, this one thing that's the most important thing of all in each one of our lives? It has to do with our purpose, our basic reason for being here in the world. Unless and until we get that figured out, we don't have much of a life.

"They were on the road, going up to Jerusalem, Jesus leading the way; and the disciples were filled with awe" (Mark 10:32a).

Jesus got it figured out, didn't he? Jesus' life was enormously powerful. Because he knew what his purpose was, his life made a huge difference in the world.

Jesus made a decision when he was up in Galilee that he needed to go to Jerusalem. And he did so, fully aware that going there would cost him his life, and yet also fully aware that that was the only way God's salvation would come to the whole world. So he gathered his disciples together and off they went on the ninety-mile journey from the north shore of the Sea of Galilee down the Jordan Valley to the great city of Jerusalem. The Gospel of Mark gives us a fascinating glimpse of this journey. It says, "They were on the road, going up to Jerusalem, Jesus was leading the way; and the disciples were filled with awe" (10:32). Other translations of the Bible say that his disciples were *amazed* or *astonished,* or in a *daze,* but I think the word *awe* best captures what the Greek word was really wanting to convey. What is so significant about that? I think the disciples were awed because Jesus wasn't holding back the slightest bit. Rather, he was out in front of the pack! He was walking way up ahead of all the others! He was almost eager to get to Jerusalem, though he knew full well that he was going to be killed when he got there! Why was he so eager? Because of his basic purpose in life, his basic reason for being, the one thing for which he felt he had been put in the world — and he knew that if he didn't fulfill it, he really wouldn't have much of a life at all!

The same holds true for you and me. There's a basic reason and purpose for which each one of us is here in the world. Our lives are not an accident. Maybe our parents thought that our coming was an accident, but no life is ever an accident. Instead, our lives are an investment — a divine investment. God made each one of us ever so carefully and ever so wonderfully and put us in the world at this precise time. God had a reason for doing that, a deep reason that lies inside the heart and soul of each one of us in this room. If we never discover that reason, never honor and live out that purpose, we really won't have much of a life!

Maybe you feel a little bit like Charlie Brown. I mean, you hear these big and lofty ideas about having a reason and a purpose in your life, and you wonder what in the heck yours might be. Charlie Brown went to see his friend Lucy. She had her famous booth set up, the one that says "Psychiatrist" on the front. Charlie pays her five cents for her expert advice. "Lucy, I need your help," he says. "I don't feel a sense of commitment to anything. I can't seem to find my direction and my purpose in life."

Lucy looks at Charlie Brown and says, "Oh, don't worry, Charlie Brown. It's like being on a big ocean liner out in the middle of the sea. Some folks put their deck chairs to face the front of the ship, and others put theirs to face the side of the ship, and others put their chairs to face the back of the ship. The real question, Charlie Brown, is this: Which way do you face?"

Charlie Brown has this absolutely blank and bewildered expression on his face. And then he says, "You know, Lucy, I can't even get my deck chair unfolded!"

I suppose all of us feel like that from time to time. We don't know what to do with such big and heavy questions about our purpose in life, our destiny, our basic reason for being. We shy away from questions like those, push them to the side and don't really deal with them at all. But Jack Palance is right isn't he? If we can't answer that one basic question about our life — that is, why we're here and what we're all about — then nothing else will really fall into place for us at all and we'll never have a life that's very deeply satisfying.

I came across a story some years ago that illustrates this point. Alfred Nobel, the great Swedish chemist, made a fortune developing explosives and selling his secret formulas to governments so that they could make bombs and land mines and all kinds of weapons of destruction. One night his brother died in an automobile accident. But the papers got the report mixed up and thought that the one who had died was Alfred. They published this long and impressive obituary about Alfred, calling him the dynamite king of the whole world. They told about the incredible fortune he had amassed, the millions of dollars he had made through developing explosives and other means of mass destruction. The next morning when Alfred read his own obituary in the paper, he was shocked and stunned beyond belief. But he was also saddened, deeply saddened, when he realized what his life had amounted to and how he would be remembered when he was gone. Right then and there he made a decision that he was going to turn his life around and live whatever years he had left creating an entirely different legacy for himself.

I believe you would agree with me in saying that Alfred Nobel did a pretty good job in that regard after his brother's death. He set up a series of major and very prestigious international awards given to people who made positive contributions to the human family. We know them today as the Nobel Prizes, one of which is the Nobel Peace Prize. They exist because Nobel didn't like the way his life had gone or the kind of legacy he was leaving the world, and he wanted to do something about it before it was too late. He found his ultimate purpose.

How about you? Are you pleased with the way your life has been going up to this point? Are you pleased with the kind of legacy you are creating, the kind of memory you're leaving behind? Are you pleased with what you have done with the one life that's been given to you, the only life you'll have to live in this world? If not, what might you do at this point to change all of that and to put your life on an entirely different course? That decision is really what Palm Sunday is all about, isn't it?

A very successful and highly respected attorney tells about the greatest Christmas gift he ever received in his life. He was a youngster when, one Christmas, he discovered a box under the Christmas tree with his name on it. The box was from his dad. "It was so light," he said, "about the weight of the box itself, and I couldn't imagine what might be on the inside. At first I thought it might be some money, but then I knew better, because we were very poor at that time and didn't have any money to share." He could hardly wait, he said, until Christmas Day when he could open up the gift from his dad and see what it was. Finally Christmas Day came. Inside the box he found a note, just a simple note, that's all. But what that note said meant everything in the world to him.

This is what the note said, "Dear son: This year I will give you three hundred and sixty-five hours of my time and my undivided attention, one hour every single day right after dinner. It's yours! We'll talk about what you want to talk about. We'll go where you want to go. Or, if you wish, we'll play what you want to play. But it will be your hour and my hour together, and it's what I want to give you for Christmas this year." "My dad not only kept that promise," the attorney said, "but he renewed it every year. It's the greatest Christmas gift I ever received, and now that he's dead and gone, it's more precious to me than ever."

His father had found the one thing that was really important — his relationship with his son.

We, too, need to realize that this is the only life we'll ever have, and the time to begin living it is right now! Again, the questions: How do we want to be remembered? What kind of legacy do we want to leave behind? How do we want to direct our life from this day forward and for the rest of our days? If we can't answer these questions, then undoubtedly we haven't found our purpose, the reason for which we've been put here on earth. We are majoring on the minor things in life. If that's true, then someday we'll be very sorry.

Jesus headed toward Jerusalem with a deep sense of purpose. Where are you headed in life? What's your purpose? There's a "Jerusalem" somewhere up ahead for all of us to face — and the only issue is whether we will move into that Jerusalem or whether we will turn away from it and move in the opposite direction.

How about you on this Palm Sunday?

Comment

The question of purpose, or finding our "fit" in the world, is growing in prominence. Unexpected job transitions have been all too frequent a part of the American experience in recent years. But Tom Peters, in his book *Crazy Times Call for Crazy Organizations* (Vintage Press, 1994), suggests that we look at unplanned visits to the job market as opportunities to better discern the special gifts we have to offer. He says that when he is doing hiring today, he distrusts anyone who does not have a mysterious gap in the "Employment History" portion of their resume. One pastoral colleague of mine refers to his long job hunt as his "sabbatical" in which he investigated and rediscovered the specific purpose God had for his life.

Sometimes the key to an answer is a very good question. In "Where Are You Headed?" Norman Neaves explores in an engaging fashion the question of finding our individual life purpose. He communicates the strategic importance of the question and reassures his hearers that God is able and willing to lead them in pursuit of the answer. Because Neaves respects the genius of God nascent in each member of his congregation, he knows better than to force-feed an answer to a question that is so particularly personal and spiritual.

Problem

Neaves keeps the central problem before his hearers by the fourfold repetition of a *leitmotif*: *"Unless and until we get that [our basic reason for being here in the world] figured out, we won't have much of a life."*

One of the dangers in dealing with such a profound topic is that those hearing it will assume this is only an intellectual exercise. Neaves deals with this in two ways. First, he keeps the problem relevant by including in down-to-earth language with each restatement of the problem the practical consequence of ignoring the problem: *"We really won't have much of a life,"* meaning a life that's deeply satisfying.

Second, Neaves' careful choice of illustrations demonstrates that the goal of discovering our life's purpose, like all good goals, is challenging but attainable. Setting up a world-famous endowed prize or spending an hour each day with a child can have lasting impact, no matter what our sphere of influence is. With his story of the boy's Christmas present from his father, Neaves reinforces the importance of finding our purpose, and reassures us that the purpose is appropriate to each individual.

Neaves' style in treating the problem is particularly instructive at the points of introduction, illustration and response. Notice how short this sermon's introduction is. There is no "round the bend" logic to it. There's just a straightforward statement of the topic. A short, clear introduction leaves more room in the congregation's attention span for the preacher's elucidation.

Preachers often try to stimulate the interest of their audience with multiple attempts at humor or bizarre anecdotes. If that is our tendency, this sermon should make us ask if we do it because we don't see our topic's relevance to the lives of our parishioners. If the topic is significant enough, we don't need to convince people to hear our sermon.

Two of Neaves' phrases are key to why this sermon's introduction works: *"Jesus...knew what his purpose was"* and *"his life made a huge difference in the world."* People wish both were true of themselves. Neaves invites his hearers to reflect on their purpose and on how they can make a difference in their world as well.

ILLUSTRATIONS

Some sermon illustrations illuminate particular portions of a sermon's logic. Others encapsulate the whole sermon. The story of *City Slickers* is of the latter type. Like Jack Palance's character in that movie, Neaves is not going to answer the question of our individual life's purpose for us. Since we remember stories much better than rational argument, we are given a handle in this story by which to hang on to the entire sermon.

But the illustration is distinctive for another reason. Both in the *City*

Slickers story and the story of the Christmas present at the end of the sermon, Neaves uses questions in his illustrations to keep the listener connected to the sermon. We wonder with the attorney-as-a-boy what could possibly be in the feather-light box. We hear the *City Slickers* story and wonder what Palance's finger means. We chuckle with Billy Crystal's befuddled response, because we don't understand either. When Crystal asks our question for us — creating almost a virtual conversation with the movie itself — we are both frustrated at the denial of an easy answer, and motivated to search more intently for the guiding purpose of our lives.

Good illustrations are not thrown in haphazardly simply because they are interesting stories. Rather, a well-used illustration catches listeners up in the story and directs their thinking in order to lead the listener along a particular path. By telling us a story about Charlie Brown and Lucy, Neaves demonstrates again that he understands how people think. Our life's purpose represents part of the image of God within each person. But that image and purpose are so distorted and supplanted by the crud of living that they seem impossible to recover as long as we live in a world of sin and darkness. Like Charlie Brown, we feel that we can't really do what is asked of us. Discovering our purpose for living seems prohibitively difficult.

For this reason, the Nobel story and the Charlie Brown illustration are inseparable. Not only did Nobel ascertain the purpose that Charlie Brown believes, like many of us, is beyond discovery, but he pursued that goal and achieved it. Years ago, Sam Hogan, preaching professor at Gordon-Conwell Theological Seminary, said to his students, "Don't dig up a snake you can't kill." He meant that we should not raise problems that we are not able to solve. The Nobel illustration in this sermon kills a particularly venomous snake, one where the listener says, "I'm too old to change; I neglected to discover my purpose earlier in life, and if I discover what it is now, I'll be frustrated by knowing that if I had only started earlier, I might have been able to achieve it."

Text

Neaves' choice of a biblical text for this sermon is remarkably short, about half of one verse from Mark 10:32. But the inspiration of the Scriptures is demonstrated in how much can be unpacked by a sharp focus on a single phrase. His sermon asks why the disciples were in awe, why the Gospel writer would bother to report that Jesus was at the head of the pack, and what the personal significance of Jerusalem is to the modern day Christian. Each question leads to the central problem: *"Because [Jesus] knew what his purpose was, his life made a huge difference in the world.... Unless and until we get that [our basic reason for being here in the world] figured out, we won't have much of a life."*

Proclamation

We could not begin to consider the question of purpose if God did not have a personalized purpose for each of our lives, springing from the attributes of God's sovereignty and God's personal nature. Neaves sees this problem and takes the opportunity pastorally to proclaim to each parishioner that they are not accidental flukes of nature. Many people, especially in the so-called "Generation X," have been convinced — by neglect, abuse or the frustration of living in our impersonal, mass-market society — that their own lives are utterly insignificant. Until listeners are convinced of their own personal importance in God's plan, they will assume the preacher is speaking about someone else, and not be motivated to seek God's purpose for their life. They may even walk out of the worship service in greater despair than when they came in.

The theology of God's sovereignty here is particularly important. Neaves communicates the challenging and reassuring message that God is able, not only to help any one of us discover our life's purpose, but also to pursue it to satisfaction.

Response

Neaves starts asking for a response before the last paragraph. After making somewhat impersonal statements about the subject of finding one's purpose in life, Neaves switches to a paragraph consisting of six questions which use the word "you" (or a variant) a total of twelve times. This emphasizes the necessity for each of us to find the purpose of our own life. Neaves will not allow the listener simply to enjoy the interesting stories he has been telling. His final illustration (the boy's Christmas present) is placed at the end of the sermon to invite our thinking about how we should respond.

By restating "the questions" near the very end, Neaves compels us to respond. He has told us throughout the sermon that until we get our basic reason for being here in the world figured out, we don't have much of a life. He avoids giving us a prefabricated answer. Like Jack Palance's *City Slickers* character, the preacher leaves us to wrestle with the question of our purpose. This struggling and persevering in prayer was once a major part of American evangelicalism. Charles Finney's memoirs, for example, demonstrate again and again the pursuit of peace with God that marked not only his own life, but the lives of many of his hearers. Anyone who turns his or her hand to a plow lightly will just as easily let go if it. If we put the sweat equity into the search for our purpose, then we will more likely apply ourselves to pursuing it with determination to the very end. The pastor secure in his or her calling will trust the Holy Spirit to lead a Christian's individual journey as well as the congregation as the people of God. The diligent pastor will not neglect the importance of prayer in the Spirit's leading of each believer and the congregation.

Suggestions

- For further insight into helping young Generation X adults reconstruct their sense of God-given personal importance, read Bernardi's and Maheny's book, *A Generation Alone* (Downer's Grove, IL: InterVarsity Press, 1994). Chapter 2 argues convincingly that the peculiar forces at work in the Baby Busters' lives legitimate the dictum that this is the first generation to be neglected rather than nurtured by its parents.

- Given the importance of discerning individual purpose, you may want to consider how you should preach/lead the congregation you serve in their discovery of God's calling in their individual lives and as a congregation. Two useful resources are Ken Blanchard's *The One Minute Manager,* and Ted Engstrom's *A Strategy for Living.* This last resource would be particularly helpful for follow-up accountability and study groups which help people in the discernment and implementation of their life purpose.

- Do you occasionally preach sermons that ask a question rather than answer it? An important implication of the priesthood of all believers is that each Christian must learn to hear and obey God for themselves. Some topics that lend themselves to the individual journey are: discerning one's spiritual gifts; the specific call of God upon an individual congregation; and the answer to a sticky community problem.

Peter J. Smith

THE NEARNESS OF GOD

ACTS 17:16–34

Dr. John Killinger
Professor of Religion
Samford University
Birmingham, Alabama

DR. JOHN KILLINGER

THE NEARNESS OF GOD

ACTS 17:16–34

It is a fact of life that what we search for most eagerly often lies so close to us that we could reach out and touch it.

Russell Conwell, whose famous speech "Acres of Diamonds" helped to build Temple University in Philadelphia, told this story. A boy he knew in Massachusetts went to Yale College to become a mining engineer. He was a brilliant student, and during his senior year he was paid fifteen dollars a week as an assistant in his department. When he graduated, they offered him forty-five dollars a week to remain as an instructor. But by that time he had got the gold fever and wanted to be a wealthy man, so he persuaded his widowed mother to sell the family farm in Massachusetts and go West with him in search of gold. He never found gold, and the last Conwell heard of him he was working for a copper mining company in Minnesota at fifteen dollars a week.

Not long after the new owner had taken possession of the farm in Massachusetts, he was harvesting the potatoes that lay almost on the surface of the ground. He was carrying a bushel of potatoes through the narrow stone gateway, when the basket caught on the posts, and he had to set it down and push it through. As he was doing so, his eye was caught by a particularly shiny stone. It turned out to be a block of native silver worth more than a hundred thousand dollars! The young man had passed through that gate scores of times a day, said Conwell, and his sleeve had brushed against that very block of silver. It was almost as if the block had said to him, "Here is something of enormous value, waiting for you to take it." But the young man never did. He went off looking for wealth in other places.

It is the same with God. We seldom realize how close God is to us. We often think, "Oh, if I only had the time or the energy, I would go in search of great books, I would listen to the great teachers, so that I could learn to pray and discover God." But the truth is, we don't have to go anywhere and we don't have to study anything. God is as near to us as that block of silver was to the young man going through the gateway. Only we don't realize it.

This is what Paul was trying to say when he spoke to the men of Athens on Mars Hill. He could see how close the Athenians were to discovering the presence of God. He had walked through their lovely city and had seen the many evidences of their search for the beautiful and the eternal. He had seen the glistening temples raised to Diana and Apollo and Zeus and Poseidon. He had even seen a monument dedicated to "The Unknown God," as if, having turned over every other stone in their attempt to earn the favor of the gods, they did not want to miss this last one! How close they were to the secret of everything! All those brilliant philosophers, from Empedocles and Socrates and Plato right on down to the men of Paul's own day! All the great artists, whose creations in stone and clay still in our day draw students from all over the world to study their beauty! All the great dramatists, such as Aeschylus and Sophocles and Aristophanes, whose plays still form the basis for Western theater! All the poets and historians and statesmen and warriors! Theirs was a golden culture, perhaps the most shining society the world has ever known. If any people ever erected a ladder and threatened to scale the very heights of heaven itself, it was the Greeks.

But in spite of all their achievements, their urge to find God had not been satisfied. They had looked everywhere, turned over every stone, and still had not found him.

Paul was filled with sympathy. He obviously liked the Athenians. His great heart was surely warmed by the beauty and symmetry of their city, by the excitement of their intellectual life. But they had not met the living Christ on the Damascus road, as he had. They had not heard, as he had, the stories of the wondrous Galilean — his wisdom, his insights, his parables. They had not dealt with the meaning of the cross and the resurrection, which, simple as they were, confounded the Greek mind and its "scientific" way of viewing the world.

"You have done what God intended us to do," Paul told them. "You have sought for God in all the places around us where he might be found. I am sorry you have not found him. For the truth is, he is nearer than you thought. You have looked everywhere and missed him. He is not far from each one of us. In fact, it is in him that we live and move and have our being, as one of your own poets has guessed. You see, we are his offspring, his children. And he has told us this through Christ, whose resurrection is the proof of his love for us."

Phillips Brooks once said of this passage, it was as if Paul had entered a room where a blind child sat, had held the child in his arms and stroked its hair and said, "Don't be afraid, my child, your father is here. You can't see him, but he is here nevertheless. He breathes in the very room with you. He loves you, and wants to take care of you. You don't have to worry any more, he is right here."

Are we any different from the Greeks? Ours too is a golden age: computers, space travel, techniques in medicine the ancient world never dreamed of, engineering feats it never believed possible. We have our philosophers and artists and musicians. We too are looking for ultimate value, for absolutes, for God. We try pleasure, drugs, business, everything, always looking, looking, looking for what will satisfy the God-shaped longing in our hearts. And the answer is right here all the time. So near we could touch it, if we only knew, if we only realized.

"He is not far from each one of us," said Paul. No further than the bowing of our heads, the reaching forth of our hands, the murmured prayer of submission, the taste of bread and wine. God is here. God has always been here. He is always at our sides. In him we live and move and have our being. We can't avoid him. We just haven't known.

What does this mean? It means that, like the Greeks, we ought to stop struggling for what we don't have. We ought to stop looking in faraway places for the joy and peace of life. It is here. It is now. It is in God, who wants to share his life and wisdom with us — who has shared them in Jesus Christ.

It means you are not alone with your problems and your pains. God is with you. He doesn't always take away your problems and pains. But he is with you in them, as he was with Christ in the crucifixion. And that makes a world of difference in everything!

All you have to do is say, "Yes, God," and live every day in the knowledge that he is present with you. That knowledge will transform you, and you will see that the things you want most deeply in life lie within your reach.

COMMENT

Rarely does one find a sermon so clear, concise and powerful as this one by John Killinger. A sermon on Paul's speech in Acts 17 could be filled with a rhetoric that would leave the listener far behind. But Killinger proclaims the message of God's nearness in ways which draw in the listener. He makes God's presence not only a proclamation but a felt experience through stories and images that appeal to the whole person. In this sermon we come to know the God who is infinitely beyond our grasp, yet always closer to us than the air we breathe.

PROBLEM

Killinger's opening story — of how a brilliant student ironically overlooked a valuable piece of silver right beside him and went off seeking precious metals elsewhere, to no avail — does an excellent job of establishing the theme of the sermon. Valuable beyond the student's dreams, the silver literally had been in his reach, yet he had not recognized it. The young man's seeking a tangible treasure in the wrong places is clearly analogous with our seeking an intangible one in the wrong places.

Killinger relates this story to our lives in the first two sentences after the story: *"It is the same with God. We seldom realize how close God is to us."* The paragraph goes on to describe how we think we have to work very hard to find God and do not realize God is already near us. The paragraph's last line repeats the problem: "Only we don't realize it." Thus, the first and last sentences of the fourth paragraph of this sermon unwrap the situation in life in which we all find ourselves. It is a situation not unlike the mining engineer who thought the real treasure was far off, when all along it was close at hand. The idea frames the paragraph and drives home the relevance of the message for each one of us.

Note Killinger's simplicity of expression. His style is straightforward: *"But the truth is, we don't have to go anywhere and we don't have to study anything."* The use of common words and simple sentences makes sophisticated or abstract ideas easier to understand. Such directness and simplicity of language also tend to increase confidence in what is said. By offering simple propositions, Killinger reasons that we, the hearers, are capable of knowing and finding the elusive presence of God. As Augustine said, "You were within me while I had gone outside to seek You."[1]

Before the biblical text is even discussed, the congregation clearly understands the problem. Like the mining engineer, we search elsewhere for satisfaction in life and fail to find God, the ultimate satisfaction.

TEXT

The same problem exists for the Greek audience which Paul addresses in Acts 17. Killinger begins by describing the cultural context in which Paul preached. We are put into Paul's shoes, admiring the works and wonders of the Greeks. Killinger underscores the wisdom of Greek philosophers and describes their achievements with respect and admiration. The list of sophisticated achievements contrasts with the simple conclusion that they were unable to find God.

In the speech at the Areopagus, Paul addresses this paradox. The Greeks have been seeking God in the wrong places. Their scientific view of the world has led them to deny the reality of God. Yet Paul uses a very rational argument to affirm the existence of God as Creator and to announce a way to God through Christ.

Killinger introduces the speech to the Athenians by noting that *"Paul was filled with sympathy."* With this simple phrase, Killinger conveys the understanding that Paul was not speaking to defend his faith in the face of attack, but was proclaiming the gospel out of love and concern for the Greeks. Paul uses an entirely positive approach by articulating his own respect for the Greeks' efforts to seek and find the true God. Although the Acts 17 speech is addressed to a pagan audience, Paul does not denounce their idolatry. Rather he praises the religiosity he finds among them. Paul uses an inscription on an altar to the "unknown god" as an indication of a hunch, a vague notion, that the reality of God may be found if, as Jeremiah says, we seek God with our whole heart (Jer. 29:14).

Killinger employs a similar pattern of argumentation for today's critical listener. Like Paul's speech, the sermon does not work from the picture of human sin and idolatry, but from the natural, ingrained human longing to find ultimate values and absolutes — to find God. To set the context for the biblical passage, the sermon points out the accomplishments and wisdom of the Greeks. Likewise, following discussion of the biblical passage, Killinger points to the cultural and intellectual accomplishments of our own society, revealing a contemporary context not unlike that of first-century Athens. In this way, Killinger, like Paul, shows respect and sympathy toward our culture and points to the same paradox: even our greatest achievements leave us unsatisfied.

PROCLAMATION

Killinger gives us ample illustrations of ways we seek but do not find that which is of ultimate value. In the stories of the mining engineer and the Greeks, the sermon builds clear comparisons for us. We are receivers, too, of Paul's message that we should have known that God who gave us life also surrounds us in the living of it. The sermon's evangelical focus is Paul's proclamation that we need look no further, for a way has been provided to God in Jesus Christ, who says God's reign is near to each one of us (Matt. 10:7).

The sermon draws out an important implication of Paul's proclamation. God is not only here within our reach, but this same divine presence sustains us through difficult times. This pastoral message is made concrete for the hearer through Phillips Brooks' story of the blind child who is unable to see the father in the room, but is reassured of his father's love, care and presence. The story not only taps into our nearly universal experience of being afraid and alone in the dark, but also provides comfort. Our identification with the boy allows us to "feel" the presence of God. This story opens to us an experiential, affective way of understanding more fully the intersection between the abstraction of faith in God and our personal experience of God.

Killinger subtly weaves into the concluding section of this sermon a series of poetic images about worship. They appeal to the senses: the bowing of the head, the reaching forth of hands, the murmured sound of prayer, the taste of bread and wine. Spilled out one after the other in this fashion, Killinger quickly refers to many ways we experience God's nearness in worship. The images offer an opportunity for the recognition of God's presence in the context of the service of worship and invite the listener to acknowledge that presence. To hear images spoken about in this way *is* to experience them.

Response

In the conclusion, Killinger turns to the congregation: "Are we any different from the Greeks?" It is a direct question, an unabashed comparison of ourselves to a civilization that flourished two thousand years ago. We come to the same conclusion reached by Paul in his speech: that which we seek is right here, if we only realize it. In this way, Killinger allows the congregation to become contemporary recipients of Paul's evangelistic speech.

The response Paul calls for appeals to the mind and intellect, as does this sermon. Yet Killinger also skillfully taps into the needs of the intuitive "right side" of the brain. Two effective stories in this sermon are metaphors for abstract ideas. A student seeks treasure in the wrong places. A blind child is reassured that his/her unseen father is there. The stories connect to our own experience of seeking and of being afraid. They touch the feeling side of us, not just our intellect.

This sermon invites us to find comfort in God. Killinger has created an experience of God's holding us as children. We can respond with gratitude and relief. The sermon reminds us that we have found God, that God is with us, and that God is never far from us, even though we may feel alone and abandoned. We are called to respond, saying, "Yes, God," and know with assurance that God is here. We bow our heads, we reach out our hands, we taste and see, we murmur our prayers. In this sermon we as hearers have been led by a masterful wordsmith and sensitive pastor to respond in praise and worship to the God who is always near.

SUGGESTIONS

- When writing a sermon which seems to be primarily oriented to the intellectual, try to include images and stories which also feed the emotional needs of hearers. Create images which appeal to the senses. Concentrate on words to connect with the hearer's own need to "experience" God in ways which may seem more like poetry than prose. If this is difficult, try the following experiment commonly used for creative writing:

    > Choose a color, either by itself or a colored object, such as an apple pie, an orange, an infant, a puppy, a kite; or as a place, such as a house or a building, a park, a memorable travel destination; or as an experience, such as a party, a reunion, a death, or a sunset. Write down in just three minutes as many things you can think of which you connect with that color. Then, using at least three of the words in your list, write a poem in just five minutes. What you find may surprise you and give you courage to be poetic at appropriate places within your sermons.

- Killinger effectively uses simple language to deal with abstract ideas. He avoids words longer than three syllables. Ideas are expressed in short sentences, where they could have become longer, complex sentences. This writing style creates a directness and can make sophisticated ideas easier to understand for the hearer.
- Look back over the sentences in your sermons to see if they are too complex to follow easily. Note your use of long or sophisticated words. Try to imagine how a child would hear your sermon. How

can you reword your ideas for a person, perhaps a visitor, who is unfamiliar with theological language and concepts?

Dixie Brachlow

Note
1. St. Augustine, *The Confessions*, trans. R. S. Pine-Coffin (New York: Penguin Books, 1961), X, p. 27.

Blessed Are the Desperate

MATTHEW 5:3

Dr. Gary W. Klingsporn
Colonial Church
Edina, Minnesota

Dr. Gary W. Klingsporn

Blessed Are The Desperate

MATTHEW 5:3, NRSV

On a cold, gray January morning just after Christmas, Debra and I were getting our girls off to school. We were in that frantic flurry that always happens at the front door just before the bus comes. Boots and hats, scarves and mittens were flying everywhere. Lunch money, homework, backpacks, and people were all converging on the front door, when suddenly, I realized our nine-year-old Katy was not there.

"Where's Katy?" I asked.

A muffled clunk came from upstairs. So I went to the stairway and called out, "Katy, the bus is almost here. What are you doing?"

"I'm looking for my recorder," came her anguished cry from the top of the stairs. "Today's the first lesson and I can't find it!"

Ah, the musical recorder — that little plastic flute they give you in school about the third or fourth grade. It took me back thirty-six years to the day I got my first recorder. And it took me back to my fourth-grade teacher, Mildred Mooney. She was a large, intimidating woman, a stern, no-nonsense field general. In that moment, waiting for Katy at the bottom of the stairs, I could hear Mildred Mooney saying: *"What? You forgot your recorder?"*

So hearing Katy's desperate cry, Debra and I both jumped into action.

There was no time for parental speeches about laying things out the night before. There was time only to look. For the next five minutes we looked everywhere for that recorder. I knew it was there somewhere; I had listened to the girls play it without the benefit of lessons for some days now. We looked high and low, but to no avail. The red and yellow flashing lights of the bus were soon at our driveway. As we ushered the girls out the door with a quick hug and kiss, Katy's last words were, "Mom, if you find my recorder lying around somewhere, will you bring it to me at school?"

Katy's final plea did it. Debra and I went into the house, and for the next thirty minutes we tore that place apart looking for that little recorder! We burrowed into the girls' closets, dug into every drawer, crawled under every bed. I just knew I was going to find that recorder somewhere under the piles of stuffed bears or among the doll clothes. I imagined our finding it, rushing it to school, and getting there just in time to save the day and spare our little girl the pain of walking in to face her teacher empty-handed.

But it was not to be. Try as we might, Debra and I could not save the day. Our search was futile. Katy would have to live with the consequences, learn the lesson. And Debra and I would have to let go of it all.

On my way to work that morning I imagined Katy walking into a large music room at school with all the other students sitting in a row with their recorders ready, and Katy alone having to go up to the teacher — a Mildred Mooney kind of person I was sure — and say, "I don't have it. I couldn't find it."

Like Katy on that January morning, we are all empty-handed. We are all looking. At times we are all desperate.

We live in a world where we have everything we need, and more! But if you strip it all away — all the external and material, all the façade — and get down behind and underneath what it is to be human, you find that we are all alike. Somewhere, somehow in our human spirits, we are all empty-handed. We are all looking.

Rich, poor, or somewhere in between, we all experience what it is to be empty, to fail, to be broken. We know what it is to hurt someone we love, or to be hurt by them; to long for someone to love; to quit loving someone; or to lose someone we have loved. We know what it is to hunger for meaning or purpose in our lives, to fail in a dream, or never to find a dream. We know what it is to lose a parent, a child or a spouse, or to lose a job or our health. We know what it is to struggle with unhappy memories, or with the daily grind.

No matter how happy or successful we are, no matter how "together" we seem to have it, at the heart of it all, down underneath our lives, we are all the same. We live in what Harriett Richie calls "the places where we are broken," "the dark holes where something is missing," "the silence of unanswered questions."[1]

We live in a world of abundance. But it's a violent and hungry world. A world of abject poverty and unspeakable wealth. A world of budget stalemates and abortion debates. A world of media violence and domestic abuse. A world where racism is an ugly reality and "ethnic cleansing" is a euphemism for genocide. A world hungering for peace but plagued by war. We all know the list could go on. Down beneath and behind all that is good is a world that is empty-handed and looking.

We are often desperate, like the old woman of whom Henri Nouwen speaks. One day she was brought to a psychiatric care center. She was wild, swinging at everything in sight, frightening everyone, so that the doctors had to take everything she had brought with her away from her. But there was one small coin which she gripped in her fist and would not give up. In fact, it took two men to pry open that squeezed hand. It was as though she would lose her very self if she gave up that coin.

Like that woman in her illness, Nouwen says, we often go through life with clenched fists, clutching meaningless things as if they were our very identity, afraid to let go. The one invited to pray, to open oneself before God, says Nouwen, is asked to open his or her tightly clenched fist and "give up the last coin," to become empty-handed in the presence of God.[2]

At one level or another, our lives and our world are constantly crying out like Katy on that January morning, "I can't find it! If you find it, will you bring it to me?" We are all empty-handed.

Blessed Are the Empty-Handed

"When Jesus saw the crowds, he went up the mountain; and after he sat down, his disciples came to him. Then he began to speak, and taught them, saying: 'Blessed are the poor in spirit, for theirs is the kingdom of heaven'" (Matt. 5:1–3).

According to Matthew, the first words out of Jesus' mouth in the first sermon of the church's first Gospel in the New Testament, are the words, "Blessed are the poor in spirit." That is: "Blessed are the empty-handed ones, the ones who are looking." Blessed are those who recognize their need, and stand without pretense before God. Blessed are the desperate ones, those waiting upon God alone for their hope and their deliverance. Blessed are those who have reached the bottom, who cannot live without God's help.

On this fourth Sunday of Epiphany, the lectionary readings shift from who Jesus was and what Jesus did as the light of the world, to what Jesus said about our lives as we walk in his light. During the next four Sundays we will hear much of the Sermon on the Mount. But today, the opening words are the key to it all: "Blessed are you, the poor in spirit." That is to say, "I am with you. I am on your side! I love you. Yours is the kingdom of heaven."

In these words, Jesus is announcing that salvation has begun. God's grace-filled presence is with those who are poor in spirit and recognize it. God has entered into a new relationship of blessing with those who are desperate. God's inbreaking rule and redemptive reign are present to those who are in need.

These simple words of Jesus are among the hardest to interpret in Scripture. They are countercultural. They set the world's value system on its head. For all around us the world shouts, "Blessed are those who have brains and bucks and beauty and body." "Blessed are the successful, the self-sufficient, the self-fulfilled, the significant somebodies."

The world promises us a thousand ways, always at a price, to satisfy our deepest hungers and fill our empty hands. The "Self-Help" sections of bookstores are full of volume after volume promising us who live with gaps and dysfunctions in our lives, that we can help or cure ourselves: "Buy this. Do that. Follow these ten easy steps to a better life. Act now — do it today — and you will be blessed!"

But Jesus comes along and the first words out of his mouth are, "Blessed are the poor in spirit, for theirs is (now, today) the kingdom of God." Theirs is the deep inner joy of participation in the fullness of the love of God.

The Beatitudes are a series of strange and holy paradoxes. From the world's point of view, they make no sense. When you look at who Jesus pronounced blessed, it's an eye-opener! There's not a strong, have-it-all-together achiever among them. There are no spiritual giants or heroes here, just needy people!

Jesus says it's the ones who spiritually speaking have absolutely nothing to give and everything to receive who are blessed. It's not the triumphant in faith, but those who mourn whom Jesus pronounces blessed. It's not the strong ones, but the gentle ones, not the righteous ones, but those who hunger and thirst desperately for God who find him.[3]

It's not the ones who judge themselves right, but the humble ones who are merciful toward others who are blessed. It's not the totally pure, but the ones who fail and know their brokenness and are pure in heart who are blessed. The blessed are ones who are longing for some peace in their lives and the world. It's not the ones in power or in charge, but the ones in pain, the rejected, the losing ones who dare to give a humble witness for God who are blessed.

From the world's point of view, the "blessed" of the Beatitudes are all losers, underachievers who have no power, no sense of how the world works! From God's point of view, they are all ones who have not, yet have it all. The blessed are those who are looking, and in the looking, finding — those who are longing and in the longing, fulfilled.

On this Super Bowl Sunday when $30 million players will take the field and TV commercials will sell for $1.2 million a half-minute, when Emmitt Smith longs to be remembered as "the greatest running back who ever played the game," the Beatitudes are a series of holy paradoxes which upset all our human assumptions about power and wealth and winning. As St. Paul says in our epistle reading today, "We proclaim Christ crucified….God chose what is foolish in the world to shame the wise; God chose what is weak in the world to shame the strong; God chose what is low and despised in the world…" (1 Cor. 1:23, 27–28). At the heart of the Christian gospel is this paradox: God chose the cross. The "weakness of God" is the power and wisdom of God — and the source of our redemption.

"Blessed are the empty-handed, desperate ones!" Jesus says. For faith is a longing of the soul for God. It's a hunger that only God can finally fill, an empty hand that only God can finally grasp. St. Augustine's words are good to remember: "Thou hast made us for thyself, O Lord, and our hearts are restless until they rest in thee." There is within each of us an eternally given restlessness, a searching, a journeying home to God. We are all empty-handed. We are all looking.

You Are Blessed

We have often misread the Beatitudes of Jesus. Most of my life I have heard the Beatitudes as rules to obey: "Be meek!" "Be merciful!" "Be pure in heart!" "Be poor in spirit!" We talk about "living the Beatitudes" and we say that the Beatitudes describe "what a Christian ought to be."

But have you ever tried to *be* poor in spirit? You either are or you are not. You either recognize that you are, or you don't recognize it. What I am saying this morning is that we are all poor and looking, whether we recognize it or not. Many of the scribes, Pharisees and Sadduccees of Jesus' day were poor in spirit but couldn't acknowledge it. Many of the sinners and tax collectors, the lepers, blind, deaf, lame, and poor came to Jesus in desperation. In Jesus' ministry they realized the kingdom they had been awaiting had dawned. To those poor, desperate ones Jesus said, "The kingdom of God belongs to you who have accepted God's will and presence in your lives." They came empty-handed, and because of that, they could receive the kingdom of God, the gift of God's own loving presence. Meanwhile, to the proud, the righteous, and the powerful, Jesus often said, "Woe unto you...."

We misread the Beatitudes when we make of them rules to be obeyed. When we try to force ourselves to become these things, we become artificial, pious, condescending, angry, resentful legalists — like some of the Pharisees in Jesus' day.

The best biblical scholarship points to a different reading of the Beatitudes. Decades ago, German New Testament scholar Joachim Jeremias argued that Jesus' entire Sermon on the Mount, with all its demands, is to be understood as teaching for the life of Christian discipleship. As such, the Sermon is preceded by something else. It is preceded by the proclamation of the gospel: "Your sins are forgiven." Jeremias contended that the Sermon on the Mount is best understood as *didache* — teaching or instruction given to those who have first heard and received the gospel of grace. The Sermon is instruction and guidance for living the life of discipleship. The "gospel" always precedes demand or exhortation. Grace always precedes Torah or instruction on the way to go. Thus, the Beatitudes, as the opening words of the Sermon on the Mount, are best understood as words of grace and God's favor which convey the blessing and favor of God.[4]

The first words out of the mouth of Jesus in Matthew's Sermon on the Mount are words of grace: "Blessed are you...poor in spirit...now/today... yours is the kingdom of heaven!"

Today a host of New Testament scholars lament the church's turning of the Beatitudes into exhortations to Christian conduct, demands and rules, goals impossible to attain, leaving us with a sense of compulsiveness, guilt, inadequacy, because we can never measure up to God's ideal.

The Beatitudes are instead pronouncements of grace and blessing to all who come out of need, statements of God's favor, promises of the future given precisely to those who are inadequate, empty-handed, looking.

The Sermon on the Mount, my friends, begins with words of grace. The first thing Jesus says is not "Do this, and you will live." Before a single instruction is given, before a single word of exhortation to Christian discipleship is set forth, — the first word is "Blessed are you...." And that is the key to it all.

If we can't hear the blessing, we're not ready for the journey of discipleship. The grace of God alone enables you and me to become what God wants us to be! Law and demand can never shape or empower us. Only grace can do that.

The Beatitudes describe the character of the community of faith, the church, as followers of Jesus Christ. These words have the power to form and shape us as people of God. It's like Debra and me saying to our little daughters Katy and Kari: "You are special." That not only says something *about* them; it has the power to make them special!

That's the good news of the gospel this morning! Each of us, poor in spirit, is pronounced blessed by God. Ours is the gift of the kingdom. It is a strange and holy paradox. It makes no sense. But it's a word of grace that alone has the power to make us the kind of persons God would have us be: gentle, merciful, pure in heart, peacemakers, salt, and light.

Let God's Blessing Come to You

Well, some of you are probably wondering what happened to Katy's recorder. I remember asking her that night, "So how was music class today?"

"Fine," she said.

"Well, what did your teacher say about your recorder?"

"Oh, no problem, lots of kids didn't have 'em — well, not 'lots' of kids — 'others'" (translate that one or two!).

"So what did your teacher do?"

"Oh, she had some extras she let us use — but don't worry, Dad, they were sterilized!"

About five days later, Katy went down to the basement to retrieve her laundry basket which normally sits at the foot of her bed. A few minutes later, we heard her coming up the stairs shouting, "Mom, Dad, I found my recorder! When I dumped my dirty clothes out on the laundry floor, there it was, in the bottom of my laundry basket!" (Of course, Debra and I always teach our girls to keep their most valuable possessions in the bottom of their laundry basket!)

But what we had searched for so desperately on that gray January morning a week before, and could not find, came to us! It came not by our efforts, but by simply letting go and accepting our poverty.

Where are you empty-handed today? Where are you looking, desperate, in need?

"In the places where we are broken, in the dark holes where something is missing, in the silence of unanswered questions, the wondrous gift is given."[5]

Can we hear the blessing? *Will* we hear it? Empty-handed, desperate, and looking — will we receive the blessing, and let those words fill our lives with God's love, shaping us into sons and daughters of God?

"Blessed are you poor in spirit, for yours is the kingdom of heaven!"

Notes
1. Harriett Richie, "He'd come here," *The Christian Century* 112 (December 13, 1995), p. 1206.
2. Henri J. M. Nouwen, *With Open Hands* (Notre Dame, IN: Ave Maria Press, 1972), pp. 12-14.
3. See Frederick Buechner, *Whistling in the Dark: An ABC Theologized* (San Francisco: Harper & Row, Publishers, 1988), pp. 18-19.
4. See Joachim Jeremias, *The Sermon on the Mount*, trans. Norman Perrin (Philadelphia: Fortress Press, 1963).
5. Richie, p. 1206.

Comment

When someone does something very well, no matter what that "something" is, we tend to elevate that person's gift to the status of art. Thus, we speak of the "artful cuts" of an NFL running back, or the "artistry in wood" of a master carpenter. When something is well done, it invites analysis, breaking down each element in order to appreciate its simple beauty.

Gary Klingsporn's sermon, "Blessed Are the Desperate," begs just such analysis, for in it we find simple truth eloquently (or "artfully") stated. This preacher understands the *"art* of preaching." The scriptural basis for the message is only one verse, but that's all that's needed. The sermon builds on this central focus to give us a poignant and memorable presentation of humanity's deepest and most basic longing: to make a significant connection with God. Let's look at each element of the sermon in order to appreciate its beauty.

Style

To his credit — as well as to the benefit of his congregation — Klingsporn is both a storyteller and a theologian, and, perhaps, not necessarily in that order. He has an ability to mix the common with the sublime. In this case, he spends the first few minutes of the sermon giving us a glimpse into life in the Klingsporn home. With a healthy measure of candor, he captures our interest, causing us to empathize with Katy, his young daughter who's lost her recorder on the first day of music class. Even more, we empathize with *him* as he and his wife desperately search to find the lost instrument. Notice the sermon title: "Blessed Are the Desperate." How better to bring us into the feel of desperation than to invite us into this moment of one family's desperation? And how well it works!

It's commonly known that "me stories" are the best stories in preaching. For one thing, the storyteller speaks with an authority that only she or he can have. We listen to Klingsporn because he was there. He lived this moment. He felt the anxiety. He faced the problem. Of all the ways he could have started this sermon, why did he choose this way? Perhaps he knew that by engaging his listeners in an emotional moment in the early going, he could draw them into the text and into the proclamation of the gospel to come.

In any sermon, the first few minutes are critical. In that brief introduction, the preacher establishes his/her rapport with the audience. And, likewise, the audience decides whether they want to listen to what follows. Klingsporn does this very effectively. Not only does he bring the audience into his living room, but he sets up a tension that keeps us listening throughout the sermon. We find ourselves wondering if his daughter's recorder was ever found. And, how did her teacher respond? Obviously, this is not Klingsporn's sole agenda here. But it is an effective device that guides us into Jesus' message to those of us "caught without" in other ways — ways that profoundly impact our faith.

Style is critical here. By way of Katy's plight, the preacher engages our emotions. And, as our emotions are engaged, so are our minds and spirits. A head-level approach to this text would not have been so effective. This small crisis in the Klingsporn home beckons us to look deeper…into the desperation caused by the most personal crises of our own lives.

Problem

Klingsporn brings us to one of humanity's greatest aches: *"Somewhere, somehow in our spirits, we are all empty-handed. We are all looking."* It's Pascal's "God-created void," or, as Klingsporn says it by way of St. Augustine: *"There is within each of us an eternally given restlessness, a searching, a journeying home to God. We are all empty-handed."* The sermon sheds light on this lingering void in every human psyche, the gnawing hunger every person has within to be attached to God and to others in a meaningful way. Like Katy Klingsporn, all of us from time to time find ourselves going through life empty-handed, looking for something to grasp that will make our way more meaningful.

Harriett Richie and Henri Nouwen are called upon to help the preacher illustrate the problem of empty-handedness. Both authors enhance Klingsporn's depiction of *"a violent and hungry world. A world of abject poverty and unspeakable wealth...of media violence and domestic abuse...a world hungering for peace but plagued by war...a world that is empty-handed and looking."* While the preacher may not require having his opinion endorsed by respected authorities, it never hurts. It's another way of showing the problem isn't limited to the preacher's opinion. Rather, it is a condition noted by others who observe society and the human condition. It's like saying, "Hey, folks, it's not just me who's noticed the predicament; these other people are seeing it, too!" Before the audience will buy the solution, they must be convinced of the need.

The Christian youth organization Young Life for years has trained its staffers to communicate the gospel to students using a simple formula: present the Problem (our sinful condition)...then the Person (Jesus Christ)... then the Propitiation (atonement as the cure)...and, finally, the Participation (how will we respond). Not only was this formula to be used in the preparation of a year-long lesson plan, it was to provide a template for each individual message. Klingsporn may or may not be familiar with Young Life's methods, but the course he follows in laying out the gospel message is similar. Notice how he covers each of the "Ps." Katy's lost recorder gives us access into our own problem of lost meaning. The Scripture presents the person of Christ and the propitiation. And, in the end, we are invited and shown how to participate.

TEXT & PROCLAMATION

There's no chance of missing the Bible's answer to our problem in this sermon. Whereas many sermons flood us with long Scripture readings, this one hones in on one clear word from Jesus: *"Blessed are the poor in spirit, for theirs is the kingdom of God."* The solution is right there! Rather than viewing our spiritual impoverishment as a curse, we must see in it the blessing. Being poor, or "empty-handed," means we are free to grab hold of the only real source of meaning, and it's found in the abundance of God's presence in the empty places in our lives. Rather than finding temporary distraction in life's superficialities — such as the hoopla of a Super Bowl Sunday — our sense of lostness leaves us ready to find lasting reward in the power and wisdom of God.

Klingsporn demonstrates a deft touch for bringing his listeners in contact with the Scripture in a natural, gentle way. No slamming the crowd with the Bible here! No showiness. No confusing verse-hopping. His familiarity with Scripture is evident in the ease with which he brings in complementary passages, such as 1 Corinthians 1:23, 27–28 and the "Woe to you…" verse found later in Matthew. That's all that's needed here. To bring in other references would only muddle things. The power of the Beatitudes is found in the individual pronouncements within them. We can do no better than to meditate upon them one at a time, and Klingsporn enables us to do so.

One of the best questions to ask of any sermon is, "So what?" In the end, no matter how well the preacher has laid out the problem, what difference does what the preacher said make in my life? How has the sermon encouraged me to change for the better? Klingsporn answers these questions well. He reminds us that the world has gotten it all backwards. *"It's not the ones who judge themselves right, but the humble ones who are merciful toward others who are blessed. It's not the totally pure, but the ones who fail and know their brokenness, and are pure in heart who are blessed…It's not the ones in power or in charge, but the ones in pain, the rejected, the losing ones who dare to give a humble witness for God who are blessed."* In a nutshell, *"the 'blessed' of the Beatitudes are all losers, underachievers who have no sense of power or the way the world works."*

Klingsporn goes on to point out that the Beatitudes are not commandments given to call us to task. *"They are not rules to be obeyed."* Rather, they are assurances of God's grace. Thus, Christianity lived out is not a matter of striving to please a demanding God or working to impress others. It is an attitude of accepting our personal desperation and brokenness in order that God can transform it, and, in the process, transform *us*. God doesn't demand that we work harder to fix ourselves. God merely invites us to absorb his restorative power. As Klingsporn admits, *"It's a strange and holy paradox. It makes no sense. But it's a word of grace that alone has the power to make us the kind of persons God would have us to be."*

"So what?" It works, that's what!

SUGGESTIONS

- Consider what a tight and effective package this sermon is. Never once are we given to veer away from the subject at hand. Klingsporn captures us from the outset with Katy's plight. Within that suspense he addresses the bigger issue of humanity's sense of lostness. By the time he returns us to Katy's lost recorder, we are still with him — in fact, more than ever. A good storyteller (and a good preacher) makes use of tension to create an unwavering desire to hear more. How do you create tension in your sermons? How can you use tension more effectively?

- Throughout the sermon, there are "handles" for the congregation. Klingsporn doesn't limit the scope of his message to an ancient sermon given on a Galilean hillside. He brings it home to us. The sermon is punctuated with references to the season (*"Epiphany"*), to the event of the day (*"Super Bowl Sunday"*), and to offerings in the local bookstores (*"Self-Help" volumes*). In addition, the story of the lost recorder has an inherent appeal to both the child and the parent within all of us. We are interested in the message because we identify with the content. It's that simple. How can you similarly use more effective "handles" in your preaching?

- Klingsporn is able to teach in his preaching. In fact, one would suspect his primary gift is as a teacher. Nothing can turn off an audience as quickly as a speaker who is eager to show off his own learning. Klingsporn is a learned person — it's evident throughout his message — but we don't come away from this sermon as impressed by his knowledge as we are impressed by our own awareness of the longing for meaning and fulfillment within each of us. The challenge every scholar, teacher, or preacher faces in the church is how to share his or her knowledge with the audience without that knowledge becoming a barrier. In most cases, this is a matter of attitude. Consider how effectively Klingsporn disguises his scholarship in this sermon for the sake of relating the wisdom of the gospel to the people in the pews.

Richard A. Davis

The Scandal in Sandals

MATTHEW 11:25–27

Rev. Richard A. Davis
Hope Presbyterian Church
Richfield, Minnesota

REV. RICHARD A. DAVIS

THE SCANDAL IN SANDALS

MATTHEW 11:25–27, NIV

In the hills along the north shore of the Sea of Galilee are situated the ruins of three ancient towns. Archaeologists have unearthed their remains, and, in the process, discovered that all three of these old Jewish cities were destroyed or abandoned not long after the death of Jesus Christ. You might know the names of these towns. They're all listed in Matthew 11:20–24: Chorazin, Bethsaida, and Capernaum.

Besides sharing extinction, these three once-thriving Galilean towns share the rather dubious distinction of having been cursed by Jesus for their unbelief. The inhabitants of these cities had witnessed first-hand more of the preaching, teaching, and miracle-working of Jesus Christ than had any other group of people, yet, ironically, they were among the least responsive to his call to repentance. It's like being unable to find anyone who's interested in art in Greenwich Village in Manhattan. It's like being unable to find anyone in Aspen, Colorado, who skis. The Chorazinians, the Bethsaidians, and the Capernaumites had realized the dream of every devout Christian to have Jesus living and working in their hometown, and what was their response? A general wave of apathy.

We'd like to think that a personal visit by Jesus Christ could remedy the ills of our troubled and depraved society, but a quick study of Matthew 11 should convince us otherwise. In this chapter alone, Jesus' authority is questioned and doubted by John the Baptist, by John's disciples, and by the townsfolk among whom Jesus lived and ministered for several months. So much for the personal charisma of the Messiah!

In verse 25, we see Jesus' response to this apathy. And it's not what one might expect. As is true so often in history, the story-behind-the-story is more interesting than the story itself. For example, we all know the words of Abraham Lincoln's most famous speech. "Fourscore and seven years ago our fathers brought forth on this continent, a new nation, conceived in Liberty, and dedicated to the proposition that all men are created equal...." Most of us know those words. But not as many know what took place before and after Lincoln gave his speech at the dedication of the Gettysburg Cemetery on November 19, 1863.

For two weeks before the event, Lincoln fretted over what to say, reworking it several times. Finally, he scribbled his text on a small piece of blue paper and stuffed it into his hat. On the day of the dedication, he wasn't in very good form. He was nervous and tired. Thirty thousand people had gathered for the occasion. Lincoln was to follow one of the great orators of his day, Edward Everett. Everett arrived an hour late, and his speech lasted for two hours! Most who were present had never seen or heard a president in person, so they remained patient, even after waiting for over three hours.

When Lincoln finally stepped forward and spoke, most in the crowd were disappointed. First of all, very few could hear him. It was in the day before PA systems, and Lincoln had a thin, high voice that didn't carry well. Besides that, he'd followed a man who was a professional orator and could project his voice for several hundred yards. Secondly, many were surprised by Lincoln's southern accent and that he read from his manuscript in a dry manner. Thirdly, the whole speech was over in two minutes. Just as people thought he was getting through his introduction, he sat down. The crowd was so shocked there wasn't even any applause.

Afterward, Lincoln turned to those near him and expressed regret that his speech had failed. And he was right. Everyone was disappointed. The president was so distressed that on the train ride home he had to lie down and have his head bathed in cold water to ease his depression. He went to his grave believing his speech to have been a complete failure. Fortunately, a couple of reporters copied his words verbatim and printed the text in the newspapers the next day. From that printing came a growing appreciation of what Abraham Lincoln said in those two minutes. It's now universally accepted to have been one of the greatest speeches ever uttered by human lips up to that time. And many argue there's been no greater message given since.

Human beings have a tragic inclination not to appreciate things until they're gone. Because of this, Jesus himself was constantly stung with frustration. He expressed his frustration with such phrases as "Only in his home town and in his own house is a prophet without honor" (Matt. 13:57) or "Do not give dogs what is sacred; do not throw your pearls to pigs" (Matt. 7:6). However, in the face of this rejection recorded in Matthew 11, Jesus doesn't walk away grousing and grumbling. Rather, he praises his Father in heaven for the stubbornness of the people. "I praise you, Father, Lord of heaven and earth, because you have hidden these things from the wise and learned, and revealed them to little children. Yes, Father, for this was your good pleasure" (Matt. 11:25–26). A failure similar to the one that sent Lincoln into despair sends Jesus into prayer.

It's important that we learn from Jesus' failure to impress the public, because we can too easily suppose that the gospel we promote should be winning wide acceptance and affecting change wherever it is shared. That is simply untrue, and there are three ghost towns in Galilee to prove it. The gospel of Jesus Christ always has been and likely always will be not only objectionable to most folks but even downright repulsive. Lest we think God blew it and overestimated his Son's ability to win friends and influence people, we need only look at this passage of Scripture. Jesus acknowledged human resistance as part of the mysterious, divine game plan. For whatever reason, God finds the warmest reception among the lowly and simple and the coldest rejection among the high and haughty.

It's not a minority opinion today that we've made a mess of our society. How and why that has happened is open to constant debate. But one thing we all agree on is that something has gone very sour in our world. To be sure, we're not the first generation in history to feel that way, but the events of the last few years — especially the last few weeks — have prompted renewed concern over the state of affairs in this country. A bomb in the heartland has caused us to ponder our future with new dread. Why does a country built on the tenets of the Gettysburg Address continually reject the teachings of the Sermon on the Mount? Christ only knows.

As offensive as the currents of our day may be, there's something of much greater offense to Americans. As much as we may fear and hate the rising bigotry of the anti-government militias or the white supremacists, there's someone who offends us much more deeply. And guess who it is — it is Jesus himself. As bad as it may get in society, it never seems to get so bad that Jesus becomes an attractive option to us. You'd think drowning people might be open to a rescue boat, but such doesn't seem to be the case. Just as he was in Chorazin, Bethsaida and Capernaum, Jesus remains the scandal in sandals for us today.

What's so scandalous about Jesus? Have you ever thought about that? Why would a Savior who teaches love and peace, who heals and resurrects the dead, who embraces the lowly and the lost, who takes all the heat for us, be so repugnant to so many people? On the surface, that's a confounding question. *Scandal* is an appropriate term for Jesus. The Greek word *skandalon* means "a stumbling block." The *Oxford English Dictionary* suggests that *scandal* is related to a primitive root *scand*, meaning "to climb," from which we get (through the Latin) our word *ascend*. A scandal is what trips up someone who is trying to ascend to a higher place. How appropriate! Isn't that what we're all doing in one way or another, trying to get to higher ground? We're financially trying to climb the ladder. We're professionally striving to rise higher and higher. We want our lifestyle to be elevated. We educate ourselves to the highest of levels. Life is like the great quest up a mountain.

Even in our moral and religious life we are reaching for higher planes of awareness. And just as we're straining with all our effort to make everything better for ourselves, we step on Jesus, and he becomes the stumbling block, the scandal that hampers our ascent. Why is this?

I'm convinced that this is God's brilliant way of humbling a prideful people. We think we're so capable of solving all life's problems by our own efforts, and so we will stubbornly and pridefully continue our relentless quest — until the ground drops out from under our feet. As long as we don't slip up, we'll keep right on striving to satisfy our insatiable desires. This is why Jesus is not only the rock of our salvation but also the rock which causes us to stumble. Pride is never progressive.

You think what Hollywood is putting out is offensive? Let me tell you, the most offensive presentations today are being made in Christian pulpits. Let me give you just one example. Brace yourselves! I'm about to utter the most offensive words you may have ever heard. So to cover myself, I'd like to point out these words were originally uttered by Jesus: "All things have been committed to me by my Father. No one knows the Son except the Father, and no one knows the Father except the Son and those to whom the Son chooses to reveal him" (Matt. 11:27). What I've just said is scandalous. I've just announced that there's no other way to know God than through Jesus Christ. How politically incorrect can a person get! I've just offended every humanist, Muslim, Buddhist, Hindu, Jew, New-ager, and cultist there is. I've spoken the offense of the cross. This is the scandal of particularity from which no Christian can escape. In light of everything Jesus said and did, there is no way we can preach a Christ who is one of a number of ways to get to God. While we can acknowledge that other religions and philosophies may have a general awareness of God, only in Jesus Christ is there found the specific knowledge of God. Others may speculate things *about* the Father, but only Jesus *knows* the Father.

The non-Christian world and even many contemporary Christians find this claim unbearably arrogant. But for a Christian to claim anything less would be unbearably ungrateful. When God gives himself at immense cost to save the world, how can we water it down by reducing him to a place on a list of alternative options? I would love to be able to say that salvation is based on sincerity rather than on one particular Savior. But I can't. I'd like to think God gives us an "A" for effort and that's all it takes. But that contradicts Jesus' own claims about himself. And so it is that Jesus remains scandalous to the modern mind.

The rubble of Chorazin, Bethsaida, and Capernaum gives evidence of what happens when a society ignores the unique authority of Jesus Christ and refuses to repent and change. Dead towns. The rubble of a federal building in Oklahoma City is a testimony to the error of pursuing exclusively political alternatives in order to change society. Before we react with vengeance and violence and judgment and fear, we'd better go back to the Bible.

The late, great Elton Trueblood gives a timeless assessment of a society in turmoil. He writes:

> It is true that our central problem is moral and spiritual. The central problem is not political, for it is clear that any political system will be destroyed if the life of the citizens has lost its meaning. It will be destroyed by war if by nothing else. The problems of world government, on which so many thoughtful people pin their ultimate hope of the abolition of war, are really spiritual problems, since it is clear that there cannot be world government without world community.[1]

Trueblood wrote those words over twenty years ago, but they ring even more true today as we contemplate stricter legislation, increased law enforcement, and more punitive counterstrikes in order to curtail urban violence.

Our Creator's concern is not political; it is moral and spiritual. Just look at the life of Jesus. For he is the single channel through which we may tap into God's agenda for humanity. In Jesus, God has revealed to the childlike and the faithful the solution to life's problems. It all hinges on simple trust. The powerful and the proud will not solve our messes. The answer won't come from the highest echelons of the elite. In the face of the chaos all around us, there remains but one simple remedy. And it is scandalous. Jesus and Jesus alone is the only answer to our predicament. Amen.

Note
1. Elton Trueblood, *The Meditations of Elton Trueblood* (New York: Harper & Row Publishers, 1975), pp. 77-78.

COMMENT

Richard Davis catches our attention from the beginning, first with his intriguing title, "The Scandal in Sandals," and then with his introduction: a description of archaeological discoveries in Galilee that point to the profound irony in the Matthean text and in our spiritual lives. Davis builds on the surprises we often encounter as we observe Jesus on the pages in Scripture. Jesus says and does things that we would not expect and certainly were not expected by his observers in the first century. Contained in these surprises is the gospel, a simple yet profound truth about God, about the kingdom of God, about life. Davis effectively uses the elements of surprise and irony both to draw the listener into the message and to drive home the truth of the message.

NEED

Throughout this sermon, Davis effectively makes the connection between the biblical message and our contemporary experience. The biblical story has a parallel with our story, our concerns. In fact, the sermon was given shortly after a national tragedy, the bombing of the Oklahoma City Federal Building, which prompted almost everyone to grapple with the meaning of that tragedy. "Is there a word from the Lord?" the Old Testament writers wondered in the wake of national catastrophes. So, too, we wonder what word there is from God in the midst of our communal tragedies. Indirectly, Davis raises and responds to that question.

Early in the sermon, Davis identifies a common wish and belief, that if only Jesus would make an obvious personal visit to us or to our world, then everyone would believe and follow him, and all problems of our lives or our society would be solved! Yet, despite our longing for the appearance of a victorious Christ and a "successful" faith and ministry, the Gospels present a different and intriguing picture, and leave us wondering how to make sense out of the dissonance. How could the people who had a personal visit from Jesus not understand? How could Jesus give thanks for his audience's stubborn refusal to believe and trust? Why would a gracious Jesus be a scandal? Why would his answers to my most perplexing questions and deepest longings be different from what I expect? What can be learned and salvaged from a national tragedy to bring back some hope and optimism? These are important concerns, arising from our deep-seated, universal need for meaning and resolution.

TEXT & PROCLAMATION

Throughout the sermon, the proclamation of the "scandal" of Christ builds through several surprises about Jesus to the primary surprise, that of the particularity of Christ: "No one knows the Father except the Son and those to whom the Son chooses to reveal him." The text and Davis' exposition draw us to the truth of the gospel, a truth that is probably not what we would have wished, not how we would have written the script, but is nonetheless God's truth. The text points to Jesus' certainty of God's authority and wisdom. It reveals both the good news of God's grace in difficult circumstances and the kerygma, the proclamation of Jesus' identity and his exclusive relationship to God the Father.

In splitting his references to a text of three verses, Davis is able to address two different but related concerns. In verses 25 and 26, Davis responds to the problem of the apparent failure of Jesus' ministry in the Galilean cities. There is something beneficial in that failure. There is a word of hope from the Lord in the lack of positive response to the demonstration of God's power, love and truth in our day. In the first point of the text, there is a lesson to be learned. In learning that lesson there is a reason to thank God.

Reflecting on the first half of the text, Davis makes a helpful transition from Jesus' apparent failure to Jesus' statement about revealing the things of God to little children. He says, *"Jesus acknowledged human resistance as a part of the mysterious, divine game plan...God finds the warmest reception among the lowly and simple."* Then, in developing the second and focal point of the sermon, the text draws us to the heart of the scandal of Christianity: the unique, exclusive, particular relationship between God and Jesus of Nazareth.

STYLE

This sermon follows the biblical text's movements from a moderately perplexing issue to the core issue. Davis moves from one to the other by setting both in the context of our experience and perspectives. And, he does it with gentle irony and humor that sets the audience up to listen carefully. I appreciate the fact that Davis shows Jesus to be frustrated. This allows the listener to connect with a real flesh-and-blood, incarnational Jesus, rather than a rigid, lifeless, unfeeling, unreal divinity. Again, this involves the listeners' own experience with Jesus and his word for us.

In his transition to recent current events (the Oklahoma City bombing), Davis connects with his listeners' frustration and concerns, and also raises an intriguing question, *"Why does a country built on the tenets of the Gettysburg Address continually reject the teachings of the Sermon on the Mount?"* Then Davis gets to the core of his message and is not afraid to make the scandal of Jesus vivid. He heightens the irony of Jesus' offensiveness and asks the question most of the listeners in a successful, suburban church might ask, *"What's so scandalous about Jesus?"*

Davis' interesting word study on "scandal" anticipates the answer to the basic question. He builds further anticipation by saying, *"You think what Hollywood is putting out is offensive?... The most offensive presentations today are being made in Christian pulpits."* Now, we are ready for the point and the text. He presents them with vividness and strength that pulls us back to the biblical context and to his opening statement regarding the three Galilean cities now in rubble, as well as to our concerns regarding the rubble in our own time and place.

RESPONSE

The Trueblood quote is interesting. I find myself questioning whether Davis is indirectly trying to make political statements as well as pastoral/theological statements. The final paragraphs of the sermon elicited several questions from me. Because I know Richard Davis, I can rest assured that these are simply "for instance" references to the contemporary scene. However, if I didn't know him, I might wonder if he wanted to imply that the bombing of the federal building is a direct punishment from God for America's *"pursuing exclusively political alternatives."* I think there is a risk in this last section for some listeners to read more into this message than is there. This could direct the listener away from the thesis of the sermon: the scandal of the uniqueness of Christ.

A sermon cannot say everything. Davis has focused on a critical issue at the center of Christian faith. It is true to the gospel, that *"Jesus and Jesus alone is the only answer to our predicament."* Does this mean that any additional response other than purely and exclusively "religious," is futile, and therefore Christians ought not to be involved in politics, economic, social work, or any other activity addressing the problems of society? Surely not. The sermon does not specifically address these issues, but it raises the question. If Jesus alone is the only answer, what then am I, as a believer, to do about these societal issues? I want to ask, "Okay, now what?" "What do I do?"

This is an interesting and stimulating sermon. It evokes reflection, encourages conversation, and most of all challenges us to face the issue of the particularity of Christ. Not an easy topic, but proclamation that is true to the gospel. We need to face the question.

Suggestions

- Davis' sermon is a good example of how to work with the text in sections and thereby maximize the wealth of a passage. He carefully builds interest in the central focus of the text. While Davis touches on a couple of related issues, he skillfully focuses on that one central issue. I have heard and read and probably given many sermons that wandered through too many ideas and perhaps got stuck in secondary points. How do you focus the central point of your sermons? Can you state the thesis of each sermon in a sentence or two?

- Davis also models the effective use of contemporary references, expressions, and concerns which attract the listener's attention and build confidence in the preacher's understanding of our contemporary life setting. His sermon title also attracts attention, and should catch the eye of someone seeing it on a church sign or in a church ad. Good sermon titles encourage the worshiper to anticipate the sermon and pay careful attention.
- Consider developing a sermon on "Jesus: The Way, the Truth, and the Life." Try to address in your own way the issue Davis has dealt with in this sermon. Possible texts: Matthew 11:27; Acts 4:12; John 14:6.

David Williamson

No Looking Back

ROMANS 6:1–11

Rev. Rick Brand
First Presbyterian Church
Henderson, North Carolina

Rev. Rick Brand

No Looking Back

ROMANS 6:1–11, RSV

I have been trying to remember just who it was that sang it. I think it was Mama Cass of the Mamas and the Papas, but I'm not sure. Maybe you remember it: "Look What They've Done to My Song." One line complained that singers were misusing the song.

The apostle Paul must have had something of that reaction when he wrestled with the questions he was getting, the responses to the good news of God's grace in Jesus Christ. "Look what they have done to my song. They have reduced the great joy of grace to a legal defense, and are using it to justify doing anything they want."

We are justified by grace, not works. We have been made right with God by his gift in Jesus Christ; by the action of God in Jesus Christ we are moved from the kingdom of the damned to the kingdom of the redeemed; God's grace has brought us joy. So, said some of Paul's hearers, wouldn't it make sense for us to go out and sin more so that we might experience more grace and have more joy?

Paul's response: "What have you done to my message of the good news of God's grace in Jesus Christ?"

Well, Paul, if our relationship with God has been established on the promise of what God has done for us in Jesus Christ, if it isn't based on what we do and what we accomplish, it must not matter what we do, and so we can do what we like. The more we sin, the more grace God has. It's a wonderful set-up — all fun and no responsibility!

In the sixth chapter of Romans Paul has to deal with this reduction of redemption to a legal verdict and the stubborn persistence of the idea that we won't change but will always be the way we are. The promised grace of God in Jesus may change our relationship with God, but we must not forget that it also changes us. When we focus on the grace of God only as forgiveness of our sin and leave out the reality of the change it brings into our lives, we easily end up accepting sinfulness as "the way we are," and we often fail to respond seriously to the ethical imperatives of the Christian life.

The Session of this church has just approved the creation of gifts to Union Theological Seminary in honor and memory of the four past ministers who were trained at Union Seminary and who blessed this congregation with their lives. We decided not to create a big campaign to get pledges and commitments. The Session decided simply to trust the generosity and goodness of this congregation. Gifts may be designated for any of the four ministers. Each month we will announce the names of those who have made gifts to each minister's fund, just as we do with the flowers at Easter and the weekly flowers. We hope that, as they remember fondly the contributions and ministry of different ministers, members of this congregation will make gifts to those ministers' accounts.

But no sooner did we establish those four accounts in the name of each minister, than we began to hear comments implying that we really haven't been changed by the grace that was preached to us by those ministers. The comments suggested that people will only give to those accounts in order to be seen. Members will get into a competition to see which minister was more popular, and certain people will be checking to see who gives what to whom.

These comments toss out the whole idea of grace — that we as a congregation have been changed in our hearts by grace, that we have been freely and abundantly blessed by the different talents and abilities of different ministers, that different ones of us at different times in our lives needed different ministers and we are grateful for that care and will make a gift in honor of that minister. Whenever and wherever the good news of the grace of God in Jesus Christ for us is heard merely as pardon, and is not also seen as medicine which cures the sickness, grace becomes cheap grace. When the grace of God in Jesus is heard only as pardon, we too often use it to escape the consequences of our actions. What we do does not matter, we say, because what matters is what God did in Jesus Christ. *Look what we have done to your song, Paul!*

In their song "Gee, Officer Krupke" for the musical *West Side Story,* Leonard Bernstein and Stephen Sondheim show us something about the dark side, when the good news becomes cheap grace. The song is sung by members of a street gang that Police Officer Krupke would like to take out behind the barn to beat some sense into them, but all of the officer's good intentions are frustrated by well-meaning social workers. The gang members mock their would-be helpers, acknowledging that any punishment they might receive would be well deserved. As the whole gang dances joyfully, they sing that all of them, even the best, are "no damn good."

These boys are refusing to be denied their humanity. They exist, and what they do matters. They refuse to let their actions and their decisions be taken away from them by a well-meaning society which excuses them because of social conditions. They would rather be no good at all, than to allow everything they do to be a result of mere "misunderstanding," or society's conditions around them.

The power of God's work in Jesus Christ does not just change our relationship with God. If we think that, Paul says, we are missing the deep down, powerful and personal consequences of the work of God in Jesus Christ. Yes, our relationship with God is changed by what God promises to do for us in Jesus Christ. But we ourselves are also changed. God's action in Jesus promises to make us acceptable to God. That acceptance brings us peace and changes what we want and what we do.

So we must not look just at the legal analogy of our sins being forgiven. We must also look at the radical conversion of the heart and the hunger of the soul which comes about as we see ourselves as acceptable to God.

Imagine someone who discovers that he has the frightening disease of AIDS. The doctor says there are some new medicines which have recently become available and the patient might give them a try. Medical research has presented him a gift of their intelligence, their compassion, their time and energy. The AIDS patient can try them and they may cure him. He takes the medicines, and by their help and his trust and faith in the doctors, is healed. I cannot imagine anyone saying that the medicine and the healing was so wonderful that a person will get AIDS again so that he can take the medicine again.

Or imagine a person who has just moved into a new Habitat for Humanity house. Do you think she would be so overcome with the joy and thrill of a new home, a gift to her from the labors of others — though she too, has worked on it — that she is going to burn it down so that she can have the joy of being given a second home?

Paul pushes us beyond the legal description of the pardon and grace of God in Jesus Christ. Yes, God has promised to accept us because of the life, death and resurrection of Jesus and not because of our own merits. The gift of that grace brings such joy and contentment that we are changed. The idea of going out to sin more so that there might be more grace is evidence that the true power of God's grace has not yet become a reality for us.

Paul tells us to look beyond the legal brief to the emotional dynamics of this redemption act. God has promised to make us acceptable, to receive us as part of his people because of what has happened in Jesus. When we are baptized as a witness that we have accepted that gift, we are united with Christ. Through baptism we participate in the cross, we share Christ's death and are buried with him. What that means is that parts of us shrivel away and die. What Paul calls our "old self" seems to become unplugged and loses power. Old desires and interests, old habits and tricks and unsettled scores, all seem to lose their hold on us. As we rejoice in the peace and contentment that come from a straightened-out relationship with God, we discover that certain activities we used to enjoy are no longer much fun. Old parts of our lives wither and fade away.

Have you seen what happens when a young couple who used to need to party every weekend starts a family? Now they begin to stay home and enjoy a whole different set of activities. "We used to go somewhere every weekend," they say, "but since we have had our baby we love to stay home and watch her grow." A new love has brought about the death of an old life.

Our newspaper recently had an article about a young man who has watched two dreams die. The boy's middle school basketball coach killed the boy's dream of basketball because he was too short — 5' 4". That squashed dream still hurts, but the young man took up wrestling and became a high school national champ. In his senior year, working as a lifeguard, he watched Greg Louganis dive, and became so inspired he decided to become a diver. The boy refused all college scholarships for wrestling. Instead, he practiced diving and is now a member of the Olympic diving team. A new love brought about a joyful death of an old way of life. What he does now reflects what he loves.

Paul sees it that way. As we are united with Christ in baptism, our old schemes, our old habits of putting ourselves first, our old preoccupation with making ourselves look good, our old need to toot our own horn — all these old pieces begin to shrink, die and fall away. The hunger for the most toys, the arguments and justifications as to why we deserve the good that we have and those that don't have it don't deserve it, are part of the old ways we leave behind. We begin to come alive in the new life of Christ. We begin to care about others as much as we care about ourselves. As we become alive in God's generosity, we can give gifts in gracious response to what we have received. We will no longer worry about what somebody might say about us, or about not giving to a minister we did not even get a chance to hear.

Isn't it still part of the old Adam's thinking when we look at the offer of God's grace and begin to plot how we can take advantage of it and use it to cover up what we do, so we can do more of what we think we like to do and so beat the system? We want to have it both ways, find a way to outsmart God and still be a winner, to get God's gift of forgiveness and not have to give up a thing. The problem is that the grace of God in Jesus Christ hasn't really hit us with its full reality as long as we are thinking that way.

When we allow the glorious reality of God's promise to truly bring us into his family, we will not only experience joy and peace, we will also undergo a radical transformation which will put to death our old self-centered life, and bring to life the new Christlike qualities. We will discover new joys of living after the manner of Jesus Christ, and there will be no looking back at our old lives with regret.

Comment

After two millennia of Christian homiletics, it's safe to say that every sermon we preach is, at best, a new variation on an old theme. The preacher's job isn't to come up with a new subject matter; it's to take the "old, old story" and make it come alive for a contemporary audience. Rick Brand provides us with a fine example of how to rework the old gospel in a way that's both in keeping with the times and faithful to the ancient truth of Christian proclamation.

If we were to make a list of the top three theological themes in the Pauline epistles, justification by faith (grace vs. works) would be at or near the top of the list. Fledgling preachers are often advised to err on the side of grace in their sermons. My homiletics professor in seminary put it this way, "Most sermons seem to contain 90% law and 10% grace. If you want to be faithful to the gospel and, at the same time keep your job, you'd do well to reverse those percentages." Even now, years later, I still find myself evaluating sermons — both my own and those of others — by that same measure. Since Brand is treading right into that delicate turf with this sermon, let's see how he does.

Theme

Given that Brand is preaching from Romans 6, he'd better get it right. If he doesn't, Paul will be spinning in his grave ("Look what [he could do] to [Paul's] song!"). The sixth chapter of Romans elaborates on the central theme of Paul's life and ministry: God's grace. Fortunately, Brand hits it dead on. *"We are justified by grace, not works."* So central is this theme to Brand's sermon that he does not once abandon it in favor of a peripheral issue. Again and again, he brings his listener's back to Paul's theme: "We're saved by God's grace, not our own efforts." I daresay a person could hear this message on one occasion and still remember it months (maybe even years) later because the preacher so clearly elucidates the theme throughout the sermon.

STYLE

Compare and contrast this sermon with messages by other preachers who often weave and bob from one idea to the next. All of us have heard sermons which take us on a meandering journey through apparently random thoughts and disparate illustrations. I call them "shotgun sermons," built on a style which leaves the congregation shell-shocked. Nothing doing here. This sermon is like a rifle shot. Brand knows what he wants to say before he begins, and by the time he's done there's no confusing his purpose. He wants his people to reconsider the pitfalls of works righteousness and to recommit to Paul's call for Christians to embrace a grace-centered way of faith and life.

Reading a sermon never does it justice. We are not privy to such intangibles as the preacher's tone of voice or his or her facial expressions. Having never actually heard Brand preach, I would suspect there is a winsomeness in his manner of presentation. If not, his style would negate his content. Even one reading of this sermon would suggest that he engages warmly and naturally with his audience. He is both accessible and relational, and so are his words. We see it in his opening with a description of Mama Cass (I actually think it was another singer) belting out the lyrics, *"Look what they've done to my song."* A little nostalgia never hurts in hooking the listener. And, later on, Brand brings his congregation deeper into the sermon with the commentary on a scholarship fund set up by their church in memory of Brand's predecessors. This would certainly command the attention of his flock; he's talking about *them!*

The topical illustrations don't end there. Brand quotes a song from *West Side Story*. He shares observations about the social habits of first-time parents. He further punctuates his point by bringing in a hypothetical AIDS patient, a woman who benefits from the work of Habitat for Humanity, and a diver in the recent Olympic games. Here is a preacher who clearly engages his listeners. He's a human being! He follows the news, enjoys the arts, and understands family life. When a preacher knows what's going on out there, it serves to enhance his message. In doing so, he develops a pedestrian style of speaking (and I mean this in a most complimentary way), as one who walks beside us over life's terrain. This does much to remove the starch and stigma from the pulpit. What could easily have been a platitudinous presentation of high-browed theology ends up being thoroughly listenable, thanks largely to Brand's warm and accessible style.

USE OF SCRIPTURE

The text for this sermon is arguably the weightiest section of all the Pauline writings. Epistles are a bit tricky to bring to life in a sermon, since they are not written in a narrative form like the Gospels. Thus, it's often more effective to take the gist of the treatise and translate it into a word more suited for the ear. Brand seems to understand this, as he immediately interfaces the text with the lyrics of a contemporary song. Then every illustration he uses does the same, each in its own way, taking Paul's apologetics and bringing them into a real life context.

Two-thirds of the way through the sermon, we find an example of Brand's paraphrasing of Paul's words: *"Through baptism we participate in the cross, we share Christ's death and are buried with him. What that means is that parts of us shrivel away and die. What Paul calls our 'old self' seems to become unplugged and loses power."* Each word is chosen to move away from theological jargon toward clear simple communication for listeners who rarely, if ever, use words like "propitiation," "atonement," or "sacramental." In doing this, Brand is saying to long-time church members and newcomers alike that the Scriptures hold truths which transcend antiquated language and hold relevance for us today. It's as if the preacher is declaring, "Do you have trouble understanding this old book? Well, try this for size. What Paul is saying is...." Often the role of the preacher is to be the translator and to translate accurately, without cluttering the way. The Scripture is the message; the preacher is merely the medium.

Response

When a preacher brings a current congregational controversy into a sermon — such as the issue of the seminary scholarships in Brand's sermon — he takes a risk. He must ask himself, "Am I using the pulpit for my own ax-grinding?" Knowing there are strong emotions on both sides of any issue like this, the preacher is open to the accusation of politicizing as well as sermonizing. Is Brand's agenda here to quell some bickering among his members over the scholarship fund? Is he here chastising certain folds for their petty legalism? And, if so, is it appropriate to do so from the Sunday pulpit? We don't know the specific context of this sermon, so it's hard to do other than speculate.

To be sure, sometimes such controversies have no place in a sermon. However, I think it is probably defensible here. First of all, it is the pastor's solemn duty to lead the flock, and sometimes this calls for strong, even stern, leadership. The pulpit is not to be a pastor's personal platform for grievance. But from time to time certain matters arise which affect the life and health of a congregation, and they must be addressed. There is nothing wrong with using Scripture to bring the people back into balance. In fact, isn't this proper use of Scripture? In the case of this particular sermon, is Brand merely expressing personal opinion at the expense of the biblical lesson? I doubt it. If the main point of Paul's original letter was to guide and correct Christians, there's no shame in reapplying it to the same purpose in another time and another place. Besides, as suggested earlier, it sure gets people to pay attention to the message when they are included in the subject!

This sermon brings believers back to the daily struggle between receiving a righteousness bestowed by God and behaving in a way worthy of that righteousness, while avoiding being prideful and judgmental. Brand calls for his people to reset their "grace meters" in the particular matter of giving to the scholarship fund. More than that, he calls for us to abandon *"our old schemes, our old habits of putting ourselves first, our old preoccupation with making ourselves look good, our old need to toot our own horn — all these old pieces begin to shrink, die and fall away."* Scholarship funds aside, who of us cannot find a personal corrective in these words? Paul, through the preacher, is still calling us back to a life founded on God's grace. Sometimes it is a general call, and sometimes it is very specific.

SUGGESTIONS

- Notice how effectively and economically Brand uses illustrations. He doesn't assume all his listeners are familiar with Mama Cass, *West Side Story,* or the Olympic wrestler-turned-diver. In fact, we need not know anything of these subjects in order to understand the illustrations. Brand doesn't clutter the stories with unnecessary details. He tells us just enough to give us the picture. He is skilled at bringing these illustrations in, getting quickly to the core and then moving on. Storytelling should never be so laborious that it detracts from the central point.
- Brand is able to see events in his church and in his world as ripe moments for teaching. On this occasion, the scholarship fund controversy provides a window for learning, and he uses it carefully. If one is responsible for preaching a meaningful message week after week, one must be looking for these opportunities for learning in the life of the congregation. If we know our people, we will sense those teaching moments when they arise.
- There is one small technique used in this sermon which proves very effective. Several times Brand returns to the song lyrics, *"Look what they've done to my song."* So simple and yet so effective, it provides a glue for all the pieces of the sermon. Repetition is a valuable tool when used rightly. It directs the listener's ear and mind back to the central focus of the message. I think it would be difficult for anyone having heard Brand's sermon to hear this song on the radio in the future and not remember the gospel lesson from Romans 6. How do you use repetition in your preaching?

Richard A. Davis

Keeping Stress from Becoming Distress

1 KINGS 19:1–21

Rev. Rick McDaniel
Glen Allen Community Church
Richmond, Virginia

Rev. Rick McDaniel

Keeping Stress from Becoming Distress

1 KINGS 19:1–21, NIV

I want to talk to you today about stress, particularly about how to keep stress from becoming distress. Not all stress is bad. We need a certain amount of stress in our lives in order to perform tasks, to get things done, to achieve our goals. But when stress is excessive or is extended over a period of time, it can become distress. It then becomes very negative for our physical and emotional health. There is a difference between stress that we all have to live and work with, and distress as extended stress.

Let me share seven myths about stress that come from two doctors, Everly and Rosenfeld, in a book called *The Nature and Treatment of the Stress Response*.[1] The first is that stress-related symptoms are all in my head, and therefore they can't really injure me. The second is that only weak people suffer from stress. The third myth says that I am not responsible for the stress in my life. Stress is unavoidable these days, so we are all victims. The fourth suggests that I always know when I begin to suffer from excessive stress. The reality is that we don't always recognize the onset of stress. The fifth myth says that it is easy to identify the causes of excessive stress. The sixth says that all people respond to stress in the same way. The seventh myth is that when I begin to suffer from excessive stress, all I have to do is sit down and relax. Oh, if it were only that easy!

These myths have been identified by doctors who have treated stress and stress-related injuries and illnesses, so they understand something about the reality of stress and its negative impact upon our lives. We need to understand how we can overcome and deal with it.

I want to share with you from the story of Elijah in 1 Kings 19 what I see as some universal symptoms of stress. Elijah was in tough straits. The issue in his life was one of intense pressure from stress — stress that can lead to burnout. You might think, "How can some story about a bearded, robe-wearing prophet living on the other side of the world, three thousand years ago, have anything to do with my modern-day realities and the stress that I am under?" But from this story I will show you how relevant and applicable the Bible is to present-day modern life.

The first symptom of stress is that we depreciate our own worth. "I have had enough, Lord. Take my life," Elijah says (v. 4). When you have reached the point of depreciating your self-worth to its extreme, you have those kinds of suicidal thoughts. You think, *I am better off dead than alive. My life is so difficult, so burdensome, that I would rather be dead than to keep living the way I am living now.* We depreciate our own worth.

A second symptom of stress is that we underrate our work. "I have been very zealous for the Lord God Almighty," Elijah tells God. "The Israelites have rejected your covenant, broken down your altars" (v. 10). In other words, "All of my work is in vain. I am the prophet. I have been trying to tell these people to obey the covenant, to worship you. But instead they have broken down the altars. They walk all over the covenant. They don't obey. They have rejected everything. And because they have rejected you, God, they have rejected me."

Under severe stress, we begin to think that nothing we do makes a difference. We punch the clock, put in our forty hours, but it doesn't make a difference. We feel that way not only about the job we get paid for, but about the other work we do — our work in the community, our work in the church, our work in our home. We begin to underrate our work.

A third symptom of stress is that we exaggerate our problems. Elijah goes on to say, "I am the only one left, and now they are trying to kill me too" (v. 10). It is true, Elijah does have problems. When a crazy queen and an evil king are trying to kill you, you have a real problem! Notice I said that we *exaggerate* our problems, not that we imagine them. Elijah claimed to be the only worshiper of God left. But later on in this story God tells Elijah that there are seven thousand other people who have not bowed to idols. In other words, "Elijah, you do have problems, but you are not the only one left." Stress has a way of exaggerating our problems in our thinking. The problems get magnified and seem larger and greater than they really are.

The fourth, and perhaps the most serious symptom of stress is that we abdicate our dreams. In verse 4, Elijah says this: "Take my life; I am no better than my ancestors." In other words, "My dreams of making a difference, of being a great spokesman for you, God, are no good. I am no better than anyone before me." Elijah is so stressed out that he has given up on the belief that he can make a difference. He has given up on the great dream that God placed in his heart to make a difference in his country, to be a spokesman for God. He has abdicated his dream.

These are the symptoms of stress, my friends. When we start depreciating our self-worth, when we start underrating the work that we do, when we start exaggerating our problems and making them even worse than they already are, and when we give up and abdicate our dreams, we are suffering from stress. And it *is* suffering.

The life of Elijah shows us that stress was not invented in the last twenty or thirty years. The reality is that the problems that produce stress are universal, and have always existed, just manifesting themselves in different situations and circumstances. Elijah's life also shows us some timeless principles that we can apply to overcome stress in our lives.

The first principle is this: To overcome stress we need to rest our bodies. Elijah had expended a great deal of energy fighting for God. In the desert, we read, "he lay down under the tree and fell asleep" (v. 5). After he rested, an angel touched him and awakened him and told him to get up and eat. In other words, I believe that Elijah did not just fall asleep. I believe God allowed him to relax so that he could sleep. Some of you have had to take sleeping pills, maybe this past week. Some of you have had to take other kinds of prescription drugs in order to relax enough to be able to rest. God wants us to rest our bodies. It is good for us to rest.

Out in the middle of nowhere Elijah found a cake of bread and a jar of water. Where did that cake of bread and jar of water come from? God provided it. You see God wants to provide for us. He wants us to rest. He wants us to replenish ourselves. Overcoming stress begins with resting.

Now let me suggest a few little ways you can rest and relax. One is to schedule a few minutes of quiet time in your busy day — a few moments of rest when you don't answer the phone or race from one place to another. For just a few minutes you shut your mind off. "But, I'm a busy person," you say. I know that. But even the busiest person can schedule a few minutes. Just take ten minutes. Lie down on the couch in your office, or sit back in your chair. Just rest for a few minutes. Give yourself a few quiet moments in the midst of a busy day.

There should be, of course, a more structured planning of restful time. I believe very much in hard work. But as much as I believe in hard work, I am a firm believer in vacations, in taking time to get away. *Work hard and play hard* is a good plan to follow. A vacation is a time to rest, to forget about your cares. Maybe some of you have not taken a vacation in a couple of years. You say, "I can't afford it." Actually you can't afford not to if you want to relieve stress.

Another way to relax is to do something you find enjoyable and pleasurable. Take in a concert, go to a museum, or take a walk in the woods. Give yourself some breaks from all the difficulties of business. Couples, go out on a date. Sometimes in the busyness of life and family, we can go long periods of time without ever doing something together. You can always find an excuse: "We can't get a babysitter," or "The kids have to do this or that." But you need to take time, to go out on a date. Give yourselves some time away to rest and renew yourselves.

A second principle we find in Elijah's story is that to cope with stress we need to release our frustrations. Look what Elijah did. Elijah poured his heart out to God. "I have been zealous," he told God. "I mean, I have been working hard for you." Then he went on to tell God how alone he felt: "I am the only one left. Everybody else has deserted you. I am the only one."

We need to release our frustrations and pour out our heart to God. Holding in our frustrations will only make us sick. Frustrations build and will then manifest themselves in some other, unexpected way.

To release our frustrations, we also need to understand their source. Sometimes the source is unrealistic expectations. One of those is the perfection trap; that is, we think everything has got to be just right, and if it isn't, we are going to go crazy. But all that attitude does is stress us out. I am not talking about doing less than our best. But there are times when we get trapped into the "everything has got to be perfect" attitude, and all that does is make us miserable and frustrate us.

We also have to be willing to give up the expectation that we are going to get everything that is supposed to come to us. We have to give up the mentality that says, "I have the right to do such and such. This is what is due me." Because life is not fair. We don't always get what we think is due us. Things don't always turn out the way they are supposed to. Sometimes the referees do blow the game. Sometimes there isn't justice in our world. There are times when we have to just say, "Either I can let this thing destroy me or I can realize that life isn't always fair."

Another way to release our frustrations is to stay in the area of our strengths. Or to put it another way, when we play to our strengths, we aren't as liable to get frustrated. When we work in the area of our weaknesses rather than our strengths, we are more apt to be frustrated. If we stay in the area of our strengths and let other people take care of the areas where we are weak, we'll find life more rewarding. When we are working with our gifts and talents, we are not as likely to become stressed out. It is when we are working in an area in which we are not gifted, or doing something we don't feel called to do that frustration sets in.

A third principle for coping with stress is this: Refocus on God. The Scripture tells us that the Lord spoke to Elijah and said, "Go out and stand on the mountain in the presence of the Lord" (v. 11). Then a great wind blew and an earthquake shook the mountain. Then, after all the violence, there was the gentle voice, the whisper of God's voice. God was getting Elijah focused back on him.

Sometimes in the busyness of life with its stress and burdens and pressures, we lose our focus. We need to refocus on God. When we put our focus on God, when we see God — the power of God, the love of God, and the grace of God — we will be much healthier persons. When we can get our focus back on God and his greatness, his love for us, his care for us, then our focus is right. When we are out of focus, not focused on God, then stress can build up.

Refocusing on God will help us develop a proper perspective on our problems, so that we attack the problem and not the people. When we attack people, we get more problems. We have got to be able to separate the person from the problem and deal with the issue. It is a matter of perspective.

How do we refocus on God and develop a proper perspective on life? By reading the Bible and spending time in the quiet meditating and praying. When our minds are filled with God's Word and we open ourselves to God in prayer, our perspective can change. God changes us. We are renewed and refreshed just by being in the presence of God.

One final principle for dealing with stress: Resume serving others. Later on in this story, God tells Elijah, "I want you to go back to Israel. You have a job to do." When we turn our attention away from ourselves, our problems and our difficulties, and we look to serve others, we will be surprised what will take place in our lives. When we serve others it is amazing how some of our problems take care of themselves. God told Elijah, "I've got a job for you. I'm not finished with you yet." Here is what is exciting. Not only did God send Elijah back to continue the job that he had already given him as prophet, but he gave him a new job, the job of being mentor to a young man named Elisha. In effect God told him, "I want you to mentor this young man Elisha because someday he is going to take your place." If you want to reduce your stress and increase your sense of fulfillment in life, mentor someone else. Pour your life into somebody else's life. Help them to develop.

"I couldn't mentor anybody," you say. You don't have to be an expert to be a mentor. As a matter of fact, a high school student could mentor a junior high student. A college student could mentor a high school student. Sometimes it is not even a matter of age. It is a matter of experience and of knowledge and of insight. Part of my role as pastor is to mentor leaders in the church so that they in turn will mentor other people. Then the leadership will grow and develop, the ministry will expand, and everyone will get the help they need. That is how it is supposed to be. The Bible says that the pastor/teacher is given to the church to equip the saints for the work of the ministry. As we serve others, we are able to take our attention off our own problems and difficulties. Then we will control our stress. When we are able to resume our life of service after resting, after releasing our problems, after refocusing our perspective, then we have overcome stress.

The exciting thing is that stress can help us. If we face it and learn how to cope with it, it can help us learn new skills — skills that, frankly, we needed and there was no other way besides the stress for us to develop them. We can also gain new direction for our lives, as we learn where we need to be going in the days to come.

Stress is a part of life, distress is not. In his Word God provides principles that can enable us to relieve the distress so that we can have a positive impact on our world.

Note
1. George S. Everly, *The Nature and Treatment of the Stress Response* (New York: Plenum Publishing Corp., 1981). Robert Rosenfeld is a contributor to the volume.

Comment

This is a good sermon — beautifully written and effectively done — and most likely well received when it was preached. But I wonder whether McDaniel fell into a trap which I encounter personally and which all of us who preach are likely to face. What I am about to say focuses only on this one sermon and, granted, treats the sermon out of context of the local church. But I must mention the "trap."

What's the trap? I think it is the temptation to preach a "self-help" sermon that sells well in the marketplace and is well received by congregations, but doesn't offer a particularly biblical, divine perspective on life. It comes in the context of a religious service but it could easily be given as a talk to the local community education class or civic club without much change. It's a challenge to avoid this trap. I've struggled with it in my own preaching. I need to constantly keep the issue in front of me as I prepare to preach. Therefore, I offer these comments concerning the issue. I fully realize that this is a provocative issue with varying opinions circulating in churches today. But I use this occasion to focus the question.

Even though "self-help" sermons are becoming common, there's more to the preaching task than coating a series of "tips" with a biblical veneer. People like helpful tips. They sound familiar. Whether from afternoon television shows or popular magazine articles, most people appreciate such tips, especially if they are general and nonconfrontive. You'll feel better if you take a pill, take a break, take a vacation, take a spiritual "trip." It seems to me that this is largely what this sermon offers as a solution to stress.

What if this advice had been given to Elijah? Would he have responded favorably to a sermon telling him, if you are feeling stress just assess the symptoms, identify the principles, follow the formula tips and life will get better? I don't think so!

It is easy in preaching to avoid the prophetic dimensions of the preaching task. Most of us naturally avoid confrontation and seek to offer comfort and help. Sometimes that help becomes superficial. Often it is only a temporary relief from a deeper issue — in this case even more profound than how to cope with stress. Just because we are trying to communicate with contemporary "boomers," spiritual seekers, or a secular culture that ignores the church, doesn't mean we can let go of the more challenging, prophetic dimensions of biblical texts and the biblical message.

One might argue that, in light of the apparent biblical illiteracy of our generation, we must pay even more attention to describing the biblical and historical context of texts, and explaining the unique, divine perspective God offers to our lives. This biblical perspective is not one we will receive from the popular or secular media and culture. That doesn't mean of course, that we have to become pedantic or boring. It does mean that we have to wrestle with the totality of a text or story in its original setting and be cautious of imposing a "modern" cultural interpretation or need on the text.

For example, the situation in which Elijah lived contains many contemporary parallels. Ninth-century Israel was living in a time of relative prosperity and peace, although they were dealing with climactic conditions they couldn't control. They were ruled by a shrewd king (Ahab) with an even shrewder, domineering wife (Jezebel). The court chaplains were part of a civil religion that used cultic practices including the equivalents of consulting horoscopes, new age channeling and even bodily mutilation (their "punker" kids must have loved the spectacle!). Baalism and idolatry were everywhere in Israel. Pure Yahwism was on the decline, in threat of extinction. Does any of that sound familiar in our modern world?

Elijah challenged Israel's designer gods in a provocation that would have made our religious leaders feel real stress. He used the public arena on Mt. Carmel (1 Kings 18) to present the power of the one true God, Yahweh, in a way that would have sent the proponents of the separation of church and state howling to their court rooms.

Elijah wasn't just dealing with personal stress, though he created a lot of stress for the worshipers of the humanly created deities. He was dealing with a condition much deeper than surface tension. He was facing a terrible crisis of meaning that filled him and his people with despair. It is a crisis faced by many people today who, when they come to church, hope to find something more than a few self-help tips. Moreover, the tension at the heart of the narrative in 1 Kings 19 is whether Elijah will be allowed to give up his prophetic task and die, or whether he will continue on as God's person. The issue at the heart of our lives is whether we will go on — and whether the church will continue its prophetic task in the world. God's question to Elijah at the heart of this story, "What are you doing here?" (vv. 9, 13), must be reckoned with.

The difficult task of the modern preacher in trying to communicate biblical truth in a contemporary manner makes it even more imperative to do the homework required. We must avoid using the Bible as a springboard for culturally confined and defined "tips," rather than offering anything that might require a radical change of lifestyle or a paradigm change of faith. Yet, at the same time, we don't have to don the hair shirt of a doomsday prophet to bring a divine perspective on our human condition. There is indeed a pastoral dimension to preaching which provides hope, comfort and help. How do we find a balance between the prophetic and the pastoral functions in our preaching? This is the most important question this sermon raises about preaching.

And here is where this sermon can be instructive. McDaniel commendably uses a structure to present his thoughts that can serve as a way to offer positive options for coping with modern maladies. He begins by identifying false myths about the nature of stress. This becomes a way of helping to rethink our commonly held views on stress.

McDaniel goes on to take the text from 1 Kings 19 and finds points of personal identification with Elijah's feelings. He summarizes these feelings in one paragraph where he describes the symptoms of stress — depreciating our self-worth, underrating our work, exaggerating our problems and abdicating our dreams. The principles of overcoming stress are simple — rest, release frustrations, and refocus on God. Finally, we are to resume serving others. Notice the four "Rs." Good pastoral advice.

The third point, refocusing on God, is McDaniel's most important. In a nonjudgmental way, McDaniel invites his listeners to redevelop a proper perspective on life by turning to God. He remains unspecific in his definition of God, but describes the power, love and grace of God as attractive reasons to refocus our attention, despite the busyness of life. To someone who may have been raised in a hellfire-and-brimstone or legalistic religious environment, God's self-revelation in a gentle whisper will be good news. To others for whom God is a distant deity, McDaniel offers a personal view of God who is approachable. In these ways, McDaniel's sermon provides some very good pastoral theology and pastoral care.

McDaniel does not engage in the extreme media preachers' tendency to focus everything narcissistically on "my story, my pain, my struggle, my triumph." Outside of a reference to his mentoring role as a pastor, he does not reveal any personal data or talk about his own journey of faith. He doesn't appear to want his congregation to pay attention to his personality. He wants them to focus on God. He wants them to see the relevance of Scripture to practical problems in life. For these reasons I affirm this sermon.

It is difficult to find the balance between the pastoral and the prophetic dimensions in preaching. However, we are called to offer both. It is one reason preaching is an art and not merely a mechanical science. The Holy Spirit must be our guide to the text and how to apply it to the lives of our listeners. We have to be attuned to our culture yet prepared to offer a message that some in our settings will find hard to receive. We have a tremendous opportunity and responsibility to preach both healing and challenge to our congregations. In the good news we preach, may Jesus Christ be our model in his manner of touching broken lives with words of both the agony of sin and the ecstasy of salvation.

SUGGESTIONS

- In what ways do you struggle with the "prophetic" dimension in preaching? How do you feel about this issue?
- In light of the above Comment, how do *you* feel about the sermon

and the larger issues it raises about pastoral and prophetic dimensions of a text?
- Do a thorough study of the Elijah stories and particularly 1 Kings 19. Prepare one or more sermons on them. What do you see as the tension at the heart of the narrative in 1 Kings 19:1–18? How does this relate to your modern hearers?

Gary W. Downing

Topical Index

Advent
    Finding Peace 183
Beatitudes
    Blessed Are the Desperate 233
Church
    How "User-Friendly Churches" Get Used 129
Commitment
    Crowd Control on Palm Sunday 101
    When We Are Lacking Direction 15
Compassion
    Unnatural Compassion 35
Cross
    How "User-Friendly Churches" Get Used 129
Discipleship
    Crowd Control on Palm Sunday 101
Encouragement
    Can I Sing When the Going Gets Tough? 115
Faith
    Finding Peace 183
    I Believe in Jesus Christ 71
Faith Journey
    Peace for the Journey 139
    Pilgrim People, Pilgrim Faith 151
    When We Are Lacking Direction 15
God
    The Nearness of God 221
Grace
    Blessed Are the Desperate 233
    No Looking Back 265
Hope
    The Nearness of God 221
Hospitality
    Martha's Feast and Mary's Portion 83
Immanence of God
    The Nearness of God 221
Incarnation
    I Believe in Jesus Christ 71
    Jesus the Word 165
Jesus
    The Scandal in Sandals 251

Kingdom of God
    Blessed Are the Desperate 233
Knowledge of God
    Jesus the Word 165
Lent
    Peace for the Journey 139
    Where Are You Headed? 207
Light
    In a New Light 49
Lord's Prayer
    Lord, Teach Us to Pray 59
Love of Christ
    Peace for the Journey 139
    Unnatural Compassion 35
    When We Are Lacking Direction 15
Memory
    Can I Sing When the Going Gets Tough? 115
Messiah
    Crowd Control on Palm Sunday 101
Offense of the Cross
    The Scandal in Sandals 251
Palm Sunday
    Crowd Control on Palm Sunday 101
    Where Are You Headed? 207
Peace
    Finding Peace 183
Persistence
    Lord, Teach Us to Pray 59
Prayer
    Lord, Teach Us to Pray 59
Prejudice
    Unnatural Compassion 35
Purpose in Life
    Where Are You Headed? 207
Reconciliation
    Finding Peace 183
    In a New Light 49
Renewal
    Martha's Feast and Mary's Portion 83
Salvation
    I Believe in Jesus Christ 71
Sanctification
    No Looking Back 265

Self-Worth
    Keeping Stress from Becoming Distress 279
Servanthood
    Unnatural Compassion 35
Service
    Keeping Stress from Becoming Distress 279
Sin
    No Looking Back 265
    When We Are Lacking Direction 15
Story
    The Power of Your Story 197
Stress
    Keeping Stress from Becoming Distress 279
Suffering
    Can I Sing When the Going Gets Tough? 115
    Finding Peace 183
    Pilgrim People, Pilgrim Faith 151
    How "User-Friendly Churches" Get Used 129
Thanksgiving
    Pilgrim People, Pilgrim Faith 151
Thirst, Spiritual
    Blessed Are the Desperate 233
    Peace for the Journey 139
Transfiguration
    In a New Light 49
Transformation
    Martha's Feast and Mary's Portion 83
Trust
    Can I Sing When the Going Gets Tough? 115
    Lord, Teach Us to Pray 59
    The Nearness of God 221
Truth
    The Scandal in Sandals 251
Vocation
    Where Are You Headed? 207
Witness
    The Power of Your Story 197
Word of God
    Jesus the Word 165

Scripture Index

Genesis 18:1–8	83
Exodus 17:1–7	139
Exodus 34:29–35	49
1 Kings 19:1–21	279
Psalm 137	115
Isaiah 2:1–5	183
Isaiah 42:1–4	59
Matthew 1:18–25	183
Matthew 5:3	233
Matthew 11:25–27	251
Matthew 21:1–11	101
Mark 10:32–34	207
Mark 11:1–10	207
Luke 9:28–36	49
Luke 10:38–42	83
Luke 11:1–13	59
John 1:1–18	165
John 4:5–42	139
John 9:1–25	197
Acts 17:16–34	221
Romans 5:1–11	139
Romans 6:1–11	265
1 Corinthians 11:23–26	129
2 Corinthians 5:14–21	15
2 Corinthians 5:16–21	35
Philippians 2:5–11	71
Hebrews 11:1–2, 8–16	151
2 Peter 1:13–21	49